DR YESHAYAHU (  
spiritual scientist, p  
vist—is founder of  
munity in Harduf  
Global Network for Social  
tor of Global Event College and contributor to the School of Spiritual Science. He is the author of *The Spiritual Event of the Twentieth Century*, *The New Experience of the Supersensible*, *America's Global Responsibility*, *The Event in Science, History, Philosophy & Art* and *Cognitive Yoga*.

# SPIRITUAL SCIENCE
# in the 21st Century

Transforming Evil, Meeting the Other, and
Awakening to the Global Initiation of Humanity

Yeshayahu (Jesaiah) Ben-Aharon

TEMPLE LODGE

Temple Lodge Publishing Ltd.
Hillside House, The Square
Forest Row, RH18 5ES

www.templelodge.com

Published by Temple Lodge 2017
First published by Virtualbookworm.com Publishing Inc., Texas, 2013

© Yeshayahu Ben-Aharon 2013

Edited by Scott E. Hicks

This book is copyright under the Berne Convention. All rights reserved. Apart from any fair dealing for the purpose of private study, research, criticism or review, no part of this publication may be reproduced, stored in a retrieval system, or transmitted in any form or by any means, electronic, electrical, chemical, mechanical, optical, photocopying, recording or otherwise, without the prior written permission of the copyright owner. Inquiries should be addressed to the Publishers

The right of Yeshayahu Ben-Aharon to be identified as the author of this work has been asserted in accordance with sections 77 and 78 of the Copyright, Designs and Patents Act, 1988

A CIP catalogue record for this book is available from the British Library

ISBN 978 1 912230 06 8
Ebook ISBN 978 1 912230 08 2

Cover by Morgan Creative
Typeset by DP Photosetting, Neath, West Glamorgan
Printed and bound by 4Edge Ltd., Essex

# Contents

| | |
|---|---|
| Lecture 1. Spiritual Science and Contemporary Philosophy in Dialogue (Colmar 2007) | 1 |
| Lecture 2. An Esoteric History of the 20th Century (Järna 2004) | 38 |
| Part 1: The World Situation at Present | 38 |
| Part 2: Impulses of Resurrection | 59 |
| Part 3: Counterfactual History | 71 |
| Lecture 3. Changing Self Love into World Thinking (Orust 2012) | 86 |
| Lecture 4. The Incarnation of the Middle Stream and Vidar (Orust 2012) | 104 |
| Lecture 5. Can We Become the Guardian Angels of our Brothers and Sisters? (Orust 2012) | 124 |
| Lecture 6. The Working of the Christ in the Apocalyptic Conditions of the 20th and 21st Centuries (Utrecht 1997) | 134 |
| Lecture 7. The Beast and the Reversal (Gothenburg 2009) | 150 |
| Lecture 8. The Christ Event of the 21st Century (Stuttgart 2012) | 176 |
| Lecture 9. Israeli Civil Society and the Global Melting Pot (New York City 2002) | 198 |
| Lecture 10. Israel in the Midst of the Clash of Civilizations (Munich 2004) | 221 |
| Lecture 11. The Global Initiation of Humanity and Education (Oslo 2006) | 231 |
| Lecture 12. The Transformation of Evil and the High Tor Archangel (New York City 2002) | 242 |
| Lecture 13. High Tor Part 2: The Fallen Angels and the Alchemical Processes in Initiation (Saratoga Springs 2002) | 273 |
| Notes | 298 |

# Lecture 1

## Spiritual Science & Contemporary Philosophy in Dialogue: Observations on the Spiritualization of Thinking (Colmar 2007)

WHAT A GREAT PLEASURE IT IS that I am able to be here with you.[1] This is the first working visit that I have made to France. Strangely enough, though I don't speak or read French, I have always closely followed the development of French cultural-spiritual life in the twentieth century and today and have been engaged particularly for many years with French thinking and philosophy. And I would like in this lecture to make you aware of the role French thinking plays in the invisible spiritual drama of our time.

    I referred to what took place in the 20th century behind the curtains of world events in my books, *The Spiritual Event of the 20th Century* and *The New Experience of the Supersensible*, both written at the beginning of the 1990s. There I described my spiritual-scientific research on the esoteric, super- and sub-sensible realities graspable only by means of modern spiritual scientific research methods. Until the 1960s very little light was created on the earth at all—and so much darkness. Not that the darkness-producing forces and events have diminished since then; on the contrary, they increase exponentially. But the good news is that in all walks of life, thought, science, art, and social life, new forces of hope started to flow in the 1960s, and in my books I described the hidden sources out of which these spiritual forces are flowing. And some of those rare and precious rays of light emanated from French creativity in the second half of the last century.

During the whole European catastrophe of the 20th century, before, between, and after the two world wars and during the cold war, there took place in France a very intense and vital debate, intellectual but also cultural and political. The forces at work in thinking, with all their ingenuity, were not yet strong enough to penetrate social and political realities; many believed them to be so "revolutionary" and radical, but they could never really break through to new social ideas and social formations. But in the field of philosophy it was different; here some true creativity took place which was indeed striving to break new ground. The last century had an enormous task coupled with the most grave and fateful results for good or ill.

This task can be described in various ways. For our purposes tonight, because we are approaching this task from the point of view of the development of thinking, we can call it the spiritualization of consciousness, or more specifically, spiritualization of the intellect and thinking. This is an expression often used by Rudolf Steiner. His whole impulse, the utmost exertion of his will and love, was poured into this deed. And his lifelong hope was that free humans would do what he himself was striving to do: truly to transform themselves! He had hoped that this would be achieved at least by a limited number of people already at the beginning of the 20th century, and that it would then be taken up by ever more people during the course of the whole century, reaching a certain intensive culmination at the end of the century. In a transformed manner it would then powerfully enter the global scene of the 21st century as world-changing creative power.

## New Beginners

It is not enough nowadays that one person does something alone even if he is the greatest initiate, because others should no longer be simply led or pushed in his steps—unless we are speaking of impulses of evil. The good can only spring forth from the depth of free human hearts and minds, working together in mutual help and understanding. And if you look at the world situation today, anthroposophy included, from this point of view, you can surely say: well, then, we are definitely only at the very beginning! We are all therefore kindly invited to begin again, anew. If we understand truly what was said above, we are asked to see ourselves as real beginners. Ever more people should understand that the Zeitgeist is now seeking new beginners, and is quite fed up with so many "knowers" who are constantly creating havoc in our social, spiritual and economic life.

This spiritualization of the intellect is the first and unavoidable step needed as foundation for further transformations of human nature and society. It is the precondition for the spiritualization of our social, cultural, political and economic life. This is our main entry point, simply because we have become thinking beings in recent centuries. Everything we do starts from thinking, and wrong thinking is immediately a source of moral-social destructive forces, while truthful thinking is a building and healing power. For this reason Steiner referred to his so-called "non-anthroposophical" book *The Philosophy of Freedom* as his most important spiritual creation. By means of this book, he said, if properly understood and practiced, each person can begin, without any former spiritual knowledge or belief, from her or his daily thinking consciousness, daily perceiving consciousness, daily moral activity and social experiences. Each can start here from where one stands in real life.

I had the experience, early on with myself and now also with friends and students in the world, that with *The Philosophy of Freedom*, if you take it in the right manner, it is indeed the case that it gives us powerful means to realize this spiritualization and bring it to consciousness. This was my own spiritual-scientific way of development from my 21st to my 35th year. After starting from Steiner's general anthroposophical work, I then concentrated specifically on his philosophical-social work. For the building of the Harduf community, on the one hand, and for my spiritual research, on the other, I searched for the hidden stream of becoming of anthroposophy, for its living supersensible continuation.

How can Steiner's starting point for thinking be continually updated, brought into the stream of the developing Zeitgeist? This was my burning daily problem. I was also aware of the retarding forces at work inside his legacy. So I was conscious early on that I must create my own way as I go, alone, and that it is not simply given out there. And when you search in this way you have to find Michael's footsteps in history and in present day spiritual, cultural and social life. This is the reason why I was intensively following the new developments in the sciences, arts, and social life, and also in thinking and philosophy in the course of the whole 20th century. Then I found, through life itself, through my work itself—and this applies for my own experience, one cannot generalize—that whenever and wherever I looked for a way to continue after 1925, after Steiner's death, the way to a further development of thinking and the spiritualization of the intellect was leading to the abyss opened with the last two German thinkers—the converted Jew, Edmund Husserl and his National Socialist pupil, Martin Heidegger—through the ruins of

European culture in the Second World War, and into the 1950s and 1960s. And it was in this following in the tragic steps of Husserl and Heidegger that I came to French philosophy, because the French thinkers were the most ardent and receptive pupils of German thought. Therefore, in order to introduce some central figures of French philosophy I will have to briefly summarize the decisive turning point in German spiritual history.

## A German Excursion

The first German thinker who was acutely aware that the time of German idealism and Goethe's time had gone forever and cannot be revived was of course the great and tragic Nietzsche. He literally lost his mind in his efforts to find new, unforeseen venues to spiritualize thinking. And as a historical symptom and clue to the gathering storm leading to the German tragedy it is significant that precisely in those years, the end of the 1880s, Steiner was working on his philosophical dissertation *Truth and Science* as a basis for *The Philosophy of Freedom*. When the latter was published in 1894, he wrote to his close friend, Rosa Mayreder, how greatly he regretted the fact that Nietzsche could no longer read it, because "he would have truly understood it as a personal experience."

Now, Edmund Husserl (1859–1938) was a contemporary of Steiner; he also studied philosophy in Vienna under Franz Brentano one or two years after Steiner studied there, probably in the winter semester 1881–82. They almost met in Brentano's classes, as it were. Karma couldn't have spoken more clearly, because Husserl was striving to develop Franz Brentano's thinking further and created his phenomenology in the direction of Steiner's *Philosophy of Freedom*. But Husserl's radicalism was not radical enough; he didn't overcome the deeper limitations of traditional, Kantian philosophy. This left in German thinking a yawning gap, an abyss, before, during, and after the First World War, which was the most decisive time for European and German history. And the year came in which German destiny, and Europe's, was to be decided: 1917. In this year Lenin is sent by Ludendorff in a sealed train carriage from his exile in Zürich to organize the Bolshevik revolution in the East; and the US enters the war from the West. Middle Europe's fate was in the scales, tipping rapidly to the worst, and Steiner initiates social threefolding as a last rescue effort. Also in 1917 Brentano dies; Steiner publishes a memorial tribute to Brentano in his book, *Riddles of the Soul*. Here philosophy, anthropology, and anthroposophy are brought together for the first time in a fully modern and scientific way, without any theosophical residues—free, that is, from traditional occult conceptions and formulations. This book states clearly that Steiner is now ready to start his real life task as a modern spiritual scientist and social innovator. But his hopes to create a worldwide social-spiritual movement collapsed already before his early death in March 1925.

After Steiner's death, Max Scheler, an original and free-thinking pupil of Husserl who met and appreciated Steiner, converts to Catholicism in 1927, the same year in which Martin Heidegger's influential book, *Being and Time,* is published. In his destiny as the last German thinker, Heidegger embodies the destiny of his people. He could not rest content with phenomenology, and justifiably so; nor could he open himself to the new impulse working in the direction of *The Philosophy of Freedom*. Instead, he transforms Husserl's phenomenology backward instead of forward, to create in German intellectual life a powerful and highly suggestive intellectual *Umstülpung* (a reversal inside out) of *The Philosophy of Freedom*. Between Husserl and Heidegger the tragedy of German spiritual life plays itself out in the late 1920s and 30s, until in 1933 Heidegger delivers his infamous *Rektoratsrede*, his inaugural address as Rector of Freiberg University, presenting himself as an enthusiastic Nazi. Later he also supports the excommunication of his aging teacher according to Nuremberg's denaturalization racial laws. Husserl, fortunately for him, dies in 1938. The decision that fell already in 1917 was now made fully visible, and with it the fate of Germany and Europe as a whole.

Since Nietzsche's and Steiner's time it has been a rather strong either/or situation: thinking can be either with the spirit of the time or be strongly against it. Heidegger's unquestionable greatness was forcefully mobilized to serve the adversarial spirit most opposite to Michael. But nowadays only an abstract intellectual, or a fanatic religious believer, would believe that he can know in advance the difference between truth and falsehood. Anthroposophy is also sometimes taken up in this manner.

Practically speaking, it is precisely the case of Heidegger which demonstrates the difficulties one faces when one strives, through real experience, to discern the difference between truth and falsehood, especially where they are reflected and deflected by the threshold. If you imagine the threshold level as mirror surface, then one of the pair would appear as a sub-threshold and polar brother, even a twin, but turned upside down to create a counter-picture, a mirror-opposite of its upper-threshold origin! Here I would like to point to a very significant fact that has served my work well through the years. By struggling with present-day thinking in various fields one is highly rewarded not only by finding true Michaelic inspirations, but also through the painful uncovering of adversarial streams. They, too, can teach us a great deal, and first hand, concerning Michael's true intentions precisely because they strive to do the very opposite!

From this point of view we may begin to understand a great riddle, namely, why Heidegger became perhaps the most influential philosopher in 20th century Europe, and for French philosophy in particular. And why Levinas said—and he was a close personal student of Heidegger in Freiburg—"we must admit, we were all unfortunately Heidegger's students."

**The French Philosophical Century**

Since the 1920s and 30s, between the wars and during and after the cold war, we find a great series of French thinkers who always begin by assimilating German philosophy. The most recent philosophical food supply for French thinking comes from the great fourfold German *Götterdämmerung* stream: Hegel, Nietzsche, Husserl and Heidegger. Let us now invite and introduce briefly a few of these thinkers. But this introduction can only be episodic and fragmentary, a flitting and momentary inscription on a narrow and rapidly vanishing path. A beginning can be made with another born Jew, Henri Bergson, contemporary of Steiner, resurrected from oblivion by Gilles Deleuze, who used as one of his major starting points Bergson's *Matter and Memory* from 1896, two years after *The Philosophy of Freedom*. Then we have the great phenomenologist, Merleau-Ponty, born in 1908; his 1945 book *The Phenomenology of Perception* is a fine study of sense perception and perceptual consciousness, and who pushed the limits of perception increasingly into the supersensible, striving to transform sense-perception and body experience into spiritual experience. Somewhat at the other pole is the "dark" Maurice Blanchot, born 1907, whose *The Space of Literature* (1955) exerted strong fascination through the later century. And then we are already with the greatly influential Jean-Paul Sartre (1905–1980).

Sartre transformed the fundamental ontology of Heidegger into phenomenological existentialism; during the war he wrote his main work, *Being and Nothingness* (1943) as a reply to Heidegger's 1927 *Being and Time*. Read the chapter on "the look of the other" in this book, and you will find a most exact and brilliant phenomenological research of the perception, being and relation of the other—something without precedent in the history of philosophy or science. After the war we see the emergence of the stream of French structuralism with Levi-Strauss and his school among others. They had a significantly fruitful influence, right up until our times, in anthropology, sociology, myth study, and ancient cultures. But this was all prologue, setting the stage for what will become the truly exciting thirty years—1960s, '70s, '80s—in which one after the other you see the most brilliant stars appear, shining over the intellectual horizon of France, and now world renowned. Then it was all beginning, but I am sure you are all familiar with those remarkable names, names like—? Names like—? (No answer and laughter in the hall.)

First let us name another Jew-born—yes, they are still all over the place, despite some efforts. I mean Jacques Derrida, a Frenchman born in Algeria. He is now rather famous, but not always truly understood, as founder of a philosophical stream that he called "deconstruction." Derrida took an opposite (or polar) path relative to Foucault and is often portrayed as his opponent; toward Deleuze he was more of a friend, from rather far away. His effort was directed towards deconstructing and dismantling the centralistic and centralizing, monotheistic father-god forces working in past and present philosophy and literature. But this was not the goal in itself, rather a means of uncovering the peripheral forces working in language and writing. Derrida discovered and described some of the formative strategies of decentralized, peripheral forces that in spiritual science are called "etheric formative forces," and he revealed the texture of the text, the weaving of text through the warp and woof of language's artistic tapestry.

Derrida was increasingly influenced by Levinas and turned his attention to ethical, political and religious investigations, studying the problems of radical alterity, the transcendental otherness of the other as unbridgeable difference. He died October 9, 2004, and has an ever growing circle of influence, felt strongly in the Americas; he is one of the few philosophers of the 20th century to become known as a cultural figure outside the philosophical milieu. The concept of "postmodernism" is articulated for the first time as a philosophical concept in Jean-François Lyotard's *The Postmodern Condition—A Report on Knowledge* (1979). Inspired by Kant's idea of the experience and cognition of the sublime (part of Kant's *Critique of Judgment*), he tried to create a non-positivist, "event-ful" concept of knowledge and art, and to apply it to social and political thought. We could name others here like the truly brilliant Paul Virilio, original thinker of modern and postmodern technology, military affairs, urbanism, and architecture. And how can we not mention Jean

Baudrillard who died in March, 2007, a sharp-minded observer and critic of electronic communication and globalized media and TV, who also wrote the short and remarkable "Spirit of Terrorism" after the attacks on the World Trade Center in New York.

And then we come to Emmanuel Levinas, mentioned above in connection with his teacher Heidegger, a Lithuanian-born Jew who became orthodox after the war and remained observant of the commandments and Torah for the rest of his life. He is beside Derrida the most widely known French philosopher of our time, and his influence is also steadily growing. His innovative and radical concept of "the other" is introduced not through phenomenology as developed by Husserl, Heidegger, or Sartre, but through such remarkable concepts as "the face of the other" and "the mortality of the other"—to which I am primordially responsible. Levinas believed this to be the only way to create a "contra-Cain" force, which he saw as the true mission of Judaism that was suppressed by western philosophy, Christianity, and middle European culture. He sought to resurrect Abel and find the answer to Cain's primordial fratricide, which he experienced as repeated on a European and global scale in the 20th century, especially in the annihilation of the Jews (as original Abel's sons) by the Germans (as modern Cain's sons), but also in every persecution of the weak wherever they are. This constitutes the essence of his thought: I am my brother's keeper! In this manner Levinas tried to bring a new religious-moral impulse into the philosophical and cultural-political discourses and consciousness of the post-Holocaust world.

The last of these great figures to be mentioned now, because our time is short, would be Alain Badiou who still lives and works today, a militant Maoist-Leninist who began as a disciple of Sartre and the French philosopher of psycho-analysis, Jacques-Marie-Émile Lacan, and was grooming himself to become the lifelong contender against Deleuze. He is the rather lonely and last star still shining in the twilight of a truly wonderful French philosophical century. Badiou wrote an excellent students' introduction to his thought called *Ethics: An Essay on the Understanding of Evil*, and he wrote the best book on St. Paul that I have read in recent literature. Yes, it belongs to the strange and audacious symptomatic of our time that a non-repentant French Maoist-Leninist writes the best book on St. Paul! These are more visible representatives of dozens of creative and original thinkers, artists, and scientists in the 20th century that lived in France. They are only the more clearly marked names, the more strongly visible planets shining on the background of a whole spiritual-cultural European and French constellation, caused by the destruction of Europe in the last century and the vacuum created by the disappearance of German thinking.

But now there was one so daring and inspiring in his originality that in a way he towered over them all, so much so, that Deleuze said: "The author who wrote *The Archaeology of Knowledge* makes it possible for us to hope that true philosophy will again be possible." And he meant Michel Foucault. "Foucault is closer to Goethe than to Newton," Deleuze writes in his fine book *Foucault*, because just as for Goethe "the light-being is strictly indivisible condition, an a priori that is uniquely able to lay visibilities open to sight and by the same stroke to the other senses," so with Foucault's new concept of language and thinking: their essential being is the imperceptible force that makes all discourse visible and possible at all. And this is the reason why Foucault could prepare and open the way for the very most significant French thinker of the 20th century, Gilles Deleuze himself.

Even the otherwise careful and rather restrained Derrida, speaking at Deleuze's funeral, exclaimed: "The author of *Difference and Repetition* [one of Deleuze's main books] is the sublime philosopher of the event." Like a sun which outshines all the French intellectual stars but also contextualizes them, giving them their historical formation and placing thinking on its way in the trajectory and direction of its future cosmic destination and constellation, Deleuze fully deserves Foucault's statement, "The whole philosophical 20th century will one day be called the Deleuzian century." And elsewhere, "A lightning storm was produced which will bear the name of Deleuze: new thought is possible; thought is again possible."

It was Deleuze, alone and together with his collaborator and co-author, Félix Guattari, who pointed out philosophy's future role and task, in all his writings. Aphoristically speaking, let us pick one statement which can be inscribed—from the point of view presented in this lecture—as a symptomatic signpost in the evolution of philosophy. We find it in his last book, written with Guattari, *What is Philosophy?* There we find this statement:

> *The sole purpose of philosophy is to be worthy of the event.*

This powerful transformation of the role of philosophy by Deleuze is a result of a common project, to which each of the above mentioned thinkers contributed, starting with Heidegger who was the first to thematize the event as a central philosophical concept. Suffice it here to say that with this concept Deleuze expresses a complicated and multi-leveled happening, which he described and varied repeatedly in his works during three decades. Translated somewhat into our words, this "event" will be understood as pulsing systole and diastole, a breathing of immanent life, the always occurring incarnation and excarnation process in every single element of matter, space-time and consciousness. Deleuze conceived life and sensibility as existing everywhere in nature, culture and cosmos with and without organic-bodily or material foundations. If we rephrase his statement in this sense we may formulate it therefore thus:

*The sole purpose of philosophy is to be worthy of the ever pulsating, breathing, vibrating movement of universal immanent life.*

## Riddles and Problems of the Spiritualization of Thinking

Over and against Guattari and Deleuze's revolutionary restatement of the meaning and essence of philosophy, we will place now some of Rudolf Steiner's statements. He says, for example, now that the role of philosophy is fulfilled (meaning, at the end of the 19th century), we must have the courage to let the lightning of the will strike directly into thinking through the wholly singular being of the individual person.[2] This will element can fire thinking and release it from its bodily fetters, freeing its wings to soar and ascend into the open cosmic etheric universe. Then it will no longer be the same "I" who thinks, but *it will be the stream of cosmic thought that flows through my transformed being.* "IT thinks in me" will become a truthful experience and real supersensible event.[3] But precisely this remarkable spiritual achievement — the "IT thinks" — poses serious problems of epistemology, identity, and of course ethics, which cannot be resolved by means of present day philosophy and science.

The main problem here is this: when "IT thinks" in me, who is this "me" in and through which "IT thinks?" In the night, when IT really not only thinks in me but also builds and shapes the foundation of all my existence, my ordinary self-consciousness totally withdraws and is wholly absent. I become unconscious in order to allow IT to take over my existence, because my ordinary self cannot yet fulfill at all, in spiritual self consciousness, the needed maintenance of my whole being. Therefore in the night, and also unconsciously during the day, I am given to ITS cosmic guidance, and healing forces, and beings. I hope I have succeeded in making this problem a bit more problematic and concrete for you: how can this *depersonalization and over-personalization process* be experienced consciously? How does the one self—the ordinary—go out, and the other—the Higher Self—come in? And who is the "one" (now already two, and it will be further multiplied the more the spiritualization process advances!) that mutually recognizes, organizes, and brings these two—and the many—into harmonic composition? And in what sort of *self*-consciousness would this "IT thinks" become conscious?

The same problem can also be expressed in this manner. Steiner said that he regarded Descartes' famous statement, "I think therefore I am," as nothing less than "the greatest failure in the evolution of modern thinking... because precisely there, where I think, I am not... because ordinary thinking is mere empty picture, image, representation, and is bereft of any real, substantial being." This statement characterizes an essential existential fact as well as experience of contemporary philosophy as a whole and especially of the French philosophers above. What contemporary philosophical thought could achieve to a certain extent and in various ways and different degrees, is part of this first aspect, namely, the "cosmicization" of thinking and the realization of "the thought of the outside" and the "IT thinks inside" (Foucault-Deleuze); but such thought felt that it must completely sacrifice the reality of the subject, the individual, to achieve this. With this complete sacrifice we cannot concur. Yet we must also admit, as pointed out above, that apart from Steiner's own lived, initiatory example, we do not have first-hand descriptions of a successfully carried-out experiential solution of this dilemma. Altogether we may say: contemporary philosophy did develop, in an original and new manner, some aspects related to the spiritualization of thinking, but stopped at the threshold in relation to the deeper problems of the "I." The celebrated though little understood statements of Foucault on the death of the subject and author can only be understood as symptoms pointing to this unresolved problem, as we will see later in greater detail.

Let me summarize briefly the first main stages in the process of the spiritualization of thinking and then indicate the full meaning of Steiner's understanding of "the sole purpose of philosophy." If the transformation of thinking through the "direct lightning of the will" takes place, and thinking becomes a singular event, and when I have come thus far with spiritualizing my own thinking, I have as a matter of fact caused the nullification and emptying of my ordinary soul and mind contents. Now because my ordinary experience of my self is nothing but the sum-total of these contents, when they disappear, my ordinary self disappears as well. I forget my subjective inner life, which as it were goes to sleep. In its stead, IT thinks flares up. IT flows into the empty, self-less place, and IT thinks through this place as a wholly other, alter-

Self. As a result the following may occur: IT now jolts my otherwise unconscious real Self—not the subjective, conscious, personal self that is already obliterated—rather IT jolts my real Self out of the physical body. And this real Self may find his way to Humanity's Higher Self, swimming and flying on the waves and in the currents of the real "world-wide-web," spread out and mingled with infinitely multiple and diverse non-organic living cosmic forces, events, and beings. But this is the central problem: IT thinks alone cannot guarantee that this meeting will take place. The force needed to enable the meeting between my real Self and Humanity's Higher Self, can only be found elsewhere. But where?

Therefore, it is immensely significant to notice how Steiner refers to pure thinking also as pure love in these words from *The Philosophy of Freedom*. When the thinker *becomes one with* the stream of "love in its spiritual form that flows through thinking," he or she realizes and individualizes this experience as a "moral intuition," conceived freely out of the spiritual worlds, and brought down to the Earth through individual deeds of love. This second side of the spiritualization of thinking has to do with the free love for the Earth, humanity, and physical life as a whole. In other words, spiritualized thinking can create a connection between the two selves—the human and the cosmic—only if it becomes an expression of love. Only then can it connect the Higher Self experienced outside the body, and the human self that receives the moral intuition and must protect it and make it real on the Earth. Now if taken from both sides, namely, from the cosmic experience of a Self as part of the non-organic world of life forces and beings, and as a source of moral intuition to be realized on Earth, Steiner's following statement may be appreciated in its full weight. He says that philosophy's future purpose will be "to save human self-consciousness" in order that self-consciousness can be remembered *at all* as humanity advances further in its present and future spiritualization process.[4] If this remembering of self-consciousness is not achieved, the spiritualization process will still continue, because the evolutionary time for it is due. However, it will lead humanity away from its true Self and its true mission on the earth and in the universe. This means that

philosophy has truly something to be "worthy about:" *the salvation and redemption of self-consciousness for all future stages of the spiritualization of humanity*, without which human consciousness will not be able to enter in a healthy way into the spiritual worlds. In the Deleuze-Guattari vein we can now finally paraphrase the statement quoted above from their book, *What is Philosophy?* We may now reply from our own side:

> *The sole task of philosophy is to be worthy of the event of spiritualization of self-consciousness and remembering of the true 'I.'*

### The Absent Great Dispute

Our characterization of philosophy's "sole purpose" resounds strongly to meet Deleuze's challenge as a *warning and admonition* from the side of the Michaelic stream. This warning is truly not given to foster pedantry and intellectualism, but on the contrary, to balance the true and real *but one-sided* impulse of the contemporary spiritualization of thinking. It is precisely because the spiritualization of thinking *does* advance further and becomes real, and because thinking has truly begun to merge with the stream of cosmic forces, that this message resounds from Michaelic spheres, encouraging the thinker not to forsake the mysteries and problems involved in the extremely complicated and contradictory relations between the ordinary earthly subject and personality and the Cosmic Ego, also called the Christ, or Higher Spirit Self. This task is something wholly new in human evolution and is perhaps the most crucial impulse of the immediate present and near future, namely, *to create a self-conscious bridge between the earthly self and supersensible consciousness*. Philosophy understood in this way will offer the only means "to save the self-conscious 'I,' that is, self-consciousness as such, for supersensible consciousness." In other words, the clairvoyant, on achieving true spiritual consciousness, must be able to look back and remember—in the first stage of spiritual development—her or his "I." And this *saving of self-consciousness* can only be achieved through spiritualized thinking, in the direction indicated by *The Philosophy of Freedom*.

Now, as mentioned above, it is precisely in connection with the concept of the "I" that post-modern thinking has the greatest difficulties, because this problem cannot be addressed by means of pure thinking alone, be it as spiritualized as possible. The "I" problem must be approached from a polar and opposite side; and this side marks the place of real absence in Deleuze's thinking also, although, as with so many aspects of Deleuze, his absent "I" is much more alive than many dead and frozen concepts concerning this "I"! From this point of view I would like to turn your attention next to the possibility of a remarkably fruitful *spiritual battle*—concerning the problems of the "I"—and *dialogue*—concerning pure thinking—that could take place, provided that anthroposophical thinking has advanced far enough that such problems become its true living problems. As I said above, I have myself been benefiting greatly from engaging in this battle for the last thirty years. And I would like to try to ignite in you also a little spark of enthusiasm for *true spiritual battle*, true dialogue of the spirits, minds, and hearts. Here a richly and mutually rewarding "disjunctive synthesis" (to use Deleuze's unique phrase) could have taken place—but never did, because what could traditional anthroposophy bring, authentically, to this field? As just described, only genuine individual achievement can stand up truthfully to this challenge and face the real power of contemporary philosophy's achievements.

Self-transforming anthroposophy benefits greatly from engaging contemporary philosophy—along with the arts and sciences, of course. This is so because contemporary philosophy grapples rather unconsciously with the same problems that one encounters if one begins to realize the actual first steps in developing supersensible consciousness. In accordance with the medieval manner of discourse—which was much more civilized (that is, truthful) than ours—we may use the term "dispute" for this rare and unique dialogic battle or battled dialogue—*for a true combat of the spirits*. The greatest of spiritual battles was preordained but never fought in history, because the spiritual battle of the 20th century, as I mentioned above, was decided for the worst early on. When in the second half of the century and especially towards its end the great culmination of anthroposophy should have taken place, only the other stream was culminating, alone. Its true opponent was simply not present out there to fight, because its decisive Michaelic battle was lost already in the beginning of the 20th century. However, this was only the first century of Michael's present age as *Zeitgeist*, with the first of three great battles, and so many smaller ones in between! Presently we are humbly striving to prepare some suitable starting points for the second great battle—the battle of the 21st century.

Now that we are seriously working on self-transformation, and with it on true spiritualization of the intellect, we are strongly attracted to our rivals, or to their legacy, because our living striving is asking for a true dialogue or battle, without which it cannot thrive and develop further. And we will have at our side Deleuze's being, leading, and the beings of his colleagues. They will serve as a strongly awakening, reminding, and truly challenging warning—and as a stark temptation as well—so that we may realize on the earth, now and in the near future, the great supersensible battle raging in the spiritual worlds closest to us, between Michael and his hosts and the adversarial—but always also helpful—spirits!

So we can say that Gilles Deleuze went farthest toward fulfilling this task of the spiritualization of thinking, but he accomplished it in a strongly one-sided way. With Deleuzian thinking we have before us at the end of the 20th century the best example of how far one could have travelled to bring this goal to a certain temporary culmination. And as I continued to study the development of consciousness through the scientific, political, artistic, philosophical, and anthroposophical developments of last century, I had to say to myself again and again: here at the end of the century we have this wonderful line up of characters, thinkers as well as artists and scientists, across the whole century, so brilliant, so shiningly original, who strive to bring thinking further. Then I looked at my own efforts, and in order to develop my own anthroposophical thinking further, I had to work through these schools of thoughts, I really had to delve very deeply, without prejudice, into the work of many individual thinkers. I really had to struggle in order to transform each stage, each person's thinking, each decade, to arrive at what these developments could offer as part of the stream of the ongoing spiritualization of the intellect: enriching, challenging, also tempting and misleading.

I experienced myself pretty much alone in this battle. Even among thinking anthroposophists I couldn't find anybody who wished to engage with this struggle explicitly, in this sense of spiritual battle. There were of course always those eager to refute each other, and also post-modern philosophy. That was always there; but I wasn't interested in refuting anything or anybody, I was trying through these thinkers to grapple with the deeper spiritual impulses at work, which either corresponded to our Time Spirit, or fought against it, or mixed the two in many bizarre ways. There I could find some important and hidden footsteps and clues that guided me on the way of the spiritualization of thinking. Of course the same non-dispute happens all the time also on the other side. One could not discover any wish to be even slightly aware of Steiner's contribution in those thinkers that I have mentioned. And their conscious un-knowing was served well by the absence of presently engaged anthroposophists!

That was, and still is today, a strange situation. I asked myself, what's happening here? It is as if I am observing a strange dramatic performance. The stage is set and some players are busy performing; they speak and act wholly unaware of the grotesque situation. They are not aware that the other players, their counterparts, aren't even there! What I see is only a half-play, a spiritual dramatic piece cut in two. The real script isn't played out, and what is played isn't the real script at all! This should have been a whole scene of battle, but we have only a half, the other group is playing no role whatsoever in the script that they themselves wrote! They wrote it bravely in spirit, with the strength given to them by Michaelic beings in the sun sphere, in the supersensible Michaelic school; but on the earth they have forgotten, and in that sense also betrayed, the roles they appointed for themselves before birth. It really should have been, from the beginning of the century to its very end, a perpetual huge battle—and a most fruitful dialogue, because spiritually seen a true, sincere dialogue is also a battle. A real brotherly dispute should take place between thinkers deeply connected to anthroposophy and the thinkers I have mentioned above. This grew very clear as the end of the century drew near. This dispute was prepared in the Middle Ages and was predestined to take place in the 20th century. But we live in the age of freedom, in which all former scripts are easily changed by the present decisions of the present players! Some eight hundred years ago, in completely different spiritual and social conditions, this battle did take place, in the high Middle Ages. Let me touch upon this particular historical as well as karmic background, in order to outline also the present and future battles that face us now.

**The Great Medieval Dispute**

In the high Scholasticism of the Middle Ages, beginning with the Platonic renaissance of the 12th century and developing in the 13th and 14th centuries, there was an enormous philosophical, spiritual battle, mainly here in France, in Paris and its university. Here the great Scholastics were striving mightily to unite Christian theology with Aristotelian philosophy, under the leadership of Thomas Aquinas, his older teacher,

Albertus Magnus, and their extended circle of students from the Dominican order. They were engaged in fierce struggle on several fronts. We shall name only one and indicate this only in outline. One powerful opposing stream comes from members of the Franciscan order. This order presents a series of outstanding religious and philosophical teachers. In the 13th century they were headed by "Doctor Seraphicus," as St. Bonaventure (born John of Fidanza) was called because of his ecstatic religious-mystical devotion and temperament. He was personally initiated through a miraculous cure at the hands of St. Francis of Assisi himself. Bonaventure was a contemporary and powerful opponent of Thomas's effort to unite and thereby transform Christian theology with his renewed Aristotelianism.

Thomas died in 1274, and for us the most interesting personality isn't a contemporary but a thinker and theologian born around 1266, who developed his thinking career in Thomas' wake. He is also not such a clear-cut opponent. In the Scholastic traditions he is considered to be a unique Realist, in opposition to the main Franciscan tradition, and he considered himself an independent pupil of Thomas and Aristotle, more an innovative successor than Thomas' enemy. Indeed, he diverged and contradicted Thomas in many original ways on important theological and philosophical matters. I mean here the truly brilliant and original philosopher, Johannes Duns Scotus, known as "Doctor Subtilis" because he enjoyed synthesizing varying and opposing elements in surprisingly untraditional assemblages. (Let me remark in parenthesis that the *philosophy of being* of Scotus, specifically his teaching on the categories and on meaning, was the subject of Heidegger's "habilitation" dissertation in Freiburg, 1915;

for the esoteric-karmic undercurrent of our lecture this is also a symptomatically telling fact).

Many differences traditionally seen between these rival streams must be significantly modified today; especially in the case of Duns Scotus they are far more complicated, and very interesting indeed. In the customary understanding, the Aristotelians or Dominicans are known as Realists. What does it mean to be a Realist in the middle ages? It meant on the one hand to be able still to experience thinking as part of the cosmic intelligence, and on the other, Aristotelian side, to experience thinking as strongly connected with the human soul and spirit, with the thinking individual. The Dominicans with Thomas at their head could still capture the last remnants of spiritual content and substance that had come from the spiritual worlds in earlier epochs, but now they were striving to grasp it firmly with their thinking as it became earthly and human. Above all they were struggling with what was already a problem for Aristotle almost 2000 years before: *the riddle of the spiritual nature of the human being and the problem of immortality.*

In the Christian High Middle Ages the question was formulated thus: religion promises the hope of salvation and immortality through faith in the revealed divine message of the Bible; but would it also be possible to think—and in thinking not only logically to prove or disprove but actually to *experience and realize*—the immortality of the individual human soul? Their Franciscan opponents belonged to the so-called Nominalists, because they could no longer experience thinking's true spiritual-universal being. Due to this inability, Franciscans trying to gain knowledge of spiritual matters, apart from established religion, were searching for it in more mystical-ecstatic ways. An interesting corollary is that this avoidance of thinking in matters pertaining to the deeper spiritual quest adorned their striving with a peculiar mystical and intuitive brilliance. It was endowed with a luster of the supersensible that, for more spiritually inclined persons, temptingly outshines the conscientious, painstaking, and seemingly dry labor and technique of thinking developed by the Dominicans—those Steiner refers to as truly loyal at heart to the cosmic intelligence ruled by Michael. Another interesting trait of some leading Franciscans was their effort to bypass Aristotelian-Platonic ideas with the help of otherwise marginalized Stoic traditions.

The Stoics assimilated a rich and diverse mixture of philosophical and religious elements right before and after Christ, drawing on Gnostic and pagan traditions. Before neo-Platonism they were already keenly attentive to the awakening inward and individual soul life of the human personality, as well as *the growing darkness* surrounding its fate on earth and after death. Steiner described this unsolvable problem in one of his karma lectures. He recounts a discussion between a young and an older Dominican. He speaks movingly and intimately when he describes this event. The younger Dominican spoke to his older teacher: *Look, master, the ancient spiritual power—originally Michael's—that still inspired the thinking of Plato and Aristotle, Plotinus and Johannes Scotus Eriugena, is dying out. People in the future will not be able to experience it any more.* And he said further: *If things continue as they are, then people will lose all spiritual substance and truthfulness in their thinking in the future. And this thinking, the heavenly intelligence, which streams from Michael to the earth, will fall prey to Ahrimanic-demonic spirits that will use it to drag humanity into the abyss of materialism and corruption. Michaelic cosmic intelligence, still administered by the gods in ancient time, will be transformed into increasingly Ahrimanic thinking in the not so distant future.* He went on to say that something has to happen now on earth through us, in the human soul itself, to prepare a seed for future transformation that will be available when Michael starts his new epoch. This seed must be prepared now in order to sprout to life in an age in which otherwise only materialistic-intellectual thinking will prevail. And he said: *For now we must hold apart the powers of faith and of thinking, but in the future this separation will no longer serve humanity. The new seed must be there at that future time to enable at least a few humans to spiritualize in their hearts and minds the fallen intelligence, and so to connect it again with true spiritual reality.*

The great champion of the Realists, the "silent ox" as Thomas Aquinas was nicknamed, tried with all his strength to prove that when a person thinks by means of the *nous poeitikos*, the active intellect, rather than the *nous pathetikos*, the passive intellect, he may unite his soul intimately with real spirit substance; then he may rightfully believe that after his death, though he will be carried to heaven on the wings of Christian salvation, he may find his individuality again, endowed with a full self-consciousness similar to the intensive, active human self-consciousness on the Earth. All this could only be hoped for and believed in, but not yet fully experienced in the individual soul. Individual immortality could become self-conscious experience neither before nor after death. It was not yet possible to experience how, through the actualization and realization of living, intuitive thinking, human individuality is transformed and immortality becomes a reality as supersensible experience, so that the human "I" can live as a conscious eternal being in the spiritual world *right here and now*, and therefore also after death. Steiner adds that indeed only the preparation for this could be made, and that Thomas Aquinas died with this burning question, this huge problem, because he could not resolve it in his time. And Steiner formulates this question of Thomas thus: "How can thinking be redeemed? How can the Christ impulse [the spiritual "I" power] enter into thinking?" But what is the so-called Christ impulse? What is this spiritual "I" power? It is the power of transformation, the power of metamorphosis working in the individual human soul, reaching also into thinking and leading it, transformed, from within, back to the spiritual worlds; and doing so in such a way that the eternal nature of the "I" will be realized in the process. In other words, if the "I" is to become immortal, it must first become so here on the Earth, through free human activity. This becoming is what is truly meant by "the Christ impulse." This Thomas could not accomplish in the 13th century, but Steiner realized and actualized this task at the end of the 19th century, when the new age of Michael began. He expressed this self-realization in *The Philosophy of Freedom* and all his subsequent spiritual-scientific work.

This may allow us a glimpse of what is working behind the curtains of human history, and how karma works from one age to the other. The 20th century was supposed, among other things, to become again a fruitful time of a great new dispute between the reborn Dominicans, together with their more platonically inclined colleagues from the school of Chartres, and the reborn Franciscans who already in the 13th and 14th centuries experienced thinking as a fallen, earthy-human element, and searched for redemption through other venues. In the 13th century, Nominalists and Franciscans said: Thinking is only a human-earthly faculty; thinking can only give names to sense-perceptible objects and to humanly fabricated concepts. If there is a universal intelligence (and many of them did believe it), it doesn't enter human thinking. Human thinking is as sinful as the whole human being and cannot partake in the grace of having an actual, presently real, heavenly origin. Divinity in its real essence is wholly transcendental, totally beyond human cognition; with thinking no human being can grasp supersensible reality nor find there his eternal individuality. Today (as contemporary philosophers) they say: the human subject, the earthly personality, has no significance! They proclaim "the death of the subject" as in the Middle Ages they denied the immortality of the "I"! Today the meaning of human personality as such is deemed unreachable and unknowable. As then it was disputed whether there are real universals, now the existence of the single object, the single personality, is denied as well. The great dispute of the middle ages was taking place in the 13th century between Realists and Nominalists, and externally-historically the Realists seemingly fought a lost battle. Inwardly, however, they prepared the ground for what was to come to light in the new age of Michael, which is now present. And we are still at the beginning of this new battle, though we are well into the second Michaelic century! Today ordinary humans like us must find the courage to become again true beginners, to try humbly but sincerely to take the first and most elementary step in this direction. Can we release the imprisoned heavenly intelligence and transform it in our hearts so that thinking can break through to a genuine spiritual reality? Can it become real *event*? Can we produce in this process a real spiritual "I"—an individual-singular being? And what really does it mean to become neither single-private personality, nor abstract-general universal being, but truly "singular" being?

### Back to the Future

Returning to what for the Realists was the future, let us go back to the end of the 19th century and the beginning of the 20th century. Steiner publishes *The Philosophy of Freedom* in 1894 as individual-singular-spiritual achievement, unaccepted and unrecognized by general middle-European culture. This is the inaugural event, laying the foundation stone on which the future spiritual life of humanity will be built. For the very first time in history a human being was individually able to realize, in and through the spiritualization of the intellect, in and through pure thinking, an actual production and creation of the eternal, moral, spiritual substance of a human individuality as a genuine self-conscious spirit reality. And he could achieve this remarkable deed as a free and modern human being, without depending on any given mystical or atavistic supersensible consciousness or esoteric traditions. It is a free deed of actualization and realization of new selfhood through cosmic thinking. The power of transformation, transubstantiation, and metamorphosis, had been so strongly individualized in the Middle Ages that an answer could now be given to the unresolved riddle and problem with which Thomas Aquinas died: *How can thinking be redeemed, and with it and through it the human self?*

This was the main theme of my 1995 book, *The New Experience of the Supersensible*, which I subtitled: *The Knowledge Drama of the Second Coming*. At the beginning of this book I placed three quotations which for me summarize the drama of the century's end, the culmination of the struggle to achieve even a minuscule individual seed of this vast human task. To these three I will now add also a quotation from Deleuze. The first quotation is from Heidegger, celebrating man's life-unto-death as expressing the essence of his being. The second is Foucault's famous statement concerning the disappearance of the human being as we know it. The third demonstrates Deleuze's real struggle with the legacy of his Franciscan forerunners, trying mightily to solve the riddle of individual immortality. The fourth is from Steiner's words written on his death bed as concise future directive. These passages are arranged in a certain ascending order—from a profound denial of everything that the Michaelic impulse of our time is striving for (Heidegger), through the two greatest representatives of contemporary French philosophy, Foucault and Deleuze, to Steiner, who was there first in time, but is and will be always the last one to be understood by our culture.

> Being held out into the nothing, as *Dasein* is ... makes man a lieutenant of the nothing. We are so finite that we cannot even bring ourselves originally before the nothing through our own decision and will. So profoundly does finitude entrench itself in existence that our most proper and deepest limitation refuses to yield to our freedom.
>
> Martin Heidegger, *What is Metaphysics?* (1929)

> It is comforting, however, and a source of profound relief to think that man is only a recent invention, a figure not yet two centuries old, a new wrinkle in our knowledge, and that he will disappear again as soon as that knowledge has discovered a new form. [...] Then one can certainly wager that man would be erased, like a face drawn in sand at the edge of the sea.
>
> Michel Foucault, *The Order of Things* (1966)

Every event is like death, double and impersonal in its double... Only the free man...can comprehend...every mortal event *in a single Event* which no longer makes room for the accident... It is at this mobile and precise point, where all events gather together in one, that transmutation happens: this is the point at which death turns against death; where dying is the negation of death, and the impersonality of dying no longer indicates only the moment when I disappear outside of myself, but rather the moment when death loses itself in itself, and also the figure which the most singular life takes on in order to substitute itself for me.

Gilles Deleuze, "Twenty-First Series of the Event" in *Logic of Sense*, (1969)

*If this were all*, freedom would light up in the human being for a single cosmic moment, but in the very same moment the human being would dissolve away. ... We are here pointing to the abyss of nothingness in human evolution which man must cross when he becomes a free being. It is the working of Michael and the Christ impulse which makes it possible for him to leap across the gulf.

Rudolf Steiner, "The Freedom of Man and the Age of Michael" in *Anthroposophical Leading Thoughts*, GA 26, January 1925

In 1929 Heidegger named the human being the *Statthalter des Nichts*—a "commander of nothingness." And he said: the whole of human existence is founded only on death, on finiteness. That was the first "statement" through which the reversal of human history was made philosophically conscious—and then politically and socially realized in so much ending and annihilating of human lives. There can scarcely be a formulation more profoundly anti-*Philosophy of Freedom* than this one. Remember what I said at the beginning: Heidegger's influence is arguably the most significant one in 20th century philosophy—at least until Foucault's prophecy is fulfilled, that "the 20th century will one day be called the Deleuzian century." Now when Foucault writes, 33 years after 1933, he says: the human subject, the 'I" as we know it, is a momentary phenomenon, caused by the evolution of consciousness in the 19th century; and it is rapidly disappearing. This is a somewhat better statement than Heidegger's! First, because Foucault isn't speaking about the essence of the human being as being finite, as Heidegger does; and second, because human essence is for Foucault exactly this: the process of open-ended becoming, of transformation—and in this sense not finite at all.

He says: our understanding of the human subject changes, it will be different in the future. So he really means: the death of the 19th century *concept of the subject* is occurring in the 20th—a fact that can also be supported from anthroposophical perspectives as I indicated above. He never meant to announce the end of the human being! The third is a typically suggestive passage from the post-modern thinker who experienced, perhaps more than any other thinker in the last century, that we are *crossing the threshold*, that great eventualities await us on the other side. But more than that, *he knew very well* that we *have already crossed* and *are living on the other side*, wholly unforeseen and uncharted, and facing infinite new frontiers. This thinker is Gilles Deleuze. In Deleuze we find wonderful descriptions of what one can experience and express in concepts and words, if one has spiritualized one's thinking to a certain extent. One experiences the essence of life: "We will say of pure immanence that it is A LIFE, and nothing else... A life is the immanence of immanence, absolute immanence: it is complete power, complete bliss."[5] The same experience has a twin, an "other" or flip side that comes organically woven with it. If one has come so far as to experience the essence of pure life, one has begun at the same time also to lift into consciousness the unconscious and real (that is, *living*) death processes that underlie ordinary thinking. Death begins to rise to consciousness, and begins to reveal its true being, namely, *the (veiled) gate to eternal cosmic life.* When one is so far on the path that thinking becomes an experience of life-in-death and death-in-life, one can experience truly that "this is the point at which death turns against death; where dying is the negation of death." And when, moreover, one experiences with one's released etheric body the cosmic, impersonal, nonorganic life forces, one knows also that "the impersonality of dying no longer indicates only the moment when I disappear outside of myself." And that means, if we turn the negative way of speaking to its positive sense: *The impersonality of dying indicates the moment in which the true I AM appears outside my ordinary self.* One comes then closest to the spiritual-scientific mystery of the "I," and only a hair's breadth, grace's breadth, separates one from being granted this experience.

While the mental image, the *Vor-Stellung*, of the "I" disappears, as we pointed out above with Foucault, and the *IT*, the impersonal life-forces of cosmic thinking, begins to think through me, then the real "I" is resurrected and comes to consciousness in and through the impersonal cosmic stream. This real "I" is a being of resurrection, and one can experience its reality at this stage neither through cosmic thinking nor through personal volition, but only through a gift of grace. *IT* is the vehicle, or chalice, not the giver of the grace; the giver of the true "I" can only be the being of humanity's "I", the Higher Self; the Christ. And Deleuze, with everything that he brings with him from former life, can advance so near—but "only" so near—to the cusp of this moment, to the threshold of this grace. And as a matter of fact it is so, when one has really spiritualized thinking so far that one can experience impersonal cosmic thinking—I really mean *experience*, not merely *think* the abstract concept—then one really doesn't find there again the mental pictures of the ordinary self, the subjective subject that "thinks and therefore he is." In this moment, that self is nothing, and the *IT* is all; and therefore Deleuze could also not find it in his authentic experience of crossing the threshold of life/death.

How close he stands there, on the threshold, facing boldly the being of death and *experiencing how death dies*. But he doesn't see really *into what death dies*; he cannot produce enough fire to concoct and conduct the alchemical combination that alone can fuse entirely—annihilating any difference in between—absolute, pure, immanent life with absolute death. He therefore doesn't see *what*, or better *who*, faces him; *what happens* at that very moment; which *event* takes this sacred place of time. He cannot experience what he has at hand, namely, how "through the grace of the real 'I' life becomes death and death becomes life"— how *in Christo morimur* or how *we die into the fullness of life*. But how movingly close he does come to unraveling His secret, when he experiences "the moment when death loses itself in itself, and [becomes] *the most singular life*... in order to substitute itself for me."

The moment when this substitution occurs is the most sacred that one can experience after ordinary death. The beginner-initiates that we can become today may be granted the grace of this sacred moment in the midst of physical life. We may truly grace-fully die and may experience in full consciousness exactly how this "most singular life"—the Higher Self—will "substitute itself for me." Only in this manner can the battle of the Middle Ages that truly took place, and the battle of the culmination of the 20th century that remained almost entirely virtual, be still realized in the course of the 21st century. This is indeed our humble elementary mission. Now *what makes freedom into reality?* Not intellectual "reality," but moral-human and at the same time supersensible *achievement?* It is precisely this that the Franciscans say is impossible in principal, and in Deleuze's case we can even see how this becomes manifest in his individual and very personal karma. Look at his fingers, and compare them with Brentano's hands that Steiner described as "philosopher's hands," and then with Steiner's own hands. Hands and fingers do not reveal primarily past karma (as the head does) but karma-in-the-stream of-becoming. If you contemplate Deleuze's fingers, what would you experience? He had to let his fingernails grow very long because he couldn't stand the physical sense of touch with his fingers; it was for him too painful! What do the fingers experience, deeply, unconsciously, when they touch? They sense our becoming, and they also experience constantly the fire that burns at the end-of-our becoming, the so called second or soul death. In other words, the fingers live and move and become, all the time, *beyond the threshold*, where our spiritual stream of karma weaves and shapes our present life out of future lives.

    The leading Dominicans knew that true freedom is indeed only temporarily impossible; they have labored hard to prepare its seed through their loyal and faithful devotion to Michael's future impulse. And this seed can now begin to take root and sprout from the earth upward in the beginning of the second Michaelic century. All alone, Steiner pioneered this individual deed through his sacrifice and toil for humanity. We are invited to be as beginners, as he was when he conceived and wrote this humble book, *The Philosophy of Freedom*, the seed for the spiritualization of thinking, consciousness, and humanity and the earth in the future. He made it possible. And even despite the fact that not his but Heidegger's concept of the human triumphed over Europe and the whole globe, Steiner's deed made it possible that, in the historical moment in which "freedom [lighted] up in the human being for a single cosmic moment," freedom will not be lost. That, in the face of the fiercest evil of annihilation, brought about by so many "commanders of nothingness" all over the earth in the course of the 20th century, "...in the very same moment the human being would" *not any longer* "dissolve away." And therefore, indeed: "We are here pointing to the abyss of nothingness in human evolution which man must cross when he becomes a free being. It is the working of Michael and the Christ-impulse which makes it possible for him to leap across the gulf." Though on the much-hoped-for large scale this battle didn't take place at the end of the 20th century, I wanted to tell you that it still may become a fruitful and joyful seed of new life in each of our hearts. This was the sole purpose of my sharing tonight, "to make philosophy worthy of this event." I wanted to inscribe it here in my first working visit to France, Colmar, Alsace: to share with you some of my experiences in the last decades of the last century, in order to encourage you, too, to begin and become beginners of the now beginning, new Michaelic century.

# Lecture 2

## An Esoteric History of the 20th Century: Forces of Death and Resurrection in the History of Our Time (Järna 2004)

### Part 1: The World Situation in the 20th Century and in the Present

I WILL BEGIN BY A SHORT description of a spiritual-scientific esoteric *method,* which has developed since the beginning of the 21st century.[6] More and more people are asking for such a method, because they wish to become relevant to the world's real social needs. Social engagement is an esoteric art of living, of being active in the real world in a wholly transformed manner. Many well-meaning activists today, even those with anthroposophical backgrounds, want to change the world but they want to do this by means of improving the soul faculties that they already possess, in order to achieve greater results in influencing the social situation. There is no question, of course, that our ordinary soul qualities must be greatly improved. This will always belong to any true esoteric work. But this improvement of our ordinary faculties is not done in order that we will be more capable of changing things that we don't like and implementing things that we happen to like, because what we like and don't like is not at all important for the real world. It is about finding the way to know in the first place what is right from the point of view of the real world, not what we believe is right because of our likes and dislikes. But what does this mean in reality?

When we face any given situation or event, our task is first to transform it into "Event," with a capital E. What changes a small event into the big Event is this: that we struggle to find a way to get out of ourselves and our habitual soul patterns of reactions, which include our desires and wishes to "change" the social or political aspect of whatever world situation we confront. The whole point is precisely to get out of our habitual soul patterns, reactions, and desires, and not to seek for a way to improve them in order to change things according to our wishes. This means, not to grasp the event and use it for whatever we want to use it for, but to reverse this attitude entirely, to turn it inside out. To be grasped by the real spirit of event is what transforms the small "e" to a bigger "E." And this is possible only if I merge with a given event, or situation, and let the Event change me, instead of trying to change the event to suit my wishes and beliefs.

Being transformed by this merging, one becomes its expression; one becomes the Event's implementation, its self-actualization through one's self. But the same applies not only for our desires to change the external social world, but also for our inner desires to develop higher spiritual capacities and experiences. Both have the same problems: they wish to implement their own wishes, desires, likes and dislikes. How do we know if anthroposophical study and meditation are real events and not just self-reflecting, inflating, subjective illusions and dreams? *Only if they take us out of ourselves entirely, if they truly plunge us into the altogether different, non-personal, non-subjective, spiritual reality of the Event.* The difference between this experience and all others is as essential as the difference between, say, the experience of being burnt by real fire and a mental representation of fire. So the person that experiences the difference will never be prone to confuse it with subjective soul experiences, feelings and mental representations of thinking. Grasping an objective event means being reciprocally being grasped by IT. This is the essential difference between the subjective and objective in spiritual cognition and practice and in social activism and its practice, and this is therefore the beginning of true, social esotericism. Being grasped by an objective event, I am becoming this Event. I don't make an inner representation about it, or indulge in my sympathies and antipathies to it. The world situation becomes self-conscious through us, as we let objective events be transformed into intensively experienced, *heartfelt questions of conscience*. These must be strongly distinguished from the subjective soul reactions that we experience in each event.

The soul reactions are natural, and sometimes also justified (although often they are not), but the point is not if my reactions are justified or not from this or that point of view, but precisely that they are my natural, habitual, characteristic reactions in the first place. Events and situations occur in the real world. Your reactions can tell you a lot about yourself, if you are truly interested in acquiring real self-knowledge, which would mean to meet yourself objectively as a world Event as well. But your reactions will certainly tell you nothing about the essence of the real Event. If I notice my reactions and wholly put them aside for a short time at least, I can let the Event speak in its own language, in its own right. And I should feel this ever stronger: that the Events have the right to speak about themselves in me, not only to hear my soul chatter about them. In our hearts, we learn to listen to the Event's language and the Event's thinking, and what we hear is transformed into existential problems and questions. The hearts begin to have real, world-related, world-imbued, questions and problems. This means that if we truly experience that the problems have emerged from the world, we will no longer be happy with our own common *answers.* Because these new problems do not come from *our inner reactions*, pleasures and displeasures with the world, so also the answers will not originate there.

As the term "dialogue" has become overly psychologised, I am reluctant to apply it to the esoteric method of working with real, existential, spiritual events and processes. So let's say that the transformation occurring between external events and inner questioning allows the spiritual world to fire our hearts and offer its own interpretation of the Event, revealing its own perspective. We are not less free, but far more free now, to actualize what we perceive, as our sense of freedom has also been transformed in the process. I say, I want to be free to truly co-create with the will and thinking of the real Events and beings of the real world. This leads to an objective inspiration or an *Inspired Event* and the result is a fully individualized and embodied moral-social evaluation and judgment, which directs our will and resolution toward the truth of the matter at hand, awakening and firing our will, pointing to what needs to be done.

Can we let the objective spiritual content take us into itself instead of taking it into ourselves to use it for our personal aims and gains? And what is experienced when we let this happen? We would experience how we are assimilated so deeply into the objective contents of the event, be it a person we meet or any other event or process in the real world, until we are ready to become what it really is, which in any case, is not our own self. What a wonderfully refreshing experience to become a wholly different and unknown self, to forget all about our ordinary self, through the other. Then to experience, not the results of the privatization and appropriation of the other person to our own inner subjective reactions, needs, desires and interests, but the very opposite, the very reverse of this. How the other person, as an unknown, unexpected, often truly unsettling and perhaps "not nice" or pleasant being, is becoming so infinitely interesting and worthy of my love. And this means that the true esoteric life of the Event begins when I experience this "not I but the other in me" as a reality.

In this way, as Rudolf Steiner recommended, real spiritual events can flow as spontaneous impulses that can unite themselves with us because we feel that this is what we truly want to become, and that these are our own immanent spiritual ideals. Michael is a spirit of action, initiative, courage and universal human cooperation, who is beyond sectarian differences of language, culture, gender, religion and ideology. Esoteric life and practice of the Event, means, therefore: reversing our common and unconscious appropriation of each event, transforming each event into a real Event, working with the world's inspiring forces, with the other's inspiration of real forces. We work in and out of the given situation, changing and shaping social reality and changing ourselves as part of the world in which we work and strive.

---

The global situation today is shaped by a powerful American imperialism, working itself out and consolidating its power by means of two main strategies that encompass global social life as a whole. First, by the manipulation of the destiny of nations through fanning the flames of the clash of civilisations in the cultural and religious sphere, and second, via the major organizations and projects of elite globalization working in the sphere of global economy. The decidedly anti-human motto of the strategy of the *clash of civilizations* is described by Samuel Huntington when he says in the preface to his book on the subject (1996) that the moral maxim of "Western Christian-Jewish civilization" is: "There can be no true friends without true enemies. Unless we hate what we are not, we cannot love what we are." This total reversal and falsification of everything human and Christian is spoken out loud today, and is repeated — usually, not in such honest words but all the more in cultural, political and economic practice! — in all of the elite circles around the globe, as the truth of western civilization. However, nearly 2000 thousand years ego, Jews and Christians were persecuted and annihilated by the Roman Empire because they believed "Love thy neighbour as thyself," which is the exact opposite of what Huntington puts as moral maxim of western Judeo-Christianity today. And now these global Huntingtons are the leading spokesmen of what they call a western, 'Christian' civilization, while in truth they are the most dedicated disciples and apostles who proclaim a gospel of a fully contemporary American Imperialism! This is the Christianity of Bush, Clinton, and Gore.

During the 20th century and its three World Wars (WWI, WWII, and the Cold War), we lived in a time period with Europe at its center. But the US has been taking over step by step. It is a work in progress, where the US gradually takes over Europe in three stages, through three world wars. Europe allowed this because it could not find its true mission and goals. At the end of the 19th century, the *social question* arose in Europe in all fields of life. One powerful example is of course the rise of the proletariat, stirred by the industrial revolutions, but the leaders and the elite ignored their cries. They sat on a social volcano, but their lack of heart forces was enormous. This led to the rise of communism and Bolshevism in Russia, and to fascism and eventually to National Socialism in central Europe. Today the situation is the same. We have a huge social question, which the leading elite are ignoring with immense irresponsibility. But unlike the end of the 19th century and the beginning of the 20th, today the question is global, and the volcano is global. The irresponsibility of the elite leads them to believe that they can *control* the starving, poor, frustrated crowds with economic, cultural and military forces. What we see today as terrorism in Islam and elsewhere is a small beginning of what could erupt. The polarisation between the North-West and the South-East is pictured as follows:

- 1/6 to 1/5 of the world use 80% of the world's resources (*the golden billion*).

- 1/6 of the world population is actually starving (*the starving billion*).

- 2/6 of the world population, some 2 billion, live on 3 dollars a day. They are kept in a state of scarcely surviving.

- Some 2 billion are between the rich and poor and struggle to join the rich.

So 20% of the population use 80% of resources and 80% of the population use 20% of resources. The 400 richest have as much wealth as about 2.5 billion people, which is almost half the world population. It is important to *feel* what this means — not just to understand it. For the intellect these are "mere facts" to be registered in the brain. But the heart forces *hear* the suffering of billions of our human brothers and sisters in these facts. And our wills may also wish to act wisely, through compassion, and not in wild rage and revenge, but in quiet, constructive, and healing ways. The global social imbalance is the result of the evolution of humanity in the last four centuries. Since the birth of the Consciousness Soul or Spiritual Soul in the 15th century, this situation has emerged rather radically and quickly. We know that this step in evolution means the freeing of the Ego to self-consciousness and self-mastery, for good and ill.

The Consciousness Soul is striving at the same time in two polar directions, to the heights of morality and toward fierce egotism. On one hand it strives instinctively to achieve *freedom* in spiritual, religious and cultural life, *equality* and justice in political-democratic life, and for solidarity, *brotherhood*, in economic life. On the other hand, and at the same time, the opposite forces of egotism and personal isolation are increasing with an intensity never known before. Indeed, these two poles can become socially untenable, as the drive for "socialism" expresses in a chaotic manner the longing for brotherhood and community, while "capitalism" expresses the desire for unbounded individualism. In the course of the 19th and 20th centuries, both have polarized and divided society, destroying human trust and plunging humanity into untold destruction and suffering.

Now as we in the 5th cultural epoch recapitulate and evolve what was historically involved in the 3rd cultural epoch, the Babylonian-Egyptian period, it must be noted that this discrepancy between rich and poor is even greater than the most infamous discrepancy in the old Egyptian times. Today it is a global incongruity and not a local one as in ancient Egypt, Babylon or later in Rome. The poor are as globalized in their consciousness and general social life as the rich elites. And what is more, in the 3rd and also 4th cultural epochs, the poor and underprivileged people had very different experiences of human value and social equity than the global poor have today. Back then, the elite leaders were experienced as god-like, as actually closer to the gods than to ordinary humans, and the folk could still instinctively feel that their fabulous riches were a part of their divine heritage and responsibility, and that they were using them for the good of everyone.

So in the course of a few short centuries the social question as a modern issue arose with vehement intensity, to break loose in the events of the French revolution at the end of the 18th century. Since then human beings everywhere have instinctively developed more and more a desire for both equality and individual freedom, and they expect that the combination of freedom and equality will produce social brotherhood as major formative power in modern social life. They entertain a natural expectation for the sharing of human fortunes and misfortunes with their fellow human beings. Therefore, the masses will continue to revolt against the elite and their measures of suppression will increase.

The Anglo-American domination of the world, considered as a matter of a purely power interest, dates back to the end of the 19th century. Before that time, Kipling's "white's man burden," still had some idealistic meaning in certain elite circles, and *noblesse oblige*, still maintained a glimmer of reality. In western occultism it was taken as a matter of basic occult knowledge that in the 5th cultural epoch the Anglo-American nations are destined, according to their inborn capacities, to master the world and are responsible for ordering human affairs throughout the next 2160 years. Therefore, they imagine that it falls to them — and *not* to the Germans — to properly "educate" the Slavic-Russian people, destined to become the carriers of the next, 6th cultural epoch that will develop in the years 3573 — 5733. As Rudolf Steiner emphasized, these western circles are convinced that this can only take place successfully from their point of view, if the Germans are utterly prevented from establishing a strong spiritual-cultural and social center in Europe, becoming the educators of Russia in a spiritual-scientific direction.

But from the moment that this world conception was articulated in this wholly one-sided manner[7], Anglo-American politics *would have to* become a question of brute power and domination. Steiner said, "We have to do here with a group of people who want to dominate the earth by means of a *beweglichen kapitalistischen Wirtschaftimpulse* (a flexible and agile impulse for commerce and a capitalistic economy)." It is here that you find the origin of the basic social programmes and spiritual-geo-political world maps that describe how in the coming 20th century this world hegemony will be achieved. This hegemony was planned and executed by people that knew very well how to use the objective historical forces, laws and rhythms of evolution in the current age. Unhappily for humanity, the history of the 20th century is nothing but an exemplary lesson of an enormously successful, anti-Michaelic strategy, which actually defeated the good forces on all fronts and established an unsurpassed domination over all walks of human life. Schematically described, their plan was implemented in a threefold step, a triple pace, using as leverage the essential time structure and division of a century into three thirds. Externally, the map of this triple pace was painted with the blood and agony of untold millions of people in the course of three world wars and so many "small" wars in between.

The First World War was the expression of the first step in putting this plan into practice. In the US, the first step was building the powerful tool for influencing US policy throughout the 20th century. This tool was created by means of the establishment of the *Council on Foreign Relations* (CFR) during and right after the world war and the Versailles "peace conference." This was a vast, internal, reorganization manoeuvre, consolidating the elite's control of the US establishment and also their germinating independence. Of course, for the next half century the US still remained in close cooperation with their elder brothers in the city of London. I described this briefly in the first chapter of my book, *America's Global Responsibility*. During the preparations for WWI and between the wars, US elite politics were closely coordinated with the most influential circles in British politics, the inheritors and protégés of the definitive founder of the Anglo-American establishment, Lord Cecil Rhodes (1853–1902).[8] Cecil Rhodes life's zeal and goal was to manipulate affairs over the entire world through the higher echelons of Imperial Britain (Steiner says that such ideas are 'as huge as the world' in *The Karma of Untruthfulness*, Vol. 2, January 15, 1917, GA 174). This concept was to ensure Anglo-American domination of the world in the 20th century and beyond through specific strategies, and economic-political tools. In 1887, Rhodes writes:

> It often strikes a man to enquire what is the chief goal in life; to one the thought comes that it is a happy marriage, to another great wealth, and as each seizes on his idea, for that he more or less works for the rest of

his existence. To myself thinking over the same question the wish came to render myself useful to my country. I then asked myself how could I and after reviewing the various methods I have felt that at the present day we are actually limiting our children and perhaps bringing into the world half the human beings we might owing to the lack of country for them to inhabit that if we had retained America there would at this moment be millions more of English living. I contend that we are the finest race in the world and that the more of the world we inhabit the better it is for the human race. Just fancy those parts that are at present inhabited by the most despicable specimens of human beings what an alteration there would be if they were brought under Anglo-Saxon influence, look again at the extra employment a new country added to our dominions gives. I contend that every acre added to our territory means in the future birth to some more of the English race who otherwise would not be brought into existence. Added to this the absorption of the greater portion of the world under our rule simply means the end of all wars at this moment had we not lost America I believe we could have stopped the Russian-Turkish war by merely refusing money and supplies. Having these ideas what scheme could we think of to forward this object. I look into history and I read the story of the Jesuits I see what they were able to do in a bad cause and I might say under bad leaders. The idea gleaming and dancing before one's eyes like a will-of-the wisp at last frames itself into a plan. Why should we not form a secret society with but one object the furtherance of the British Empire and the bringing of the whole uncivilised world under British rule for the recovery of the United States for the making the Anglo-Saxon race but one Empire. ... What has been the main cause of the success of the Roman Church? The fact that every enthusiast, call it if you like every madman, finds employment in it. Let us form the same kind of society a Church for the extension of the British Empire. A society which should have its members in every part of the British Empire working with one object and one idea we should have its members placed at our universities and our schools and should watch the English youth passing through their hands.

(John Flint, *Cecil Rhodes*, Hutchinson, London, 1976, pp. 248-52)

Note the typical nationalistic and racist arguments Rhodes uses, that advocate population displacement, so the master race will have enough room to live and prosper, as well as complete control of the 'despicable specimens' of humanity by the master race. The German scientist and intellectual prophet of German Nazism, Oswald Spengler, in his *Decline and Fall of Civilization in the West* (1918), described the spirit of colonial expansion which possessed Rhodes as something, "daemonic and immense, which grips, forces into service and uses up mankind." Here is the clue to the careers of both Rhodes and Hitler: that at a point in their lives, they both encountered something "demonic." Rhodes met a 'ghost' soon after becoming a Mason, and Hitler met the 'new man' in an ecstatic experience in the early 1930s, according to Rauschning's *Hitler Speaks*. In the years after the end of the First World War, Rhodes began to receive attention from the European political right wing precisely because his career showed such an elemental will to power. Spengler regards Rhodes with almost mystical awe, as a prototype of a new sort of leader: "Rhodes is to be regarded as the first precursor of a western type of Caesar. He stands midway between Napoleon and the force-men of the next centuries....in our Germanic world, the spirits of Alaric and Theodoric will come again — there is a first hint of them in Cecil Rhodes."

The goal of WWI, as the first step in shaping the whole course of the 20th century, was to help Bolshevism to power in Russia, while developing National Socialism in a demoralized and humiliated Germany, and allowing the US to enter forcefully into European affairs. In between the two world wars, Old Europe was then left alone again with its own deteriorating moral and social resources, while the weakened and frustrated Germans accomplished their own total national collapse. Europe was destabilized as a whole.

The Second World War was the external expression of the second step taken to shape a new map of Europe and the world, and specifically to transfer world dominion from the British Empire to the US. The war ended with the final destruction of Germany, both morally and as a politically sovereign nation, and the division of Europe between the US and the Soviet Union, setting the terms for the coming cold war in the last third of the century. The rise of Hitler to power, from the point of view of realities, and not the *fable convenue* of external history, has yet to be told. Let it suffice here to point out that behind all the stages, from the failed Putsch in Munich in 1923 until the outbreak of WWII in 1939, it was a well coordinated plan, orchestrated by the western powers. They knew well that once Hitler's madness was set loose, he would never stop, and they could rest assured that Germany, as in WWI, could not survive a war waged on two fronts. Nobody in the inner circles ever believed in the longevity of the Molotov-Ribbentrop pact (promising non-aggression between the USSR and Germany). Indeed, from the beginning they counted on a prolonged, mutual annihilation of Germany and Russia, which would delay the US led invasion of Europe until after the Russians had already bled the Germans to death. In coordinating these plans, the inheritors of Rhodes' influence, assured the division of Germany and of Europe as a whole, the consolidation of Stalin's hold over Russia and Eastern Europe and the establishment of the Iron Curtain for the next half century. They helped build Stalinist Bolshevism in Russia to the level of *The Great Satan*, which stirred both fierce competition and economic expansion in the US during the Cold War.

Furthermore, just as the *Council on Foreign Relations* was established directly after WWI, as a long hand to direct domestic and world affairs according to the elite policies of the US, likewise, during WWII, the infamous *Bretton Woods Conference* took place (1944). In these meetings, the *International Monetary Fund* (IMF), the foundations for the *World Bank* (WB) and the first elements of the *World Trade Organization* (WTO) were formed, to set the terms of commerce, loans and development, according to the "Washington consensus," for the coming second half of the 20$^{th}$ century. Today we see the results of this consensus. These three evil brothers cooperate to control and parasitically suck the life forces out of the world. For example, the WTO requires open borders, a "free market," and the elimination of tariffs and taxes in order to maintain their global economic hegemony. But while the US and European forces dominating the WTO speak about a free market and a 'free' flow of goods, services and capital, at the same time they subsidize their own agricultural production with billions of dollars ("Government support for agriculture in the mostly rich countries of the OECD amounted to $252 billion in 2011, or 19% of total farm receipts," *The Economist*, Sept. 2012). The spending on agricultural subsidies in the rich nations is only exceeded by military spending, which amounts to almost

1 trillion dollars in the EU and the US alone. This leads the farmers in the rich nations to dump their products on poor countries at prices which are unrealistically low, destroying the economy and social life of developing nations. The farmers in the poor countries become desperate and many commit suicide; there were 20,000 suicides among Indian farmers alone reported for 2003. In the WTO negotiations in Cancun, Mexico, a leading Korean farmer committed an honorary suicide to show his solidarity with desperate farmers in the world.

Thus the WTO completely undermines the basic social structures in poor countries, and so a vicious circle begins. Farmers cannot live off their farming; they move to the city slums and become part of the huge urban problem. This leads governments of poor countries to borrow money from the IMF in order to solve these social problems. But then the IMF imposes socially devastating "structural adjustments," which inflict severe budget cuts in these poor nations and essentially undermine public education, health care, and infrastructure. In other words, they undermine all those things one wished to expand by taking the loan. Now, obviously, the poor country cannot pay back the loans or survive under such a heavy debt burden. The same scenario applies to many undertakings of the World Bank. For example, in my book, *America's Global Responsibility*, you can see detailed examples of how the Asian economy was destroyed during the economic crisis of 1997-98.

Now, the WTO should become a global economic association, in which consumers, traders, and producers regulate economic life themselves. The World Bank and the IMF really both belong to the third, cultural and spiritual sphere. Handling capital and banking is a spiritual and moral matter, and must be entrusted to the free, third sector of society; for in Europe and elsewhere, the third sector has entirely become a state supported appendage. Even most anthroposophical institutions have become state supported, so we must look for free human spirits, who can again begin to think and act in the original sense of threefolding. New moral forces are needed in order to decide what to develop for human existence. Any alternatives to the IMF will not work as long as they are within the political framework. They must be made *free*, and go into the cultural sphere.[9]

As we continue looking at the 20th century as a whole, it should be clear that the third world war was the cold war that led to an atomic "balance" of angst, which contained humanity from the beginning of the '60s until the collapse of the Soviet Union in 1990. Only the problem of Yugoslavia remained to hinder the US domination of Europe. There, under the somewhat moderate and independent Tito regime, real seeds of cooperation were developing between Christians and Muslims. This amounted to a stark violation of the clash of civilizations theory. So with the help of Europe, especially Germany and France, who were working as Washington's accomplice, in ten short years Yugoslavia was demolished and divided. A policy of 'divide and conquer' was practiced with much excellence by the Clinton administration and was brought to bear on Bosnia-Herzegovina in the Dayton agreement in 1995, which divided the nation into three artificial cantons, ruled since then as a western protectorate. The last action of this war was the US led destruction of Serbia by NATO, for the first time without UN authorization, setting precedence for the Bush administration's unilateral strategy and military policy.

Having achieved its 20th century goals by conquering Europe, the American Empire can now continue to its

21st century strategy, where they can encircle Russia on all sides, from Asia to the Persian Gulf region. In Brzezinski's classic book, *The Grand Chessboard* (1997), which is a manual for practicing imperial geopolitics in the 21st century, you will find that:

> The last decade of the twentieth century has witnessed a tectonic shift in world affairs. For the first time ever, a non-Eurasian power has emerged not only as the key arbiter of European power relations, but also as the world's paramount power. The defeat and collapse of the Soviet Union was the final step in the rapid ascendance of a Western Hemispheric power, the United States, as the sole and, indeed, the first truly global power. Eurasia, however, retains its geopolitical importance. For America...the chief prize is Eurasia.
>
> (pp. xiii-xiv)

The geopolitical tool created to achieve these and other aims in all parts of the world, including Israel-Palestine, the Persian Gulf Region and the former Yugoslavia, is Islamic terrorism. In an interview given to the French paper, *Le Nouvel Observateur*, Brzezinski felt he could finally speak openly about the covert US support for the Mujahideen in Afghanistan in 1979:

> Le Nouvel Observateur: Former CIA director Robert Gates states in his memoirs that the American secret services began six months before the Soviet intervention to support the Mujahideen [in Afghanistan]. At that time you were President Carter's security advisor; thus you played a key role in this affair. Do you confirm this statement?
>
> Zbigniew Brzezinski: Yes. According to the official version, the CIA's support for the Mujahideen began in

1980, i.e. after the Soviet army's invasion of Afghanistan on 24 December, 1979. But the reality, which was kept secret, is completely different: actually it was on 3 July, 1979 that President Carter signed the first directive for the secret support of the opposition against the pro-Soviet regime in Kabul. And on the same day I wrote a note, in which I explained to the president that this support would, in my opinion, lead to a military intervention by the Soviets.

Le Nouvel Observateur: Despite this risk, you were a supporter of this covert action? But perhaps you expected the Soviets to enter this war and tried to provoke it?

Zbigniew Brzezinski: It's not exactly like that. We didn't push the Russians to intervene, but we knowingly increased the probability that they would do it.

Le Nouvel Observateur: When the Soviets justified their intervention with the statement that they were fighting against a secret US interference in Afghanistan, nobody believed them. Nevertheless there was a core of truth to this...Do you regret nothing today?

Zbigniew Brzezinski: Regret what? This secret operation was an excellent idea. It lured the Russians into the Afghan trap, and you would like me to regret that? On the day when the Soviets officially crossed the border, I wrote President Carter, in essence: "We now have the opportunity to provide the USSR with their Vietnam War." Indeed for ten years Moscow had to conduct a war that was intolerable for the regime, a conflict which involved the demoralization and finally the breakup of the Soviet Empire.

Le Nouvel Observateur: And also, don't you regret having promoted Islamic fundamentalism, and helping future terrorists, having given them weapons and advice?

Zbigniew Brzezinski: What is most important for world history? The Taliban or the fall of the Soviet Empire? Some Islamic hotheads or the liberation of Central Europe and the end of the cold war?

Le Nouvel Observateur: "Some hotheads?" But it has been said time and time again: today Islamic fundamentalism represents a world-wide threat...

Zbigniew Brzezinski: Rubbish! It's said that the West has a global policy regarding Islam. That's hogwash: there is no global Islam. Let's look at Islam in a rational and not a demagogic or emotional way. It is the first world religion with 1.5 billion adherents. But what is there in common between fundamentalist Saudi Arabia, moderate Morocco, militaristic Pakistan, pro-Western Egypt and secularized Central Asia? Nothing more than that which connects the Christian countries.[10]

On the economic and social side of this twofold strategy, the three evil brothers, born during the Second World War, have had an immensely detrimental influence on the global situation in the last third of the 20th century. As a result, the world has become a sick social and ecological organism. The *head system* (the rich countries in the North and West) sucks all the life from the *metabolic system* (the poor countries in the South) and the middle *heart and lung system* suffered a heart attack, heart failure, or even a heart transplant in the 20th century. The head cannot think properly, because of the overwhelming amount of unnecessary life forces that it greedily sucks into itself from the rest of the world. The head system is vegetating up there and the people are transforming themselves into Ahriman's puppets; he works through them, planning and organizing social life. Instead of developing a fully human, heart-felt intelligence, we see instead a dreamy consciousness engulfing the North, which is not *awake* to what is going on in the world. The multitudes in the South are robbed and deprived of their life forces and are thus forced to awaken in an erratic and immoral way, through the pain and frustration, to which they are subjected. In the East and South, the nations are condemned to rebel against the West and North, and to also succumb in this way to the other, more Luciferic, forces of evil. The balancing and harmonizing middle system, the heart and lungs, the global rhythmic system, should have been centered in middle Europe. But Europe was taken over by the Ahrimanic forces of the West and was assimilated into the US Empire. Europe has thus left the East and South to themselves, and has become simply an appendage and tool of the western, Anglo-American forces.

This is where humanity stands at the beginning of the 21st century: there is an increasingly destructive polarization and division between all of the hemispheres, the rich and poor, with no regulating, harmonizing, global heart and lung system in the middle. It cannot breathe. This is the reason why the 21st century starts with a sick planetary organism. The poor are all too conscious of the global reality, and their pain and frustration increases as they see the rich western and northern nations wallowing in wealth. The rich are stupefied by their affluence and their heart forces decline and become stunted. The proletariat is now not only a European group, but a global situation concerning two thirds of humanity. The rich and powerful in the North-West, dream away their responsibility for humanity, trying to isolate themselves far from realities of the poor.

We need to create the heart and lung system everywhere in the world, in order to heal this sickness.

These are, therefore, the stark realities and challenges facing humanity at the beginning of the 21st century. It faces anyone that honestly seeks to become part of a true contemporary spiritual movement. Now global civil society, if we may use this term, will only fulfil its role if it becomes involved in such true spiritual life. Civil society truly understands itself only if it really seeks to connect itself to real spiritual life, and to not the traditions of our spiritual and cultural institutions. It will succeed only if it connects to the presently active and creative spiritual experience and research and through them, with the spiritual worlds and beings that guide humanity's evolution in our time.

## An Esoteric History of the 20th Century (Järna 2004)

Part 2: Forces of Resurrection at the End of the 20th Century and Today. The Mutual Relationships between Humanity's New Social Impulses and Spiritual Science

The situation in the world today is not a chance happening, but a result of a well planned strategy.[11] It is portrayed as chance and chaos by the media, but this is only a mask created so that one can allow the strategies behind it to develop undisturbed by public interference. However, enough is published and discussed in the open to reveal what the real plans are. Of course, the good forces also have their divine, long term plans. Rudolf Steiner described these forces, and how they can be used for the best for humankind as a whole.[12] But the same knowledge is possessed also by those who use it to benefit only small groups of human beings, causing thereby untold damage and suffering to humanity and the earth. In reality, there are plenty of resources on the Earth for everybody, if we only worked in a compassionate and hence economically and politically balanced way.

The good evolutionary forces could hardly find anyone to listen, let alone to do something, during most of the 20th century, until its very end. The ruling elite felt extraordinarily triumphant the more we drew close to the year 2000. They saw their work of global dominance near completion and felt they could progress undisturbed. After Europe's spiritual defeat in the first and second thirds of the last century, the West had its chance during the third section, starting with the 1960s. Despite the fact that anthroposophy was not spiritually reactivated, much was truly happening in the peripheral fields. There were remarkable developments in North and South America, Europe and Asia, with the human rights movement, struggles against the Vietnam War, student revolts, and a strongly felt change of consciousness and values on the part of the younger generation. However, the older generations remained passive and feared the new ascent of future forces. They preferred to protect the old establishments and allowed the elites to come back online quite quickly in the 1970s and '80s, "correcting" their errors of the '60s. In the US, for example, they did away with the two Kennedy brothers who entertained (at least in their higher selves) other ideas about the war in Vietnam, relations with Russia and East Europe and some social and economic issues that were not well received in Wall Street. "*Ich bin ein Berliner*," declared JFK in his famous 1963 speech in Berlin, upsetting his elite mentors a great deal with his suggestions that the cold war could soon be over, quite contrary to their plans to continue it until the end of the century. They also did away with Martin Luther King Jr., who could have become a candidate for presidency, bringing with him a deep and powerful moral, human, and spiritual element into politics. The good forces were brutally suppressed, of course. *But the law is that impulses from higher spiritual and moral forces cannot be entirely eradicated, only suppressed and hence postponed.*

The real issue here is that, the general evolution of human consciousness and the growth of new moral and spiritual forces, must find their way into spiritual science. But only real spiritual science can relate to them, not only externally, but by finding the inner, fully conscious entry into the spiritual worlds that nourish them unconsciously. Until this happens, no true advance will be possible for humanity as a whole. This is the cause of the catastrophes of the 20th century. In each third, a new impulse was given, coming directly from the spiritual world, guided by the powers of *Michael and Christ* (this is what we can call them in our western, anthroposophical, Judeo-Christian jargon, for want of better names). They sought the hearts of human beings, in which this supersensible Event of the 20th century, and its impulses flowing through multiple offspring in all fields of life and thought, could be consciously grasped by spiritual scientific cognition **in real time**, that is, in each moment of history. Only if the impulses coming from Michael and Christ, living and active in this very historical moment, would have been experienced and embodied as individualized, spiritual scientific experience, and then transformed into strong and vital thinking and feeling and applied in practical social life, could they have been able to unite with the same impulses which flowed into humanity in a more unconscious way. With each new third of the century (and with each new day), they could have entirely changed the destiny of humanity in the course of the 20th century, but in the first and second thirds, they were almost wholly suppressed.

At the beginning of the third segment, during the 1960s, something escaped total suppression, something was beginning to grow, but it was coming from the unconscious, beneficial, positive growth forces of young people, who brought these energies from the spiritual worlds indirectly, from the life before birth. The youth were looking unconsciously for other people that could achieve the same experience here and now, in the physical world, who would be connected here and now in full and active cognition and consciousness, with what they brought with them unconsciously as young people from the same spiritual being and impulses. At the end of the last century (and even more today) these youthful individuals were striving to become more mature, they were striving to spiritualize themselves and achieve spiritual experience and perspective, as real active social inspiration. Then they could have entered the new 21st century, already united with the conscious, spiritual scientific centre. But the necessary coming together of the peripheral (unconscious) and central (fully conscious) impulses and forces of the time, was not accomplished on any grand scale. Rather, as we shall see, it only took place in a small and distant site, but nevertheless in a seed-like, potent and positive way.

The first seeds that sprouted after the long winter came from the periphery and not from the "mother field" (the Michaelic school and its impulse), which was still mostly asleep and dormant in the '60s. These seeds developed somewhat in the '60s, but without the support of the mother field, they could hardly become what they were intended to become, because the forces that young people bring with them from the spiritual world before birth die out in the middle of their own earthy life. There, in the middle of earthly life, they either die completely or become institutionalized, normalised and politicized. If they are merely connected consciously with spiritual knowledge in abstract form, already traditional and institutionalized, the forces die out. It is only with real living people who embody conscious spiritual experience and practice real spiritual research and its social applications that these youthful forces can continue to develop.

Now the time of the final test of this possibility in so far as the 20th century was concerned, came at the very last minute, at the end of the '90s. The '60s generation, who still remained faithful to their original moral experience, were tested in this regard. Many, of course, had already left the path long ago, but some continued on into the '90s and for the first time in the whole 20th century there was a moment of real objective chance. This is conditioned by objective karma, and what I am telling you here is only possible because of this objective karma. It was possible that, at one, rather peripheral and remote place (as I said, the mother field was dormant in the central regions and organs), such a meeting would take place, where the unconscious moral impulse, flowing through what became known as "civil society" would meet a consciously creative, contemporary, spiritual science. It was seeking — again I emphasize, in a very remote and peripheral site — to find connection to a spiritually real and conscious Anthroposophy. You know that according to the former Michaelic plan, which I call plan A, described by Rudolf Steiner in his karma lectures of 1924, it was planned that Anthroposophy and the Time Spirit should converge consciously and creatively on a grand scale by the end of the last century. We will study this in more detail in the next lecture.

This did not happen *as planned*, and although it is also not seen nor understood today, it is still important to point out that it *did happen*...but only as a small, invisible, yet nevertheless true, vital and vibrant, peripheral seed. This seed exists and it still works today, although it is mostly unrecognized by the streams and traditions of social activism and anthroposophy. This mighty transformation that was hoped for did become operative. It was, however, not the formerly planned global culmination of the 20th century, but, being a seed of this culmination, it did become a linking thread between the two centuries, between the two Michaelic plans, A and B. It is a first glimpse, a quintessence of what was started by Steiner at the beginning of the 20th century and what the spiritual leadership of this stream is intending today, at the beginning of the second Michaelic plan for the 21st century. Being small as it truly is, this seed is yet incredibly potent, and has already changed the real course to human history for the better, though again, externally speaking, this is hardly visible.

This seed is so powerful because it is the true Michaelic, Anthroposophical seed for the 21st century that faithfully carries the past in itself, without sacrificing the real, living, contemporary, supersensible stream. It unites both, for this is the essence of any seed, after all, to be the bridge between past and future plants. Some people, as single, isolated individuals, representing the best '60s generation, were working in cultural and social activism and innovation and were at least striving to become spiritually conscious. Through them, in some respects, it is true to say that Civil Society really matured over 30 years and began to change world affairs in the '90s. Some of the leaders of Civil Society were of the '60s generation — no longer flower children, but more mature and serious bearers of the voice of humanity's moral conscience. And karma did prepare a real meeting, right at the end of the century, at the very last moment, between them and authentic, living spiritual science. But before I describe this meeting, let us look at the struggles and achievements of socially and politically orientated Civil Society at the end of the last century.

For example, in 1992 at the World Summit in Rio, Civil Society made its first visible appearance on a large scale, influencing world powers to sign the Kyoto agreement. Then came the Battle in Seattle against the WTO in 1999, as a result of the careful preparations and sacrificial activity of millions of dedicated individuals and organizations in the Civil Society movement. The collapse of the WTO in Cancun in 2003 was the final result of the whole powerful impulse of the 1990s. The poor countries had endured enough of the lies and empty promises. So 22 countries walked out of the meeting and thanked Civil Society for their support and help.

One little known but immensely important victory of global Civil Society, took place at the very end of the century, right before the victory in Seattle. This was the stopping of MAI (Multilateral Agreement on Investments) by various NGOs. These secret processes, directed by the most influential circles among the OECD countries, would have given unlimited legal power for foreign investors over national sovereignty and legislation. It would have cemented the lid over world investment and finances. Work on MAI was totally secret and not covered by the 'free media.' It was necessary to keep it secret because the elite knew that MAI would not be accepted by anyone who could see the consequences of such an agreement. In 1941, where plans for a preliminary WTO, IMF and World Bank were worked out, it was not necessary to keep such secrecy because everyone was engaged with the war. Now the situation was totally different and it needed to be top secret. But, God interfered, speaking through the voice of conscience. It was only because a high official felt moral shame for what was going on and leaked the plan of the MAI to a Civil Society organisation, that the relevant information was spread widely. And this was the death blow for the MAI, because free access to information and knowledge is what these powers detest the most. Now the greatest enemy to the elite is Civil Society with its conscience and morality, and the feeling of shame in the face of the global injustice and corruption.

Another aspect of this time must be mentioned here as well, because it is directly connected to any phenomenological-historical study of the end of the last century. At the beginning of the 1990s, a paper delivered at the Prince of Wales Economic Forum introduced the notion of Threefolding for the first time, via the concept of "tri-sector" society, into the world of elite circles and organizations. In this study, Civil Society was represented as the third, cultural-spiritual sector. Soon the UN adopted the tri-sector approach and created a vast network of "tri-sector partnerships." The World Bank (WB) followed suit, and since then, former WB president, James Wolfensohn, will not give a public speech without proclaiming the gospel of cooperation between business, governments and Civil Society. The WB has invested large sums in such plans and projects ever since. In the '90s the good forces did arrive to prevent a total catastrophe. Certainly Civil Society was asleep in Yugoslavia, but it was awake in the economic sphere. The elite wished to seal their work, and cap it with a stone to ensure that it would proceed as they wished. But the grave is still open, the stone is not there, and new possibilities for resurrection exist everywhere.

In the period between 1995 and '99 when the MAI would have augmented the WTO, it was global Civil Society which put on the brakes. Precisely in this very crucial time, there was a battle against the emerging WTO in the Philippines and southeast Asia in which an anthroposophist and Alternative Nobel Prize winner, Nicanor Perlas, played a role. Much became possible at this point and much was at stake. But yet again, it all depended on the extent to which its task could be raised to real, full, spiritual scientific consciousness.

At this moment, I received an e-mail from Nicanor Perlas with an invitation to participate in a conference remarkably entitled: *Globalization, Threefolding and Anthroposophy.* Perlas asked me to give the keynote lecture in this conference in October '98 in Manila. I asked myself, naturally, if this could be a hopeful sign that something was changing within the anthroposophical movement, at least in the far periphery. I wondered if this change would for the first time make possible a real connection between a conscious, supersensible experience and research and some contemporary social activism. I was aware of the fact that at the very same time the MAI was collapsing. In the last years of the 20th century, hope was there for the connecting of the mother field with its peripheral offspring, which could express itself also in Civil Society.

Now what I stressed repeatedly in my lecture in Manila in October, 1998, and have emphasized ever since is this: only if actual spiritual research — not traditional knowledge and repetitions of old forms — is brought to fertilise social activism, will we see a new spiritual-social movement arise in the 21st century. In this respect not only social activists but also anthroposophists entertain many illusions! I have seen it again and again in social life, for example, when people strive to implement what they understand as "social threefolding" and other, related spiritual scientific concepts. What is misunderstood is that it is not about learning new concepts and implementing them. First, spiritual science itself, which gave these concepts to the world a century ago, out of the creative, actual work of Steiner, must be experienced and transformed within ourselves. It must first become a real, creative and fruitful spiritual and human activity now. We need to learn a wholly new, creative and free, spiritual and social activity if we are to realize social threefolding in practice out of the needs of the real, contemporary, spiritual world.

However, the aftermath of the Manila conference proved that most human souls and hearts were not yet really willing to open themselves to receive the new spiritual impulses and revelations and implement them in new social practices. The courage is simply lacking to face the real spiritual world, the real spiritual practice, and the real meeting with ourselves through the meeting with our fellow humans. But there were hopeful signs. Let me offer another historical example of this now from a far away site: Israel. Symptomatically, this event took place immediately at the beginning of the new millennium and the 21st century.

I share this as an example of the new resurrection forces working through some Israeli Christians and Muslim Arabs, who initiated and realized a remarkable expedition to Auschwitz (May 2003), which also a group of Israeli Jews joined. These Arabs and Israelis, led by the Catholic Father, Emil Shofani, and the ex-communist, Muslim journalist, Mr. Nazir M'agali, came to such a moral intuition because of their deep and heartfelt carrying of the fate of the state of Israel and the Jewish people. They took this courageous step at the time in which the suffering of their Palestinians brothers and sisters in the occupied territories reached inhuman proportions. They said: *if we want to find the way to the future, we must now carry the wound of the Jewish people, otherwise, all our efforts for peace and cooperation will continue to be shattered. Until now, each side represented its own wound, and tried to listen the best that it could to the story of the wound of the other. But this approach doesn't work. It's too weak. What can we do beyond this?* They described how they underwent a long period of doubt and helplessness. But they never gave up the will to achieve the good, even when everything seemed to fail, and past achievements disappeared under waves of violence and bloodshed. Indeed, at the moment of greatest doubt and pain came this inspiration: we must now take on the wound of the Jews, if we want to understand the coming into existence of the State of Israel and our own Palestinian fate connected with it in such a painful way.

What a great example of moral intuition, imagination, and technique, which came into being as a result of an inspired dialogue with the supersensible worlds! What an inspired example of a practical, intuitive-moral realization of such an impulse on the earth! The Palestinians made this sacrifice, moving from the natural and justified identification with their own personal and national wound, to embrace and carry the wound of the other. Thus they joined hands and hearts with the Time Spirit and the modern Christ Impulse, demonstrating the universally human as a reality and producing forces of healing in one of humanity's most burning historical wounds, namely, the intertwined destiny of Muslims, Christians and Jews.

So you see, at the time in which Arabs, Palestinians, and the Islamic religion are branded by such representatives of "Christianity" as Clinton, Bush and Huntington, as being outside of the "western Christian civilization," the true Christ Impulse works through a group of Israelis-Palestinians-Muslims-Christians-Jews. The time is now here, when Rudolf Steiner's words, with which he closes the intimate esoteric lecture cycle about the mysteries of the Holy Grail, can indeed come true:

> Shall the light of the East meet the Light from the West…? Let us [in Europe] make ourselves ready and capable to understand the Christ — that we shall not misunderstand Him — when He shall perhaps in the future speak to us, when the time for this is ripe — when other confessions of the Earth shall be inspired by His impulse!" (*Christ and the Spiritual World: the Search for the Holy Grail*, GA 149, January 2, 1914)

When I met Father Shofani in Nazareth, I asked him the same question I had raised in Manila, 'How do you see the continuation of this impulse in Israel?' He looked at me with his wisdom filled eyes and smiled, 'This is God's will. He will inspire us as he did before, and what will happen is not in our hands.' Now, don't think I didn't realize the truth of his words. Of course I did. And yet, another truth was just as clear to me as he spoke. For, the aftermath of both the Manila and the Nazareth impulses (and other similar ones, like South Africa's remarkable moral strides) has demonstrated that in our modern times, even the most significant moral impulses will necessarily die out if they are not taken up consciously by spiritual-scientific activity. But this activity must be able to penetrate **consciously every day anew** to the same sources out of which these impulses are presently flowing.

We must emphasize again and again that special impulses are given by the spiritual world — thanks to God! But while we experience the truth and greatness of such Events of grace, and admire the people that sacrifice their lives in order to realize them, we must also be clear that spiritual science can only become productive if it becomes an ongoing, daily, active and creative work. More and more people can learn to consciously experience the spiritual sources of these impulses and can tend them physically on the earth. Only such a spiritual science will bring us forward, and whatever is flowing into humanity by way of the graceful social and moral impulses described above, must be united with actual — not traditional, not theoretical — spiritual scientific research and its various updated social implementations. It all must be become fully conscious in our age, in order to become truly fruitful in the cultural and social life of humanity in the course of the 21st century.

## An Esoteric History of the 20th Century (Järna 2004)

### Part 3: The History and Counterfactual History of the Anthroposophical Movement and Society in the 20th Century

Let me start again by emphasizing the esoteric method that should permeate our exoteric work today.[13] We should let events and realities speak to us and our inner heart forces, and our conscience should contemplate, shape, and reflect on them in order to transform these realties into destiny questions. Our questioning activity then becomes a dialogue with the spirit of the real world, and not with our own concepts and mental pictures. This prepares the ground for an objective spiritual activity and judgment that comes neither from "outside," nor from "within," but from the spiritual world, in which we are living, moving and becoming together. But we should be aware of the old concepts, phrases, social routines and well established habits of spiritual work, which keep popping up in us. Our being as a whole, through the mutual interchange with the essence of the other as Event, in continuous dialogue with the real world, as described above, will make new, socially shared, thinking, feeling and acting possible. We should put old things aside and let experience speak, let ourselves be renewed by the spirit of the living, actual incident, on all levels of soul, spirit and practice; we must let the new spiritual Event of our age alone be our guide.

Our human understanding and realization of spiritual science is still new and immature in the physical world, and of course, we must make mistakes time and time again. However, we should be proudly conscious of our mistakes (the little child is proud when she falls, because she is so immersed and happy in the process of learning something new). We should not hide them because we are ashamed that we are not yet 'perfect!' We must be humble enough to be proudly imperfect, because those "perfect" imitations of what the living, ever changing and creative spirit of Rudolf Steiner left behind in the physical world, are responsible for the most spiritually and socially retarded forces that have worked over the last hundred years. To imitate and perpetuate the finished forms that he created in the time, space and cultural-social conditions applicable a century ago, is to hinder the true advancement of spiritual science.

But we can learn to work more honestly and fruitfully with each new Michaelic century. So now we have a new opportunity to learn how to work with the basic forces and dynamics of spiritual science. Historically, the consciousness soul is also still new, the global situation is new, and spiritual science as a free spiritual, cognitive and moral activity is new. Therefore we have a long path of learning ahead of us and it is no wonder that we do things wrong. We are all as little children learning to walk. But are we aware of this fact? Do we know that we are children exploring a new territory? Because children also learn very fast, and are open and fresh, seeing the world constantly with new eyes and hearts.

We can compare the 3 full centuries of the present Michaelic age (the whole age is 354 years, 1879-2234) to the first three years of a child's life: these centuries are the first three earthly stages of the development of the consciousness soul. The seeds of all future development are planted there and this time will end with the first experience of the spiritually independent individuality. When the Michaelic age ends, humanity should have developed the strength of a spirit-filled and inwardly guided self, consciously connected to the spiritual worlds. This will be needed in the coming age, because between the 23rd and 26th centuries the Time Spirit will be Oriphiel, who is the very opposite of Michael. Michael is the Christ Sun Power. Oriphiel is a Saturn power, wholly separating humanity from any external spiritual guidance and revelation. He is the darkening spirit, who eclipsed the sun at the time of the mystery of Golgotha, a force of complete darkness. The only power we human beings will have in his age is that which *we create within ourselves*. Therefore it is important that at the end of the Michael age there shall be some human beings who can actively, creatively, and independently actualize the productive powerful forces of Spirit Self. Today we have the 20th century, the first full century of the present Michaelic age, behind us, and we need to clearly see what has happened and what we need to prepare for the second and third Michaelic centuries (the 21st and 22nd centuries).

A truly spiritual scientific history of the 20th century has yet to be written, both for humanity as a whole, as well as for the anthroposophical movement as part of humanity. We shall call what spiritual science had to accomplish in the course of the 20th century, the first Michaelic century, Michael's **plan A**. In this plan, spiritual science was meant to be developed as the freshest, self-updating, creative spiritual stream throughout the whole century, starting gradually from the centre, and working towards the world periphery until the end of the century. It was then to undergo a metamorphosis, a reversal inside out, an inversion of centre and periphery, a real *Umstülpung*, to become a global spiritual-social movement. However, this plan failed to materialize, as nobody but Steiner really carried it, and it came to an end with his death. Therefore, when we look around us into the physical world, embodied in the institutions and cultural forms, norms and habits that have been handed down through three generations, we only see the remnants of plan A.

Rudolf Steiner created and embodied a centre under his leadership in the Christmas Foundation Conference, because all his previous efforts from 1902 until 1923 to encourage his pupils to become independent co-workers failed. He expressed his final hope very clearly during all of his lectures in 1924: that a living community of free humans could carry this new spiritual and social impulse with him as partners. The Christmas Foundation conference only sought to help his pupils realize this hope. He was waiting for a sign that the new impulse was understood and could be carried by his pupils as they became true partners. So, after remaining in the periphery of the Anthroposophical Society for so long, not even becoming a member, and hoping that his pupils would be able to create a true society and community, he finally took it upon himself (by default, because he was left alone in any case).

Now he had to decide, as he explained in 1923, if he should leave these people and work alone or if he should found a society by himself, carrying the whole on his shoulders. When he chose the 2nd option, which meant an immensely painful sacrifice on his part, he really decided to take the failures and shortcoming of his followers upon himself. He did not choose this option to do their work in their stead, on the contrary, but to help them do it in a new way. Of course, he had to start his new impulse, as any foundation must do, with one teacher, one geographical space in middle Europe, the hill in Dornach, and one spiritual-social structure that he founded all by himself, the new General Anthroposophical Society. If plan A would have been realized, this centralization would have been gradually and organically transformed in the course of the whole 20th century, and today we would have had a totally different, that is, inverted, form and substance.

Spiritual science was initiated with the intention that it would grow energetically and creatively as a social-cultural impulse, from one third of the 20th century to the next, from one generation to the next, reaching a stage of maturity and transformation, that Steiner called a 'culmination' at the end of the century. But world karma took a different, opposite, course. This caused the premature death of Rudolf Steiner and furthermore, the development of the movement essentially stopped. Speaking purely spiritually, in regard to its true esoteric development and external world mission, spiritual science didn't even take a single step forward. It had been intended that spiritual science should be a force that would take deep root in middle Europe, and become influential in guiding Europe in external social, political, and cultural aspects.

As I indicated in my book, *The Spiritual Event of the 20th Century*, counterfactual research of the history of the 20th century reveals that Steiner should and could have reached his 72nd year precisely in the most significant year of the 20th century, 1933. This would have enabled spiritual science — if it had become a living, active movement and community of free and creative people — to confront the new powers of evil with the new Christ forces. Then it could have continued to grow into the 1950s and '60s, expanding from Europe to the whole world, to reach a culmination at the end of the 20th century as in plan A of Michael. At this culmination, new impulses would have been given for the 21st century. The movement would have united itself with other kindred spiritual movements and individuals, reversing itself inside out and outside in, finally becoming oriented towards the first truly global century of humanity.

It was as Steiner repeatedly emphasized, that was the main task of spiritual science to prepare Europe for what came up so powerfully from the 1930s onward, the new, etheric, Christ Event and the simultaneous confrontation with its evil opposite, the so-called apocalyptic "Beast" (which is essentially our own lower self as humanity). Humanity was now already far beyond the threshold, and the question was whether we would become conscious of this fact or not. Unfortunately, humanity did not. If the threshold would have been crossed consciously through spiritual science with the conscious recognition and social application of the new Christ forces, then one could have confronted the evil in oneself in the real time of its historical emergence. This was the good Michaelic plan, which Steiner described in 1924.

But human beings in our time have a wholly new relationship to the divine plan, because we live in the Michaelic age of freedom. We are free either to understand and consciously work with God, or to reject His ideas altogether and do the very opposite of what He kindly suggests. For the 20th century, humanity chose the wrong path. Humanity rejected Michael's plan with an overwhelming dedication to evil, bringing about catastrophes beyond the worst that could have been imagined in the past. It may help if we consider this situation more objectively, that is, not only as the result of this or that person's failure, but really as part of humanity's karma. So it came to pass that in 1933 there was no difference between what happened among those representing spiritual science and what happened inside humanity as a whole. In Dornach, as in any other place, humanity was entirely confused in the moral judgment concerning good and evil. Evil was called good and good was called evil, not in Germany alone but also among anthroposophists and throughout the whole world. In Dornach and Germany it was especially tragic because of the special mission that this society and this people had in the 20th century. After all, the Germans chose Hitler instead of Steiner, to put it rather drastically but nonetheless accurately (just like two thousand years before, when the Jews, who pioneered all modern historical reversals, chose the Roman emperor instead of Jesus). We know that spiritual science should have been spread far enough in Europe and in Germany especially, in order to enable humanity to understand *that if one is on the other side of the threshold without conscious spiritual understanding, one experiences a fatal reversal — things become their opposite.* Christ is seen as evil and the evil forces and beings are perceived to be Christ and his angels.

The karmic task of the German people had been to accept spiritual science, for which they had the right preconditions. But they took the opposite course in the 20th century and will have to first come to terms with this fact, in order to be able to legitimately approach their mission in the 21st century. In 1933, the second coming of Christ was neither seen nor understood, and therefore was transformed into its opposite. This is the basic law of reversal: the historical expression of the hope of freedom and love on the one hand, and the tragedy involved in misuse of free will and the truly unlimited modern human capacity for error and betrayal on the other.

Now, there is also some good news. As I experienced and researched at the end of the 20th and the beginning of the 21st centuries, I found that what did not happen on earth did indeed take place in the spiritual worlds in the second third of the century, especially in the 12 years, 1933-1945 (see *The Spiritual Event of the 20th Century*). What was prepared there **is a wholly new Michaelic plan, Plan B, for the 21st century**. Our task now must be, first, to awaken from the traumatic sleep and forgetfulness of the 20th century to understand what actually happened then; and second, to wake up in *the real present and immediate future*, in order to uncover the basic outlines of the new Michaelic plan B, for His second century.

Let us recapitulate how the 20th century could have unfolded, by tracing its arc in a counterfactual history (a term and method introduced by the historian Niall Ferguson).[14] Steiner indicates that this is how history should be studied from a spiritual perspective. This means that we study what actually happened, not as if it were linearly caused by previous events, but instead what *should and could have taken place.* This study is absolutely necessary if you are to begin to understand the real spiritual history of humanity and the anthroposophical movement in the 20th century and today.

Now, Anthroposophy was founded on Earth in the beginning of the 20th century as a **centralized** impulse: one founder, one society, one location. This form was natural and necessary at that time. All initiatives started this way in the past, but it was not meant that they should linger on and end this way! As any plant can teach you, if the species is to continue to thrive, the individual plant must undergo a perpetual, organic metamorphosis, which culminates in the dramatic process of "die and become" through its flowering, fruit production, and the dissemination of so many new, life giving seeds. In this process the old organism dies out and gives birth to a whole multitude of independent, peripherally interconnected, seedlings, sprouts and new plants that grow and flourish in their own locations. Such anthroposophical sprouts could have been networked together as an independent, global web of diverse, richly differentiated, new Michaelic impulses. In this counterfactual, ideal, scenario, Anthroposophy would have prospered inwardly and outwardly, expanding its sphere of influence and deepening its spiritual substance, maturing through the crisis of the second third of the 20th century, until the culmination and reversal of centre and periphery at the end of the 20th century.

As we pointed out above, in this case, Steiner would have lived and worked at least until 1933 and with him a growing community of awake and independent, loving, and mutually supportive, sisterly and brotherly co-workers. They could have understood and applied in real time the new Christ experience, with its necessary confrontation with the lower self or Beast. They could have transformed this evil through love and self-knowledge into a greater good. This form of Anthroposophy would have then spread from the '60s to the '90s from Europe to the world, with all the good forces strengthened by the recognition, healing and transformation of evil through our higher and new spiritual and social faculties. Long before 1933, an unknown, mentally deranged painter would have committed suicide in Vienna, and Steiner, fulfilling all his plans for the new formation of the Anthroposophical Society and School of Spiritual Science, would have been surrounded by a creative community that could have continuously evolved to meet all future impulses. Then, he could have peacefully departed, knowing that such a vibrant community of creative spirits would naturally be able to maintain and strengthen their independently achieved, supersensible contact with him and the supersensible Michaelic school after his death. During the second third of the century, a community of people would have sprang up, inspired by spiritual science, who were developing new faculties of supersensible cognition.

After 1966, this creative community would have developed organically to become an open, world embracing, free movement, integrating hundreds of newly seeking souls each year. The new generations of the '60s and '70s would have naturally united their new spiritual and social faculties with the creative approach and realization of spiritual science, for which they were preparing themselves in the supersensible Michaelic school before their birth. This would have demanded an organic change of the structure and substance of all the anthroposophical organizations and institutions and above all of the centralized legacy left by Steiner himself at the Goetheanum. But this upheaval would have been felt as something entirely natural and organic, and people would have realized this change consciously and with great enthusiasm, because it would have been felt to express their growing maturity as modern and free co-workers. The centralised organism would no longer have been felt to be adequate; it would have progressively become more decentralized and modern, as befits a spiritual association of freely striving human beings in this age of freedom. As such a self-transforming movement and institution, it would have accomplished the first real meetings and mutual integrations with the real shaping forces of the world periphery already in the '60s and '70s, reaching the culmination and new beginning now as we speak these very words in 2004!

In reality, Rudolf Steiner died in 1925 and the forces of conservation and survival took over. Yet, the spiritual world does not stand still or conserve anything. The Time Spirit moves on, pragmatically adjusting itself to human failures in the age of freedom. The supersensible Michaelic school, with the real, living Steiner at his head, has not stood still since 1925. It has moved on, and today it is seeking people whose hearts and minds are open to listen to what they have to say!

If Steiner had died satisfied at the right time, he could have quickly reincarnated with all the others who were with him on the earth and all the souls who would join them for the first time. At this point the Platonic stream, which had not yet incarnated in the 20th century, would have come to earth and united with Steiner and all of his Aristotelians, who immediately reincarnated. It would have been a huge metamorphosis, if as in plan A, Steiner and Alanus ab Insulis from Chartres would have worked physically together for the first time! What a world event that was planned and prepared for! And think about the thousands (and indeed, millions) of fine Michaelic fighters giving us *new* impulses, making the Michaelic movement into a global impulse, capable of entering world politics, economy and culture as a mighty, creative force!

At this fruitful point of the 20$^{th}$ century, metamorphosis would have taken place as naturally as in the case of any flowering plant. There could have been a powerful spiritual rejuvenation and fructification of spiritual science from fresh supersensible experience and research, carried and nourished by hundreds and thousands of mutually connected and supporting co-workers from all nations and races. Many mature fruits of the 20$^{th}$ century would have become available for humanity, and many new seeds and sprouts would have come to life everywhere around the earth. The centre of the Anthroposophical society would have become peripheral, in other words, spiritual, free, open and active in the real global world. In addition, social, economic and cultural impulses would have been generated, directly changing and influencing world events in external, day-to-day history.

But all this **did not** happen.

So Michael had to draw up a new plan for a second chance in his second century, as it was already clear at the time of Steiner's death that plan A was obsolete. Now, the 21$^{st}$ century is the first *global* century and Anthroposophy should have become a creative global movement, directly involved in the inner and outer shaping of world history. It should have shifted long ago from a centralized, middle European society into a world society and from mere survival to the new Michaelic strategy. Therefore, **Michael's plan B** is to work out of a periphery without a centre. Plan A would have connected a self-transforming, vital centre into the world periphery, but plan B instead creates a scattered periphery without a centre. The new movement therefore has no physical centre, but what tremendous new Michaelic powers are working in the periphery, if we open our hearts to them! This new movement must grow out of the individualized work in each one of us, and each person is at the periphery as her own centre, and then many centres will be formed everywhere. There is no one centre, but many, no one teacher, but many, and this is valid for all institutions. It is the creative homelessness of the true spiritual movement!

Let me describe a personal-impersonal moment in connection to the history of the Society at the end of the last century. At the end of the '80s and then again a few years later, I was asked to found and lead an Anthroposophical Society in Israel and to serve as its general secretary with Dornach's blessing. I explained why I had to decline such a nomination from the centre, since such an act would contradict the real demands of the Time Spirit. I told the authorities that since Steiner's death, his seat should have been regarded as a "peerless seat," like in the round table traditions, allowing a free circle, and a peripheral, free spiritual movement to develop. Of course I knew that there would be a "price to pay" for this. I wasn't naïve. My refusal to possess the central seat of the Israeli society was a purely personal decision on my part, but even today, some 15 years later, I am just as convinced that I made the right choice.

Obviously, what is said here applies also to all and each anthroposophical field of thought and work, not only to the Anthroposophical Society itself. I use here the example of the Society, but if the mother has not changed, certainly most of her "daughter movements" have not gone further than their mother. The real renewal of spiritual science *from its very foundations* still has to be done and then only will it be possible to implement new cultural and social impulses that will transform the "daughters." But first the "mother field" must be resurrected in our hearts and deeds.

If the Anthroposophical Society and its daughter movements and institutions transformed themselves into associations and networks of free people, then local and temporary centres would arise to give expression to real and specific needs with no command or control room. A "periphery" would arise in the hearts and minds of free people, who strive to work spiritually in social forms that respect and foster an utterly modern freedom. Anyone who wishes could then recognize and apply the best practices from these peripheral forms. Such free associations do not depend on being recognized or suppressed, acknowledged or condemned, by centralized authorities who decide for everybody what is right and wrong in spiritual life. This independence would allow them to develop freely, as should happen in free spiritual life, and they could address real human and spiritual situations and needs. Such a **free spiritual life**, which is wholly new and the most modern of all things, does not yet exist anywhere, but it is the goal of a truly creative future.

For it is the quintessence of a modern spiritual and social life, to be alive as long as it acts out of true impulses, and to die out when its time is over. **Peripheral and individualized centres like these are kept alive by a spiritual reality, and not by outer forms that subsist and are conserved long after the real situation and needs have expired and died out.** In such peripheral centres, a spiritual intention clothes itself with a physical, social and economic body, when it is incarnated to do its job, and then this body dies when the spiritual intention excarnates after it has completed its allotted task.

Now tremendous new Michaelic impulses have begun to flow from the spiritual centre of the 21$^{st}$ century. This supersensible Michaelic stream has not found any hearts and hearing in the centralized anthroposophical institutions. Nevertheless, the facts must be spoken out seeking those hearts that are open and courageous enough to truly listen. The future spiritual and social movement is beginning to form in so many places, and we all are called to be its planners, doers, and co-workers. Also here in Sweden there are promising new seeds and sprouts. Let human beings hear this!

## Lecture 3

### Changing Self-Love into World Thinking; The Three Paths that Use the Forces Freed from the Head and Heart
(Orust 2012)

WITHOUT THE SPIRIT we can do nothing. It is only our arrogance that makes us believe that we create, we think, we do.[15] We don't even walk by ourselves or speak by ourselves — nothing — it's all by the Spirit. But arrogance is a very positive and important force for the modern person, for without it all the achievements of modern culture and civilization would never have come about. It started from the first moment that Rene Descartes experienced: "*I think myself. I create my own thoughts. I think, therefore I am.*" The 17th century was the first time human beings had this illumination. Up until this point, people still looked upon thinking as a Cosmic, Spiritual Revelation. Thinking comes from the stars, from the hierarchies or from nature. It is definitely NOT *'I create my thinking out of my being.'* This new discovery and experience of the soul, is a bit more than 2 centuries old, only a short time since this big scandal. In relation to this, 1721 is an important year, to which we will return below. Before the middle of the 18th century, the scandal intensifies and becomes a world drama. Goethe and then Fichte participate in this drama, and then a 'totally unprofessional and non-academic' book appears: *The Philosophy of Freedom.* Steiner creates a tremendous scandal by writing this philosophical text!

We should understand from the author of *The Philosophy of Freedom* that the modern revolution, which started almost 200 years before him, was already beginning to reverse itself entirely inside out. Steiner is not saying: *After Descartes, let's relax for 500 years, to take it in, understand and work with it.* No, he not only reverses thinking, but he also immediately develops Anthroposophy, and shows how it can be realized practically. In a very short historical time, not more than a fraction of a second of evolutionary time, we have to first go from the Cosmos to the human to consolidate thinking in personal consciousness, and then immediately reverse it into a cosmic experience again. This is like one process with no interruption, from the cosmos to the human, and back to cosmos in one movement.

In 1919, the author of the *Philosophy of Freedom* stated with courage and audacity, in the opening lectures to the teachers that founded the Waldorf school, that the greatest mistake in the modern world conception was: "I think, therefore I am." Because in everything that we call ordinary thinking, the being "I am" is completely lacking. This thinking is totally dead and abstract and has no real substance. It should rather be: "When I think, I am not. When I think, I am nothing with a hole in it." This stream of empty, dead life that signifies modern thinking is completely lifeless and cannot perceive anything alive, but only the dead in the human and the world; not to speak of anything of a soul or spiritual nature. It cannot perceive life, only what is falling out of life as dead. If we are to make something alive out of this dead thinking, we have to use our human life forces, our heart forces, and stream them into the dead thinking to bring it into a time of resurrection. But we must take these forces from our body, from our limbs, from our digestive system, from our metabolism, and from the heart and blood. We have to take the life forces where we have them and stream them into the head, so that thinking will become alive and will go all the way to the far cosmos.

Because the head is totally dead, containing dead substance, it can only produce dead thinking. Life should come from the body, the blood and the heart. There we have enough forces, though we are not using them for thinking. We have thinking forces that are dead and living forces which are going through instincts and desires; so we have to cross them with one another. It's up to us to stream the forces from the heart and the body through the head, take thinking with it, resurrect thinking and go with it out into the cosmos. And when it goes out, it becomes spiritual perception, if it is animated by the love that is streaming out of the life forces from the heart. Because what we call spiritual perception in spiritual science (Imagination, Inspiration, and Intuition) is the expression of the natural power of human self-love, transformed into spiritual activity. When we transform this natural love into spiritual activity, it becomes higher consciousness.

If I take the life forces, the forces of love, which in ordinary life I take in to nourish and love myself, and instead send them into objective thinking, the subjective becomes objective and the dead thinking comes alive and becomes spiritual perception. Our thinking is objective, but dead. It can perceive the world objectively, but only the dead part. The most it can produce is mathematical and mechanical concepts, but not more than that. On the other hand, in the body we have lots of life, but it is subjective life, so we have to let it stream into the head to get objective life. If I use the self love and connect it with objective reality, and love it with the same love that I love myself, thinking becomes alive and becomes an expression of love towards the world. That's why the spiritual scientist can know so much about the world, because he has so much love for it. Spiritual knowledge is practically applied love.

Now we can ask how the human came to be built like this. How did evolution bring us to this place and what are the future prospects for this situation? So we ask Rudolf Steiner about it, as he is someone who has researched the case. What is the problem with the head, how did we end up with the head in this situation? He tells us that the etheric life body of the head separated from the physical head already at the beginning of the Ancient Greek civilization. In the even older times of Lemuria and also in the first post-Atlantean people, the etheric body was still coming down and entering into the head, making it into this big brain that we have. But around the time that Christ came to the Earth, the process was reversing. The etheric body was released from the head, and this is why abstract thinking was born in Greece. People began to be able to think in concepts for the first time; before this they were thinking in pictures and imaginations. Modern philosophy and natural science started in Greece, because they were the first people that had released etheric heads. Thinking became more and more human until, in the 17th century, it was finally expressed as, "I think therefore I am." This idea is coming completely from the physical body and not the etheric anymore. Modern thinking is dead simply because it is a product of the dead brain; it doesn't have the etheric life forces of the cosmos working in it.

At the same time another process started in the year 1721. The etheric body of the human being started to be released from the heart, and it will be completely released from the whole physical heart region by the end of the 21st century. Mind you, we are now in 2012, so this means only 380 years for the whole process to take place. Can we really believe this? It is an amazing fact and a very short time. The etheric body is released not only from the head, but also from the heart. It is falling out. The process will then continue all the way down through the limbs, and in a very short time the etheric body of the whole human being will be released. The good news is that, because the etheric body is released from the heart, human beings can be working freely with their heart forces. If we are inwardly active and creative with the heart forces, we can really do some work. For example, if we don't remain passive in our life of feeling, but make it into an active power to work in the world and make organs of perception and cognition, we have the possibility to control, move and exercise our feelings. But if we don't, the opposite will take place: the heart region will become like the head, empty and dead. Humans will experience more and more that they are dead in the heart; lonely, deserted, and thrown into the world without a protective aura. Empty souls.

This is actually a fantastic new step, because without this feeling, humans could not become active and do the real work. Nobody is forcing them, but if they want to, they can say, "Wow! What a joy! I was the most terribly lonely person in the world. I'm so happy! What a progress and potentiality." For, in my loneliness there is the greatest potential for spiritual development. My forefathers could not utilize it, because they were not lonely, but were instead part of a family, of nature, of the stars and the cattle. But there is a competition for this empty, dead, etheric heart, as there is a competition for the dead thinking; a race to fill the empty wishes, longings and desires. We are not the only ones interested in this empty space. It is a *Loch* or hole that many beings are interested in. All the luciferic and ahrimanic beings are very happy that this is happening, saying, "We already took over the human brain, now we will take the heart, then we just have to add the limbs, and we have got the whole human."

I will mention two basic ways this is done, first from the ahrimanic side, and then the luciferic side. From the ahrimanic side, this is what Ray Kurzweil has been speaking about as the technological singularity and the coming merger of the human with infinitely intelligent machines. 2045 is the year that Kurzweil predicted for the singularity, this total merging of humans with Artificial Intelligence. In esoteric terms, this means that the human's free etheric body from the head to the heart will be totally taken over by ahrimanic, infinitely brilliant, wise and powerful intelligences. I would recommend Kurzweil's movie, *The Singularity is Near*, to everybody interested in the coming future, as an introduction to open your mind and eyes to see where we are going from the ahrimanic point of view. I call this the building of the kindergarten of Ahriman, in preparation for his school that he will build in the 23rd century in America. He will build a school that will work with the etheric forces taken from the rest of the body as well: the head, the heart and the whole thing. So there is a Waldorf kindergarten and Ahriman kindergarten.

The singularity people promise a new kind of immortality. Human beings will be identified with Infinite Intelligence through super computers and so on, and they will experience a sort of immortality for their earthly consciousness, an indefinite life. Your whole soul life, including everything you were thinking and remembering, which you already invested externally in the infinite virtual reality, will be preserved forever. Even if you die physically, it will be preserved and it will continue to evolve and develop through Infinite Intelligence. The idea is that people will not die physically or at least live hundreds of years, since the new technology will overcome the illnesses that medicine could not conquer. But after long years, if they still die at all, all their life will remain as a virtual personality in a tech reality, continuing as it were, a second life. But this will really become the primary life, the life of this individuality as his avatar in virtual reality. If you don't know this world very well, it will be hard for you to create a picture of it. Look into it; the children already know all about it.

This is the ahrimanic side, because everything is accomplished through Infinite Intelligence, working through virtual reality. In the future a huge intelligent machine will have been merged into the human body, a supercomputer with flesh and blood. It will not be me and the computer, rather I will be the super intelligent machine itself with this consciousness within myself. I will be the Internet. That's the idea and it's a step not far away. I recommend that you study it further yourself in Ray Kurzweil's books and in anthroposophical literature. Steiner said things about this that are very difficult to understand, because he speaks about a future that is far away, but with these new developments, the gap between Steiner and reality in this respect is coming closer. So you will understand Steiner better if you read Kurzweil, and you will only understand the spiritual aspect of Kurzweil if you read Steiner. Steiner said a few words about how the school of Ahriman will come in the 23rd century, more or less clearly; however now, if you follow the recent developments, you will begin to have a concrete sense of the kindergarten, which then gives you a better idea of what the school will be like. Time is moving on; we can understand better.

But there is also the luciferic school plan, where people are doing great things! There are many streams, many people. It's a huge work that's been going on for a long time and they have a specific knowledge of how they want to use the released etheric forces for their own purposes. On the luciferic side, great spiritual streams are working to create spiritual immortality by training people in spiritual practices, meditation and so on. We all know the more popular ones, but there are also more serious ones where people learn in depth how to live spiritually outside the physical body, in the astral world, developing astral travel and astral projection. This is all about using the released etheric body and connecting it with spiritual beings that fill the empty etheric body with their forces and give you a strong sense of life outside of the body. This life is not yours, but you still enjoy it a great deal. These two kinds of immortality or virtual life are exact mirrors of one another. In one, the virtual internet intelligence of Ahriman will be physically inside us. In the other, there will be a luciferic spiritual immortality in which people learn to live outside the Earth. In both types, the second life you receive will become your first priority, your primary life. Your internet life will become your own, and there will also be a spiritual practice that will create an immortal etheric and astral body which will become your 'true life' outside the Earth.

Not all of you may have heard of Second Life. It is a virtual reality game where people create a second life with an avatar-personality, which is your personality on the internet. You play with it and live your life there. Under the ahrimanic influence in the future, this will become your first life, and what you still have here on the Earth, will become a second life. There you can be whatever you want. You invent any personality, you invent any biography, you can play any role, you can choose your body, and you can have lots of bodies, lots of personalities. There you are free to use the power of metamorphosis, which is the power of the etheric forces of the heart. But you are using this power in a technological virtual reality, where many people already spend most of their time. When it becomes part of your body, it will simply become your real life, and without the need of an external machine. The same thing will happen with the creation of a freed astral body that will be using luciferic astral bodies: people will see this increasingly as their true life, and will forget their life on the Earth. Let us now look at this picture in greater detail.

This is already the real life of young people today. The younger generations are highly spiritual people and come into incarnation with very powerful memories of the life before Earth. They experience spiritual things as children like never before. But the young people say — *The humans that I see are terribly unspiritual and boring; they will never understand my spiritual life.* So the children plug into a technological 'second life,' because this is the most spiritual thing they can find. This tech virtual life is the most similar to their life before birth, because it allows them to undergo continual metamorphosis. They are not going to look to adults or teachers, they won't even count you. They will come from the spiritual world directly and go straight into the web. We will entirely lose the future, if things continue like this, no question about it. The children of today are in another place; Waldorf educators already see this. But how do I reach them? The teachers and the students were once able to understand one another, but now the teachers and adults really don't know how to talk to young people. If we say that the children are the problem, we are already missing the real issue. The children have moved on. They went on with life, and we stayed behind. So now there is a difference between us.

The younger generations are not the problem, we are! We are the problem, because we fell asleep! We have slept half a century. Can we wake up? If we wake up, we will find them and they will find us. But the change must come from us, it's not about the children, they're okay. They're moving with the time. We stopped and fell asleep a hundred years ago, like Rip van Winkle. For the children, the older generation is a waste of time. It's dead people. It's dead salt. They can learn nothing from us. Wake up and change yourself, and come back to our real time. We have to change as humans, because right now we are terribly uninteresting. We are boring creatures. We are not creative. We are not part of humanity or part of the time. Why should they follow us? I totally feel with them, I totally understand them. Most adults are totally uninteresting people. They are busy with nonsense; they don't care about life, and they are not creative, not free, and not adventurous. They are terribly asleep or they worry about their pensions, for heaven's sake. Dead souls. Children are alive and they want nothing to do with dead souls.

So we have to be so very alive. We don't even begin to know how alive we must be, for our children to become interested in looking at us, even from the corner of their eyes! If we wake up, we can ask — *Wow, how long was I asleep?* This is very important, because there is a difference between sleeping 20 years or a whole century. When was the last time I was in contact with what science or technology or art are doing in the real world? Reading my new book, *The Event in Science, History, Philosophy and Art,* can be an indicator of how long you have been asleep. Was it 30 years? Am I stuck in the 1920s or '60s or '70s? This investigation will help me come back to life. This will help me realize that I am very weak and uninterested in life. I hope you feel this. If you read the book with all your heart, you can have this experience. You can say to yourself — *When did I fall asleep? When all those great ideas have passed me by, what happened to me? Where was I?* This is a possible experience and I have heard this reaction from people who have read the book, and I'm very happy, because this is also a part of the whole endeavor. In the future, if we want to have any connection with children at all, we will have to wake up and become adventurous. Of course, we can still force them to go to a class and we can lock the doors, but we will only have this power for some time, not forever.

During the course of the 21st century, the etheric body will be completely released from the heart. By the century's end, we will have billions of human beings who are living in complete unity with the virtual physical reality and millions and millions who already have this luciferic spiritual consciousness we talked about. It is so easy today, spiritually, to give people some exercises, because they can go out of their bodies very easily; millions of people today live more outside of their body, whether consciously being awake or dreaming in conscious, astral projection. Millions are already doing it worldwide and the number that will achieve this by the middle and end of the 21st century will be many, many millions. I know, for example, some people who work very seriously with the meditation school of Clairvision (a huge movement based on Samuel Sagan's work, which has a strong presence on the Internet). Thousands of people are successfully working on this worldwide and they are making tremendous progress. They look down on your anthroposophical meditation with loving compassion, just like you look at the children in the kindergarten playing with sand. This is a very powerful, luciferic movement, but only one of hundreds of streams of the like. This movement even refers to anthroposophical knowledge and recommends that people read Rudolf Steiner. This is an important picture and it's all about the released forces from the head and the heart. When this is complete, the two distorted possibilities will be realized in full force.

In 1721, the etheric forces started to be released from the heart. Why 1721? When you get older, you notice that the etheric body starts to separate from your physical body until you are dead altogether, but this is a gradual process that begins from the middle of life. It's the same with the evolution of mankind — humanity is getting old and reaching its end. Since the etheric body is getting released, it means we are finishing our physical life and will have to create a new spiritual life (or a strong ahrimanic or luciferic life). Hopefully a small stream can achieve something a little bit better than these two alternatives. I'm not sure about this middle stream, but I am sure about the two others! Actually we have a very short time to still live in full incarnation on the Earth. You don't understand how short it really is, and this is why our time is so crucial and why these two streams are trying to use this time as much as they can now. In 3,000 years, we are not going to be incarnated physically as we are today; all humans will be out, perhaps coming to visit every now and then, but not really living here anymore. It's over! The human story of life on the Earth, that's over, but the big question is how it's going to be over! This is crucial, because the time we have left incarnated in the physical body, which we are already exiting very strongly, is the only span where we can develop the true power of love! Now is the time to do it, and in the coming centuries and millennium THIS WILL BE THE TASK. The true power of love can only be developed here on Earth, and this is precisely what these other two sides are trying to stop.

This is the background to the work of our Global school, which we discussed earlier. **The only good way to actively fill my empty heart, my empty etheric body, is through the being of the other person. This is the only thing that will give meaning and a reason to be incarnated in a physical body.** People that do not find this community work to be a lot of fun will go to the ahrimanic or luciferic spiritualization and immortalization. Only the people that have experienced the mystery, the greatness and the beauty of meeting the other person this way, will want to continue with the evolution of the Earth. If what you really want is to develop your spiritual perception and widen your experiences, the stupidest thing you can do is to come in contact with other people. This is what will stop you most in your development: other people and social life — it's terrible! Considered from either the ahrimanic or the luciferic side, this is the stupidest thing you can do. What we do here in the Global school is totally stupid. Think about it. Why waste your time to take the life and being of another human being into your heart? What is this nonsense? It's a total waste of energy. What for? If I want to be spiritually developed, I should do it by using other people, and not the other way round. And if I want to be a materialistic leader, if I want to reach the singularity, I should do it with machines or whatever. No, this is totally a waste of time, according to their points of view.

Truly any meeting with another person, even on a very elementary level, already hinders my inner spiritual development, and if I really take this being into my own, then this immediately kills all the possibilities for a certain kind of clairvoyant development. It just kills it. *Because with the free etheric body that I have, I can bring in a powerful spiritual being, a luciferic being, with superhuman forces.* This being will fill my empty heart with forces of vanity and pride and faculties, and I will quickly begin to see, hear, and experience the most vivid dreams and astral travels. These forces are mutually exclusive: true love pushes this being away, but when this being comes in, it pushes the other person away. But "I" am not interested in that, because I want to be developed and I like my astral travels; all this is such ecstasy. What bliss! People who haven't experienced it yet, don't know what bliss it can be. Many, thanks to God, don't know yet what it is, for if they experienced it, they would never withstand the temptation. But in a short time, everyone will be able to have it, and the temptation will be enormous and most human beings will run with it. It is very, very powerful, no question about it. The temptation will be so strong (and is strong already), that people will say, "You can press this button and have experiences out of the body and you can do this exercise and make astral travels." Can you imagine someone responding, "No thank you, I have to meet another human being?" No one will say this; only very few.

Some people are wondering about how the elemental beings play into this whole picture. Quite a few individuals are trying to communicate with them today, but it all depends on why we want to approach them at all. What's the idea behind it? Why is it important to communicate with the beings of nature? If it's really to learn from them, to work together with them, and to understand them in order to do practical things for the Earth and nature, then it can be very good. But if the goal is to use this to escape the Earth, then it's not good. If it increases the love of nature, then it's exactly what we have to do. Yet also among the elementals, one finds the same two groups of luciferic and ahrimanic beings, for they also work in nature, but with goals different from humanity. Choose your friends wisely. You can learn from any being, no matter what name you call it, but first you have to know which being it is. If you consciously recognize the being, then you are immune from the danger. You can learn a great deal from the ahrimanic beings, because they are incredibly smart, and the fact that they exist is not evil in itself. They are only bad if you think they are good. If you know that they are bad, then it is okay and they can teach you quite a bit. They remind you to be a better person. But many times, people overstep the mark and become fascinated. They begin to enjoy this learning process for its own sake.

You can recognize the good beings to communicate with, because they are the ones not trying to tempt you. The upright beings are not trying to pour information and knowledge on you in great quantities, on the contrary. The really good ones will always first try to stimulate you to become creative. They will give you an idea of how you can know or accomplish something, but they don't pour finished information into you. They will say, "Do you want to know this? Okay, I'm not going to give you the answer, but the answer will be how you can get there yourself." This is a good example. If you ask the being a question and you get 30 volumes of books of knowledge about love and light, then this being cannot really help you, because it just wants to express itself and doesn't care about you. In this case, you can just exercise the ordinary judgment that you have in daily life and you will see what's right and what's wrong. Just remember that for the true beings, it is much more important what humans can do themselves. They want us to produce something that only humans can create on the Earth. They don't want to give out of themselves, but instead they want to help us give something to them. They recognize the dire necessity for humans to begin to create something spiritual.

So this is the picture: a big black hole in the heart where the light bulbs are not working anymore and this empty space can either be filled by my own activity, or it will be filled by technology or by luciferic spiritual experiences. Our social yoga is there to give an answer on the level of the heart. We are trying to find a way in which we can work with the forces of the heart in the right way. Not egotistically, but through the other and with the other person. When we participate in the school work, we do some of the first exercises of cognitive yoga. These concern some of the more scientific processes of working with the forces of the head itself, and how to transform the forces of the head through this cognitive yoga. We work with the forces of sense perception and thinking, in order to, through the senses and through thinking by means of spiritualized work, direct them through the body. So we will have yoga for the head and yoga for the heart, and the released etheric body will be taken care of as a whole. This is necessary for the next stage, when in the 22$^{nd}$ century and beyond, the etheric forces of reproduction, of sex, of metabolism, and of everything that is connected with the lower part of the body will begin to separate as well. The reproductive and sexual forces will be totally controlled by human beings. If there is not the purest love that has developed in order to work with them, you can imagine how these forces might be used through science. It's coming very soon, and the whole school of Ahriman will be eventually based on using those forces, because they serve the highest spiritual forces that we have in the physical world. These sexual forces would be used for great, great things beyond the kindergarten, up into the full ahrimanic school.

This world would be terrible in the spiritual sense, because those forces would be used to increase the one-sidedness of the technological evolution and to alter spiritual evolution. In this way, you can totally estrange a human being from its true evolution. When you can use those forces to live outside of the body, it's over. You are disconnected and you never return to the Earth, so Lucifer wins a total victory over the human. Remember that when the etheric body is released altogether, you are actually dead. So you are not coming back; you have full life in an etheric body outside of the physical body, with all the forces animated by spiritual beings. That's it. You're done. You're finished with evolution of the Earth. You don't need the Earth. Bye-bye, Earth.

When you control the forces of reproduction, you control incarnation and excarnation. Ahriman uses them so that people never excarnate, so they stay here on the Earth. Lucifer uses the same forces for excarnating and not coming back. *This is what happens when you control those forces — you stop reincarnation.* It's over. Think about it: there will be a time in which all humans will be able to stop reincarnation, to stop karma, either by staying indefinitely on the Earth, or by leaving the Earth indefinitely. If this comes to pass, there must be some humans left on the Earth, that through their power of pure love **choose in freedom** to continue to reincarnate, to continue to bring new souls to the world, to continue to build communities, and in this time it will be almost impossible. Only a very few humans will have the strength and the power to do it, in a time where humanity as a whole is totally taken by those forces now reaching all the way to the basic bodily level. This will be in the dark age which is coming after the Michaelic age. In the 23rd century, when Ahriman will open his school big time, we start the so called Oriphiel age. He is a dark archangel who will come to bring to the Earth everything that we have been speaking about. We have two short centuries of the Michaelic age remaining. Think about how little time we have to give humanity the strongest forces and impulses in this direction. To overcome Oriphiel, we will have to work with the forces we have developed by then. So, this is why I tell you, dear friends, it's time to do some work.

# Lecture 4

## The 21st Century: The Possible Incarnation of the Middle Stream and the Impulse of Vidar (Orust 2012)

LET US LOOK AT THE LAST lecture and make a short recapitulation of its main ideas.[16] We said that the human head already became devoid of real cosmic forces 2000 years ago. This enabled independent human thinking, which is based on the physical brain, to come about, with its motto, "I think, therefore I am." It's important for Rudolf Steiner to explain that thinking, precisely because it's dead, is also free. It is free in the sense that it is not bound to the spiritual world and the cosmos. Because it's dead, like a dead body, it is no longer connected to the forces of the universe. So it cannot force us to do anything, because it's empty. It has no real life content and no moral content, so it cannot compel us to do anything. It leaves our will free. I can think about whatever I want; I can invent whatever I want to invent, for in my thinking there are purely pictures, representations and empty concepts. In older times, when thinking was part of the cosmos, when people experienced thinking as revelation, it always played a part in directing our wills. As a behavior of the whole, people could not separate the two and say — *I think it, but I will not live like that or do it.* If they had a certain impression, they lived and acted according to its content, out in nature, for example. So what we can do is to make thinking alive again, enliven it with the forces out of our own body and being, let it stream through the head to once again make it cosmic, and therefore able to receive moral substance without impairing our freedom.

I have to choose freely to do it, because I want to use some of my self-love to love the universe. Then it goes through the head, in an objective way. Then this thinking that becomes spiritual again can be filled with cosmic forces, without me becoming less free. I am already free enough to remain free. What makes it possible to connect the forces of the heart with the head and with the cosmos, is the fact that the etheric body, since the middle of the 18th century, has also been releasing itself. It is actually almost totally released; starting in 1721 and finishing by the end of the 21st century. So we are almost there. This means that all the forces of the heart, in the etheric body, the astral body and the "I," are also free from the organic body and thereby depend on our activity. Again, the question remains whether we will fill them with activity or not. If I don't fill the heart with objective love for the world and for other people, it will remain empty and I will feel increasingly empty and lonely and deserted. I will essentially ask other forces to come and fill it for me. This will take me to the world we described with the luciferic and ahrimanic ideals of evolution. The empty etheric body is falling down all the time and Ahriman will always take the forces from the head, to create the singularity, the merging of the human with the machines, including physical immortality. He also takes the forces of the heart as well as the head; because people who are dreaming are fired by enthusiasm and have strong desires to achieve immortality, healing and all the 'good things' through this technological singularity. So the connection of humanity to the supercomputers, which will take place inside our own bodies and not outside, will first use these etheric forces which are dead or empty. Because they are empty, they can be used for whatever you want, and anybody can use them.

Lucifer would also take the forces of the heart to create astral immortality. He takes the etheric forces with him to his astral soul world and out of them creates the most beautiful, rich, and fantastic experiences for people. So this picture will be fully real by the end of our century; the forces of the heart will be totally released, and from then on, will also be totally dead. These forces can be manipulated in both directions as they are entirely free. In the 21$^{st}$ century, we see that much is already possible and this is exactly what gives us the greatest chance to develop independent heart and head forces that will be strong enough to take human evolution into the middle course, in the right way. We are also preparing for the next short period, beginning in the 23$^{rd}$ century, when a totally different Spirit of the Time, Oriphiel, will rule from then into the 24$^{th}$, 25$^{th}$ and 26$^{th}$ centuries (c. 2230 to 2580). It will start with the foundation of the school of Ahriman, and lead humanity into a real dark age for three centuries.[17] During that time, in the middle of the 5$^{th}$ cultural epoch, there will be no spiritual help given from outside at all. Today, during the Michael age, we still receive a great deal of help from Michael. He doesn't do the work for us, but he opened the way, and he helps us to become free and creative. But with Oriphiel, help will not be given. Then, only people who already have it totally in themselves as free creators, will possess a spiritual life of their own.

So we have to think creatively on the Earth now, for in the age of Oriphiel there will be only as much life as humans can create out of their own incarnated soul and spirit. They will have the Christ source here on the Earth, only to the extent that they have individualized it in their head, heart, and will. Not more than this. So this is to help us understand why the present age of Michael is so important. His age extends from 1879 to around 2230.

These are the three and a half centuries of the Michael age, which we have to realize this impulse. One century is already behind us, so the important thing is to understand that we have to use this comparatively short time to become spiritually independent. We can use the freedom that we have, through the forces of the heart that are released, to become much more creative in the right way. The second and third century of the Michael age must become much more resourceful and much freer and humans must become much more able to do the work themselves than in the last century.

This is the right feeling for the Time Spirit of the century, to sense the need to become more free and creative in our spiritual work and to expect ourselves to lead the way. Anthroposophy was given at the beginning of this age, so that humans could prove that they could use it in a creative and independent way by themselves. The spiritual world is making the best of plans, but free human beings decide if the plans will be realized or not. The Michaelic forces of this age are the strongest spiritual forces that support humanity. Everything is possible if humans really join the work and do their part. As Steiner indicated in the last year of his life, the rules of reincarnation could even be changed during the Michael age, so that a powerful group of people in the anthroposophical stream could be incarnated at the end of the 20th century. This did not happen, but it is the best example that we have about the age in which we are living. We have to think about this example all the time and imagine that the equivalent could happen today. Everything is possible; it depends only on our initiative, courage, and freedom. We can truly realize things and the spiritual world makes everything possible today, if humans do their part. Moreover, this was never the case before in human history; it is a first time possibility. In other periods, in other ages, human beings were told what to do. They received the impulses, and what had to happen, occurred with the right timing. But this is because the timing was not dependent on human free will. Now, everything depends on human free will. Indeed, whether or not humanity will even reach its goal of evolution depends on human free will. Humans can fail in the whole thing, all the way through until the end, if they prefer not to develop. They can decide — *We don't want it, we will just go with the other alternatives.* It's definitely possible, because nobody will force them to do the right thing.

From the last years of the first decade of this century, I have become aware more and more of the spiritual influences coming from the future. For me, especially the years 2007 to 2010 were the beginning of experiencing the future possibilities. There is a whole new setting, a whole new plan, and a possibility for the course of the whole of this new century. And it's really increasingly important that people open their eyes toward the future and begin to understand, what the new goals are and what the new possibilities are for this century. First, what happens from today all the way to the middle of the century, will decide its second half. But first, the way to the middle; if you look at the century, you see a certain structure of time and evolution. A century is kind of like an organism, when you look at it; it has a middle point. Around the 2030s, '40s and '50s, you have the spiritual world giving the main impulse for the whole century. This impulse is streaming from there to the beginning of the new century. They are already starting in the first, second, third and fourth decades. You have a small wave in the first decade. In the second decade, you have a greater one and in the third an even greater one. Finally, it becomes a real tsunami towards the 2030s, '40s, and '50s.

In the first 10 years that we have already experienced, we had a very small wave. In the time we are living now, we will have a greater wave. You can feel it already in the beginning of the second decade. The waves are the creative forces of the future, the Christ forces of the future which are there to be used in the right way. So these are the forces that, in the right way, can fill the human heart and the human head with the greatest possibilities of new creativity and new spiritual development. This is the meaning of the singularity, 2045. This is the actual meaning of the middle of the century. People on both sides, the ahrimanic and the luciferic, with their various technologies, know these things and they know that they have to prepare the tools now to receive these forces and use it for their purposes. This gives them a tremendous opportunity to strengthen their ahrimanic and luciferic projects, and they will take away incredible amounts of energy for this and that.

It is significant that Ray Kurzweil's worldwide campaign, with his movie and books, started in 2011-12. This is very significant, for you can see that this is guided by real spiritual impulses, because it is exactly 33 years between 2012 and 2045. He says that you should prepare yourself now, because in the coming 33 years the singularity will be fulfilled. So, this is why I also started my new phase of work this year, beginning with publishing *The Event in Science, History, Philosophy & Art* in 2011 to prepare for this, and now, going out more and more to give lectures and workshops, because I felt that this is the right timing, from a spiritual point of view. I was actually surprised to see how precise and exact some of the guys on the left and right are! Because I came from my own inner experience, and found that I was not alone in the field, as far as Lucifer and Ahriman are concerned. They also know something that I thought maybe only I knew!

There are also the brothers on the luciferic side, who are counting on using those forces by the middle of the century. They have already started and will continue to use them to lead millions of forces across the threshold into the luciferic world, to disconnect them principally from the Earth on a big scale. Both sides, of course, are aware of the new forces that are streaming in; both of them know that the new forces will culminate in the middle of the century, and both are working now very consciously to build what is needed as preparation, so that by the middle of the century they can realize their aims. So, I think this already shows us what our task should be. We should also start with this year, 2012, and should prepare the vehicle, create the chalice, to receive the forces of this century, through the real, free moral activity of the human being. Then some of these forces will also fulfill the real goals for humanity, from now until the middle of the century.

By the time of this spiritual singularity, this moment in the middle of the century, there must be at least a small group of human beings, who can consciously find the right impulse to act here with the right thing in real time, to keep a certain balance between the very strong achievement of the luciferic and ahrimanic forces. Those achievements are going to be very strong; we can already see this today, if we understand the world. I am not concerned about the success of those guys. They are very successful anyway and they will do what they have to do. My concern is about the work being done with us, because I feel that this is still very weak, in comparison to what is coming from the future. So, I decided to go and try to find and speak to as many anthroposophists as I could, to tell them about this, and to look for partners among them. However, it's pretty difficult to find a way to speak about these things today, because the resistance is very strong. So we have to find better ways to be able to speak to more and more people, because anthroposophists have the knowledge, they have the background; they have the depth, the possibilities and the experience. They should be able to provide a certain foundation for the new century, the second Michaelic century. This is their task.

This is why I'm so very grateful that exactly here, in Sweden, I have found the first openness in the whole world. In Sweden, we had this great opportunity, thanks to all of your work here. I think this is also a sign, that there are certain forces that are trying to work here, that have a certain measure of freedom of expression, which will take time in other places to develop. I have been told that I need to learn Swedish now! But the real important thing is that we learn the language of our time, the one that more and more human beings around the Earth should learn to speak. We must be very serious about this, and feel the responsibility and the related opportunity, especially when we look at the contribution of the north, which I hope other countries will join. This is an immense responsibility to give a firm beginning to anthroposophical work in this century, along with the possibility of incarnating a development of the certain freedom that the north possesses.

This freedom must be understood as something exceptional, something that is not to be taken for granted, and something that must be actively protected and developed further. Otherwise this openness can also close down. That's the only place from which something new can eventually stream down to middle Europe (but not overnight). This is of course the most important question for the middle of this century: how much will be able to be realized in middle Europe again? It's a new chance for middle Europe, and for the people overall to reestablish their mission after the catastrophe of the last century. But this they cannot do alone, for they must be supported by what is coming and today it can only come from the north.

So because of the special mission of the north, especially in Sweden, I would like to look more at the anthroposophical background of this and take a greater look at what stands behind this situation. For this we need to take a glance at some of the basic anthroposophical concepts in this connection. I mentioned the fact that in our time of evolution right now, we are living far past the middle of evolution, and everything is developing further. Everything, all the kingdoms, natural and spiritual, are in transition to the next step. Everything is in movement; nothing is defined any longer by its place, by its number. Everything is actually already halfway to the next level. So the angels are on their way to becoming archangels, humans are taking the place of the angels, and so on, from the minerals all the way through. This is now a process of what we call becoming. This becoming is the transition of all creation and hierarchy to the next level. For example, if we look at the minerals really closely, we will see that they are becoming much more alive than they used to be. They are much more filled with life forces and this so-called 'dead kingdom,' the mineral kingdom, is not dead anymore.

In addition, the plant kingdom is also coming to life. You could see it already in the *Lord of the Rings* and *Harry Potter* movies: the plants are listening and they respond. They are becoming sensitive, and developing the beginning of a soul element. You can feel it when you go out in nature. And also, any owner of a pet will tell you, there is a spark of ego that is very strongly working in the higher animal kingdom today. All around the globe, there are many human beings who are developing new faculties for spiritual experience and spiritual sight all over the planet. Human beings are developing the next level of angelic faculties and even beyond that. So this is a general course of evolution, but there are, of course, so many exceptions. You know this from Anthroposophy; there are many beings that are not progressing, but are standing still and even going backwards. There are retarded beings from all the hierarchies in all humans. This really makes it interesting! Furthermore, there are those who stay behind and even dip lower than where they used to be. But there are also exceptions for the good, because the good must be prepared in advance. So, there are always the great teachers of humanity who proceed much faster than the rest of humanity, and prepare the future in advance as single individualities. The last example is Rudolf Steiner himself, who actually performed a fulfillment of the goals of humanity for a long time in the future during his incarnation. This leaves an impulse for humanity for a very, very long time to come, because he can already go today through the stages of evolution that humans would gradually go through only much later.

Now he spoke in this connection about another individual and its mission, and this is very interesting for our connection here. One of the greatest spiritual teachers of humanity was Gautama Buddha, who reached the Buddha stage in the 6th century before Christ. When a human being reaches the Buddha stage, he is actually reaching the angel stage. The interesting thing here is that then his own personal angel can become free from the work. This angel, Steiner says, who was working with the Buddha throughout all the ages, like our own personal guardian angel is working with us within each incarnation, was known in Atlantis later by the name of the Nordic god, Wotan or Odin. Wotan was the spiritual being behind those gods of Nordic history, through some of his Atlantean appearances. This being became free when Gautama became a Buddha. Now naturally, in the course of history and evolution, this being was ready to become an archangel, for he had finished his work as an angel. The human being who was given to him to protect and to guide had become an angel. It would be a natural decision on his part to move on as an archangel. We can also say it differently, because he actually had become the stage of an archangel in any case, since he had been developing as the Buddha was developing. So when Gautama was developing throughout many incarnations and becoming a Buddha, his angel was becoming an archangel already.

For this reason, he could have become an ordinary archangel and taken his place among the archangels, which are the folk spirits who guide nations and groups of people. Yet, he was very closely connected to the Christ being, since all the work he was doing with the Buddha was always connected very strongly to the Christ Being. Therefore, he decided to connect himself even more intimately with the being of the Christ, who had incarnated just a few centuries after Buddha on the Earth. He decided to remain with the Christ on the Earth and not go to the rank of the archangels. He has been serving the Christ since then, but because the mystery of Golgotha and the Christ Impulse up to this century was still working more in the hidden, unconscious, esoteric way, this being has also been working on the hidden, esoteric path. He actually resigned from working externally through nations and cultures, as he could have done as an archangel, and remained only connected as *an esoteric impulse of the Christ, completely hidden from any external work.*

This archangelic being wanted to wait until the second coming, when he could work externally once again with the Christ, as an external force in evolution and civilization. He waited 2000 years, focusing only on the inner work. Here we have to bring into the picture another being that is a servant to Christ: Michael, the archangel. He has been working, since the mystery of Golgotha, as the real forerunner of the Christ, as the one who opened the way for the Christ, and clears the way for the Christ to walk. Michael was preparing the time for his new age, which started at the end of the 19th century here. Because in the new Michael age, the second coming of Christ would start. It's been starting since the last century and Michael is making this possible. But, Steiner said that Michael is moving with evolution in the normal way, and he is joining the movement of the archangels who are becoming Archai or Time Spirits, in our own age. So Michael is really becoming the Time Spirit of our whole age, and not only of his three and a half centuries, which he rotates with the other main archangels. Michael, the closest servant of the Christ, has already become the Time Spirit of the whole larger age in which we live. So his position as a very personal individuality, who opens the way for the Christ, is now becoming free, because he is not an archangel anymore.

But recall that we have this being waiting, who was the angel of the Buddha. He is an archangel, but he didn't take the job. He said, "No, I will sacrifice my job as an archangel. I am waiting until the right place becomes available." So he became known as the hidden or the silent god. As a silent god, he did not speak in the last 2000 years, because he was waiting for the new Michael age, and the new Christ impulse, in which he would become the very foundation. He would give his being, now becoming a rightful archangel, and would give all his life spirit forces to serve the new impulse of Michael and Christ. He was waiting for this. Therefore, this being has begun to fill the archangelic position that Michael left vacant at the end of the 19th century. This former guardian angel of the Buddha has become the closest supporter of the new Christ impulse that is now working into external culture. So he is finally beginning to speak with the new revelation of the Christ.

In Norse mythology, which is the only one that really knows this being very well, he is known as Vidar. We can understand this through our anthroposophical research. It's the being Vidar, the silent, unknown god, who is now coming to his new position, and he is beginning to speak, which means he is now working with the evolution that is moving into a new phase. As Vidar is taking a new position and beginning to fulfill his new role now, he is carrying specific forces, which are very important to understand, because these are the forces that we need to use in order to fulfill the mission that I have been describing here. If human beings begin to work in an active way, by developing the heart and head forces as I have described, they will be able to receive the *life spirit* forces coming from Vidar, and work with them in a very unique way. **These are the forces of life that through human activity will replace the old etheric forces of the heart that are dying out.** So we are talking about the Vidar forces, when we are talking about the new yoga process of breathing in the cognitive sphere and heart sphere, in the way that can allow human beings more and more to exchange with one another and work with one another. When we speak about the goal of our time, we are speaking about these forces. This is the way to make them active in our culture, in our time, and in our future. Vidar will become stronger from century to century, as a source of the new forces that support the whole new Christ revelation. What is more, the impulse of Michael and the impulse of Vidar are always connected.

When we speak about the Christ impulse today, we have to imagine the Christ being, surrounded by the aura of Vidar. He is actually incorporating himself in the Vidar being, and He's working through this being into the world. Vidar gave himself as a body, as a soul, as a chalice, for the Christ being to work through. He is now speaking. Vidar is the voice and the power through which the Christ speaks to us. His new forces can stream into the place where our etheric forces from the head and heart are being released, if human beings prepare in the right way. So in this way we can create the central stream, and maintain a certain balance between the ahrimanic and luciferic ideals, which I described before. I have been recommending Kurzweil's film about the technological singularity, which shows the ahrimanic impulse for the middle of the century, because our own spiritual alternative to this impulse must also become very strong by then.

Indeed, this conflict is spoken about in Norse mythology. It is said that all of the old gods tried to overcome the Fenris wolf, a new, powerful evil. But none of them could do it because this new, powerful evil, which is really ahrimanic, is greater than all the old gods. Only Vidar can do this, because in this way he can serve the Christ impulse. This means that, if human beings will understand and take these forces into themselves in the right way, and implement them into social and cultural life correctly, they will find the force that can overcome Ahriman around the middle of the century. This is the modern appearance of the real Fenris wolf. The god Loki could come to terms with the wolf, in one way or another, but nobody else could, because it is a totally new phenomenon. Only the modern Christ impulse can overcome this particular technological-ahrimanic evil. This is why it is said that only Vidar can fight the war against the Fenris wolf. It is also said that Vidar wore a certain shoe or boot made from all of the leather pieces that were thrown away when others were making shoes. He used this boot to break the jaw of Fenris during Ragnarok.

Vidar's boot is a very important clue to the whole nature of this being and his work. It tells us that the forces of the Christ that he is serving are the ones that our civilization completely rejects. We live in the Fenris civilization. Our civilization totally rejects the Christ impulse. But Vidar now possesses strong forces, because for 2000 years he remained with the angels though he was an archangel, and remained silent all that time. They are doubly strong forces and he can also make use of all the forces that are thrown into the garbage by our civilization. He has been going around the world to the periphery, looking for the scraps of the best forces that the Fenris wolf has devoured and thrown out. From those forces, he is making shoes for human beings who have to walk the talk. No ordinary shoes can lead you through the field of Fenris, because your legs would be torn to pieces by the thorns. Only the shoes made from those Christ-forces can let you walk this road. We have to walk the path with the forces of the heart. The shoes are made from the new life forces of the heart. This is the leather, from which the boots are made. It's going to hurt in the beginning. But then, as it continues, it will be that much more joyful.

Of course, we must understand that the Fenris forces actually came to believe that they won in the 20th century, and they are harboring a very strong belief that basically humanity is already theirs because of what happened then. So they have a tremendous confidence and power that they never had before. This means that the fight over this century is not going to be an easy one, because humanity is going to be promised healing, salvation, and redemption for all human life by materialistic means. Everything that you want will be given to you freely. You just have to write the signs on your forehead and your hand, and socially and culturally you have to make the sign that you are accepting the deal. Because eventually it will not be possible to produce, to buy or to sell anything outside of the social, economic, and spiritual order that is already being created. There will be a new image of the human being that will appear, founding a new religion. This human being will be immortal and will overcome all illnesses. If you sign the contract, you only have to sacrifice all the forces of love, true morality and freedom. And you will get, in exchange: eternal life, eternal youth and eternal power.

This will become a real temptation for all humanity. Humanity will serve this as the new god and the new religion. The Fenris forces actually speak a language of salvation. They speak of peace, love, abundance, and healing; which is why all of humanity is totally taken by this. Nobody will be able to withstand the temptation — it is huge. You will be able to close the wound of mortality. Nobody will say no to that. Humans will already serve this as a new religion by the middle of the century; humanity as a whole will work with the beast. So, when the new Christ revelation happens, it will be completely covered by the new beast. Therefore, other people should be there, who can represent true love and true brotherhood in such a really strong way, that this can compete with the fantastic image of the human who is totally complete, who is made totally whole, but is nevertheless the total reversal of the human. You can read in the second chapter of *The Event in Science, History, Philosophy and Art* about the reversal mentioned in *Revelations* that is already coming to fulfillment in the 21st century. It is the beginning of a greater cycle, but it's already happening: a total reversal. The reversed, opposite human being will become the average human being.

In connection with this, people have been speculating about the incarnation of Ahriman. This will not take place completely until the 23rd century. Right now, we have the formation of his kindergarten; in the next century, we will see his elementary school, and then, in the 23rd century, the incarnation of the headmaster himself. However, all of humanity is already possessed by Ahriman today! Can you find someone who is not? There are only a very few exceptions, and they are possessed by Lucifer, so the middle stream simply does not exist. Our government, economy, education and medicine are already Ahrimanic. Then you have Luciferic alternatives: the 'spiritual' route and its various streams. However, Lucifer is also a good help against Ahriman, so it's not always bad, but we just have to understand that this is the spiritual map of where we are.

The real thing, the Michaelic stream itself, is still trying to incarnate and has not been able to do so. Consider the true meaning of what I said at the beginning: there was a possibility that the Michaelic stream could reincarnate in the 20th century. This possibility did not happen. So it's not on the Earth, it's in the spiritual world. It's our task to prepare a new possibility for this incarnation, to prepare the soil for later on in this century. First, we have to do our jobs as ordinary human beings, who have to take the basic steps. Steiner was waiting for anthroposophists to take this first step and they did not do it. This step must be taken first before he can continue.

We have to prepare the ground. Humans must do their part. Steiner did his part, but he remained alone. Nobody understood what he was talking about in the practical sense, in connection with creating the social impulse. He needed partners for the social impulse, but nobody could understand this. He is still waiting for the social impulse to start and only then can he come again. He is not here with us on the Earth.

Rudolf Steiner can do his own work very well. I think he proved himself, right? But he cannot handle the social question alone; he can only do it with real independent coworkers, who create a society, a community of free people. He depends on us now. He is keeping everything of his own work, but the rest is up to us — it is our work. In this field, we haven't moved even one little step since he died. Not the smallest one. We are still at the very same place. It must begin with our own independent work that he cannot do for us. We're still trying to take the first step, our step. I'm just pointing out the facts, not any opinions about it; just the facts. That's where it is. I remember those discussions about the end of the last century. I could see how people refused to admit the facts.

I remember that it became, at a certain time, a trendy thing for people to say that they were reincarnated anthroposophists from the beginning of the century. They even began to have memories. I remember a discussion with a prominent anthroposophist, who was convinced he was a reincarnation of someone from the beginning of the century, and you could do nothing to change his mind. He even knew the name of the person that he reincarnated. The important thing to understand is that we are in the beginning of the same task, with new conditions of course, but still the same task. Until enough people do this, there will be no new wave, no new great effort of the Michaelic School to incarnate, because there is no place to incarnate. There are not a lot of human beings who can take it in.

So, dear friends, if we do our work today, then we have something to give to the next generation who will be able to move with it into the middle of the century. Otherwise it will not happen by itself. Remember what is said in the book of *Revelations*: human beings will be totally fascinated by the new miraculous science, it will become their religion, which promises to make you immortal, to make you healthy, and to make you wealthy forever by purely external means; you don't have to do any inner work. Humanity will be duped by this new religion, with its enthusiasm, hope, love, brotherhood, God, and spiritual experiences. In any lecture of Kurzweil, you can see how he speaks about his plans: they are a new 'spiritual' message to humanity.

In conclusion, there must be a real alternate to these plans, so the true human being can also become possible. Only the forces of Vidar can make this true. That's the mystery of these forces, which means we have to do this. In 33 years, by 2045, the beast, Fenris will come with all his might, with all his forces. Then a question will ring out: what can come from the north to answer this? What can come as the real Christ impulse that will make it possible for at least a small group of humans to be able to educate themselves and the new generation? What can rise up now, so that around the great time at the middle of the century, and already in the 2030s and '40s, there will be some alternative to this huge war coming from both sides? I wanted to add all of this background to our work here, so you understand that, though we are spending our days doing some funny little exercises, behind it stands a far-reaching picture. This means there is a lot of potential, but also a lot of responsibility for the future.

# Lecture 5

## Can we become the Guardian Angels of our Brothers and Sisters? An Introduction to the School of Spiritual Science
## (Orust 2012)

WE HAVE BEEN PRACTICING real dialogue for several years now with the friends in the Global School (or 'Elementary' School of Spiritual Science) here and in many parts of the world.[18] Through this work we have experienced that it has a certain validity and a practical value in bringing down spirituality into real life, into day to day situations, as we try to make it more concrete in our social life, the life that we are living most intensely all day long with other humans. Most humans are with other humans all day long. There are some people who try to get away from them, going to the forest, to the mountains or the jungle...until they run into humans there too, who were also thinking about escape! You go to the moon, more humans! Now to Mars! There is no way to escape anymore, humans are all over the place and they are multiplying, and 7 billion or so are incarnated all over the planet Earth. Never have so many human souls been incarnated at the same time in recorded history. This is huge and dramatic, and has to do with the spiritual signature and challenges of this age.

The important thing today is to be able to look someone in the eyes and be true to the image of the other human being, to be loyal to the images of the humans that come to us through our friends and colleagues and any acquaintance that we meet in the street. How can we be true to the human, to the element of humanity as such? What does it mean to be loyal, true, and responsible for your brother? What does it mean to be honestly able to say, "I will be my brother's keeper!?" What does it mean to be my brother's keeper, and also to ask your brother or sister to be your keeper? This should extend in both directions, as a conscious social contract, an interpersonal contract. How can we make each work situation and each social situation into a place in which we begin to experience such things as a most elementary need? It cannot be abstract or an idea, but rather it must be a feeling, a need or an instinct. It must become this deep. Maybe this is not true for all humans now, but in the future it will be felt like the bodily hunger or thirst we experience today. The need will be very clearly experienced and felt: "I MUST be your keeper, your guardian angel."

When I look at you, I see that your guardian angels are leaving you. Not because we have done something wrong. It's a good sign, not a bad one. But it is a huge challenge that we must face if it is true. It is a spiritual fact that the guardian angels are leaving us, because they have some other things to do and because they know their timing and ours. They know we have to take their place. We are becoming angels, they are becoming archangels. Everything is moving, even God is becoming a kind of Super-God now, something more than God. Everyone is moving up; in fact, don't tell me that you haven't noticed this with your pets! They will be taking your place very soon. If you don't move up, they will take over! Many pets are commanding their humans like angels did in earlier times; you know that. It's not a secret, it's like an omen. With pets and their owners, it's very clear who is in charge. So if you are not beginning to move to the level of an angel, your pet is there to take you over.

If I look at a person today, an ordinary person that is not conscious of the spiritual movement of our time, in the aura around them there is a feeling that speaks about profound loneliness: a being thrown down, deserted, as if his spiritual aura, which was carried by the angel in earlier times, is gone. It used to be there, even a century ago it was there; until the middle of last century it was still there. Just think about what is really happening as we speak. You feel this desertedness, this loneliness, objectively speaking, like this person doesn't have protection anymore. So this is where you feel you are called to be his guardian angel. But it is coming from very deep places within yourself; you have to feel it and experience that you are called for this mission.

It cannot be a social law or regulation by the state. Can you imagine? We would have to sign a paper here: "Each participant of the seminar must be the guardian angel of each other." We would first sign it and then this would be checked and monitored. No doubt the state would try to regulate this, but not in a spiritual sense and not in a free way. But the spiritual situation is really significant. I should feel that I want to be your guardian angel, that if I don't ask you to be my guardian angel, I am lonely and deserted. I cannot really be my own guardian angel; I can be yours, and hope that you will be mine. **Trying to be my own guardian angel will only end in a very unbalanced, egotistical position.** In that case, I would be thinking only about my own good even more than I do normally. Physically, I have to think about fulfilling my needs socially and so on, like we do all day, it's quite justified. But if spiritually we add to this the worry that I have to be *my own* spiritual guardian angel, then even the spiritual life will be about myself. So this cannot be a very healthy situation. I have to think about *your protection* as you should think about mine; if this is practiced more and more, then this creates the right, healthy, social atmosphere and a life which is simply a reality, and not an ideal. The reality in this sense is that the angels are leaving. Now what do we do with it?

Of course, technology is also coming into the picture and replacing the angels. Lots of ahrimanic and luciferic angels are all around, taking the place of each good angel that is leaving. But only humans can take the place of the angel in the right way. The place does not stay empty forever: if the space is left by the right angel, it is filled in by other angels, other beings. If I don't step into the empty space left by your angel and say — *I will fulfill this role*, then some other beings will come who are not the beings we want to guide human evolution. I tried over the years to understand what should be the foundation to rightly cultivate Anthroposophy, and what would be the right soil to cultivate spiritual science in our time, in this century? What should it be? I was asking these questions, because I was aware already as a very young person of the fact that the world was tremendously changed. I had already perceived that the end of the 20th century was profoundly different from how it was in its beginning, and even its middle years. We are living in a totally different world. In the beginning of the 21st century, it is even more changed.

So for me it was always, again and again, using different methods, to work at finding new truth to answer this question: what is really updated and really connected to the Spirit of this time? I was not searching for what was right 100 or more years ago. It has already been a hundred years since Steiner created Anthroposophy and all of its forms and branches, a hundred years from our time! **This must be felt!** I am not speaking from ideas coming out of my head; I am speaking to you from my inner experiences. For me a stretch of 100 years today is like a 1000 in earlier times. Let us say a miracle happens in your life and you become a spiritually creative person, and you create the forms that are connected to your needs and the spiritual impulse for today. Let us say you are Steiner himself and you have created forms that are connected to the real time, today. But what are you going to do with them tomorrow? Do you understand the problem? In long past times if you created a social form, you could relax for a thousand years! It carried its own momentum; it was sanctified by the laws of religion and the stars. Fixity, preservation, and tradition were the rules then. You had to have this element of fixity and rules, because you didn't want changes to be too rapid, you wanted to keep them all for hundreds of years: these social forms, religious forms, thinking forms and feeling forms.

This was essential when humanity was young, and it is still essential for our young children. We should keep a daily rhythm and a certain form for their growth that we don't change every day. For a time a young humanity in the past needed protection in this way. But today it is all upside down, turned inside out — the reverse became as true as what was the strict law in those times — now the opposite is the law. Many people feel this happening and you should feel it (or maybe you will feel it tomorrow or need another incarnation), but the time is ripe now. Many people do, even though they don't allow themselves to say it. In many people you can see they feel it, even if they don't know it themselves, because they suppress their feelings. They are afraid to admit it because of the consequences, not that the consequences are bad. But they are afraid nevertheless, because they are afraid of change. Change is not bad, but they are afraid, because they are secure in their old forms. For many years already the time has been ripe and around the world many people are experiencing it consciously.

I will give you a radical example of what I mean. If I now go out of this room and come back even after just a minute, I am shocked and feel bad about the fact that the room didn't change on the way back in! I come back to the same room, the form remains the same! I am shocked by that and feel very uncomfortable. I actually feel that the external form should immediately change as I am changing. Even more radical: I feel quite uncomfortable that I wake up each morning in the same body! It is getting older and there are some diet problems, of course it is changing in this way, but it is not in this sense I mean. Not in the sense of less or more external beauty, but inwardly to feel that as I go through some strong experiences or great changes, lo and behold, it stays the same! I've been transformed, in many respects I have a different soul, but the box I'm living in couldn't care less! It's a scandal! It must be felt as a scandal, something that doesn't belong to this time and age at all.

Many people feel it and they are changing their bodies, and changing sexes every day, Saturday this, Monday that, and there is all the plastic surgery. These are external motivations people have, but there is also definitely a deeper issue. People feel not only that their bodies are not sacred anymore religiously, but also that it really should change with them! They feel it is not right for the body to hang on in the same way, so they try to fix it externally, which I would not necessarily recommend under all circumstances, every day. But we have to understand that these people feel it instinctively, and this is why it goes to the body directly. **Other people are beginning to feel more spiritually, that if I create a form today, tomorrow it is totally obsolete. And to feel this is the beginning of an awakening to the**

**social question.** Put the social question first and out of the social question all these institutions will be transformed. But it must start from a place in which we have the greatest freedom to change. It is true that I cannot change the shape of my body through my soul experiences immediately.

In connection with this, let us consider architecture. It is true that we have some great problems with architecture, the most horrible of the arts. Huge problems. As we are rapidly changing inwardly and still don't have the technical means to change the exterior surroundings, this is a case of profound disturbance. When we go out in the streets, everywhere we are terribly affected by the fact that the forms stay. The same houses, some of them standing there for centuries or thousands of years (these are often more beautiful than others) but in any case, the fact that they don't change with me every day, every moment, is a problem. It IS going to change much faster than we believe, because the new building technologies will allow for a much greater change and variety, the new materials will become intelligent and AI, so this will express itself also externally very soon. But it is not the physical architecture that is our topic now, I was thinking about the social architecture — here humans have great freedom to change the social forms every day, and they don't do it. So let us speak about the place in which the feeling is justified and where I can do a lot about it, but don't do it simply because I'm afraid to change. I'm used to this way. But I CAN do it; it's a form that can be changed! I'm not speaking about state regulations and laws; these are not the places we begin from, because they are very difficult.

First we have to look at the places in which greater freedom is possible and this is first and foremost the space between you and me, the human space. In spite of all the external forms, regulations, laws and astrological star conditions, we have a freedom to create and to recreate, transform and metamorphose our social conditions every day according to our needs. So, this is why I think we have to focus there, because that's the greatest thing. If we realize we have freedom, if we make it real and learn this social art, the Manichean Royal Art of the future as Steiner called it, where the temple is going to be built and all the good things are going to happen. If we learn it there, it will spread naturally to all social forms and institutions, because people will have created new social life, new social processes and forces and this will of course work into their social conditions everywhere. They will have completely changed their social institutions, but it must come from within, it cannot be forced or compelled from the outside; it must come from the real change of heart within the community. And when this change of heart in the community is really strong and creative, it will create totally different social institutions, simply because this will be an expression of an inner change. People will see it and say, "A school? A school cannot look like that!"

Here we are not speaking about changing the external form, such as the size of the windows or the color of the walls; the essential issue is to deeply feel the following within the community: 'Among us, the co-workers and teachers, we have created such a social life, that out of it an entirely new social setting is coming to life and now a whole new school structure, rhythm, and curriculum wishes to emerge from it, as naturally as breathing.' Only in this way will it be truly real. Trying to change the social structure is futile; it's completely false, because it doesn't have any authentic human forms. But I can have a true feeling that — *I want and know that the time is ripe for everything that happens around us to reflect the immediate present life between us.* This feeling is becoming more and more real and is increasing everywhere, and will increase every year as we go towards the future. The right source is the community, the place in which the element of the human soul really exists; here is where the practice of what I call social yoga is both real and necessary, in the social breathing between you and me.

The source of this can rightly be called the Christ Impulse of our time, the present and future Christ Impulse. Because that is where he is expressing himself, that's where he is working, in a way that is truthful and healthy for us. This is right. It is not mystical, not anything occult; it's completely available to any human meeting in any human work in the present. That's the most secure and most profound place in which spiritual science can be based today. But to make an effort, a serious, honest, humble effort to do it, one has to really want to do it — not as another goal among 20, 30, or 100 other projects, but to say that this is the heart of it all! If you cannot work on this, who cares about the rest? If the heart is not functioning, the body is dead! Why work so much to manicure this dead body?

Who wants to make a real effort, to put first things first, and to say 'this is the foundation?!' No more excuses, no more saying, 'After work if we have time, or during the holidays after we finish our work.' First things first, before everything else, this will be our foundation. Unless we give it all of our attention, who cares about the other things? They will come second and third when this happens first, but not the other way around. If this is put in the second or third place, it will never happen! If you let people begin to give lectures and talk about social questions and social problems, many different and strange solutions will arise. You'll get abstract threefolding. That's your punishment, to get lectures about threefolding; that is the total dead end of everything social, when you even have lectures about it! No, we have to really mean something very concrete about it, otherwise we cannot move forward a single step. This is why I said to myself, there can be a new start for creating a foundation for Anthroposophy from this place of social breathing. This is why, wherever I can find people interested in it, I'll work with them. I'm trying to find people who feel similar to me. I'm travelling around the world now looking for such people. If you find someone let me know. They look like us! They have those bodies that stay more or less the same! If you look at their aura, they are more lonely and deserted than others. So they might be here, you never know, always be positive!

# Lecture 6

## The Working of the Christ in the Apocalyptic Spiritual Conditions of the 20th and 21st Centuries
### (Utrecht 1997)

WE ARE STRUGGLING STILL to find a language of the soul that can approach the spirit, and a language of the spirit that can speak to the soul.[19] The soul cannot yet speak to the spirit, and the spirit has not yet learned to approach the soul in the right way. So we are divided even here; we are split in two. This also happens on the geographical and political level, with consequences for the whole world organization, the map of the whole world. The question of the Western European, English-speaking people and the central European, German-speaking people, and all the way to the East is very important; it is crucial for the future.

My intention is first of all to give a general outline of the 20th century as a whole and what it means for the evolution of human conscious awareness on the Earth in this time. I will then give some indications concerning the overall transformation of the human constitution that occurred in the 20th century and the basis for psychotherapeutic work.

Let me draw (in Figure 1) a line that expresses the time spirit of the 20th century. This is an aspect of the evolution of the time spirit of the last century. It is clearly paradoxical. For if we start in 1899, with the end of the Kali Yuga, as it is called, this actually meant that there was more light; there were more values from the past for the social life of humanity than what came later. The paradox, for many aspects of life, is that following the end of the Kali Yuga and with the beginning of the 'new age of light,' the line of development for culture, civilization and social life went below the Kali Yuga level.

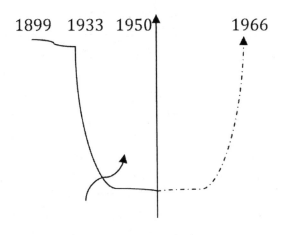

Figure 1

This then is the first great paradox of our time. Drawing it like this, I indicate the line of civilization in general, not of the individual human being. The line then moves upward from this abyss. It is somewhat less clear and I use a broken line to indicate that the way up is not as certain as the way down. The way down to the abyss is a world fact. It happened; it is happening; we are there. The way up is a possibility, something not yet realized and perhaps not even realizable at all for the future in this form.

If you permit me, I will interpret Figure 1 as follows. The events that happened when humanity went down into the abyss can of course be explained in many ways.

What I am going to say will obviously reflect just one possible approach. But I will make it very clear. I think we live in times when we have to speak clearly, more clearly than we may sometimes be used to, about the realities of the 20th century, for otherwise we will not be prepared for the 21st. We have to call things by their names, which means that I shall have the pleasure of using concepts, designating the spiritual, human and social experiences of this time, taken from Anthroposophy. The choice is not arbitrary, but the result of an inner struggle, which is part of both anthroposophical experience and of human experience at this time. Anthroposophical terms cannot just be applied to all of the events of the 20th century, without conscious consideration, as a matter of course. For whatever came up to the year 1933 in the world was conceptually prepared for, while we do not yet really have anthroposophical concepts for everything that came in the second third of the century, from 1933 to 1966. The words, the concepts of anthroposophy, the research results communicated by Rudolf Steiner were given up to 1925. Only the realities of that time could, of course, be called by their names.

As to the future, only indications could be given, and indications are something different compared to the reality that is already present. If you consider the way Rudolf Steiner spoke about the future, you find that he always spoke of possibilities. He always said that I-development in the age of the spiritual soul would depend on human freedom. Looking at the future, you can therefore only say that it could be like this, but it will depend on the way human beings freely choose to go. It is quite clear that Rudolf Steiner spoke of possibilities in a different manner than the way he spoke about things that had already happened. Then he would speak directly, characterizing them from different points of view, but these would be things that had happened, that had become realities. Today, as we look back from the end of the 20th century, we have Rudolf Steiner's indications, but much greater freedom of perception as regards things that have already happened. Out of this knowledge we have to call things by their names and we have to stand behind our judgment with our inner authority, our inner experiences. We can no longer hide behind the known judgments of Rudolf Steiner. If we are uncertain about our own experiences or cannot bring them to full knowledge, we will also be unsure in looking back on the 20th century, and in our ability to judge in a sense that will truly lead to concepts. We need anthroposophical concepts based on knowledge that will fit what is happening in our time. This uncertainty, of course, is not something intellectual. It is the question of the human heart. It is a moral soul question, a psychotherapeutic question of the highest magnitude in our time.

The human soul, the human I of the present time, has grown uncertain of its own existence. For, it has experienced something that has never been possible before in human evolution. Here we move to the central event of the 20th century, to this deep abyss. Let me characterize this in very simple terms. I am not going to be too anthroposophical about this, but if you look at the available anthroposophical literature you will find many possible explanations. What happened in this time is a total transformation of human I-evolution. There is the abyss, and in the abyss we have the physical body, ether body, astral body and I of human beings, their human constitution. Looking at the abyss experience, we have to say that there was a complete transformation, metamorphosis, of I-development or evolution. It happened in such a way that the following became possible: Firstly, the human being can now lose the I completely. The bodies no longer hold the I tightly in incarnation. This is the simple result of the fact that humanity has begun its dying process. Humanity is physically dying. This began with the end of the Kali Yuga, and even before this, from the beginning of the age of the spiritual soul and indeed the Mystery of Golgotha. Humanity is dying, or, as we usually put it, humanity is crossing the threshold. When we die, the bodies begin to loosen. The first thing that happens as we grow old is that the ether body loosens and separates from the physical body. This is happening very intensely in our time.

Two thirds of the time Rudolf Steiner said it would take for the ether body to be completely free of the human organization have already passed. He spoke of 300 years for the process in which the ether body separates from the human heart to be complete. The head, he said, had already separated. 300 years is a very short time; it consists of the first two centuries of the Michaelic age, at the end of the 20th and up to the 21st century. In a hundred years time, the ether body will have completely separated from the heart. We can say, therefore, that the human I is no longer bound etherically, but also it is no longer bound astrally to the physical body. The I is no longer bound to the physical body — neither etherically nor astrally. The human I is free from the forces that hold it naturally in incarnation. I use the term 'naturally' in the good sense of evolution.

The good powers have been at work from the beginning of Earth evolution, bringing together the composition of the human nature and creating the physical body, ether body and astral body, then adding the I, the divine spark of the human being. These have ceased to work from the middle point of the 20th century, though it was a long process until this point was reached. But as Rudolf Steiner always said, from now on all things of the past will be done with and they will decrease. 1950 is the absolute end point. This marks the end of the past. The past falls into the abyss and is destroyed. Divine guidance through the blood, through heredity, through norms, through concepts, through religious values and beliefs — all this falls into the abyss. Everything that holds the I at the human level, and even the level of the Kali Yuga, is destroyed in the abyss. The 5000 years of the Kali Yuga now appear to be very human because of everything that goes on below this level. In the 5000 years of the Kali Yuga, called the years of darkness, human evolution was still carried by divine spiritual tradition if not direct inspiration; until the watershed came in our time and the past ended. The human I is thus free to incarnate or not to incarnate but also at the mercy of powers that are embedded in our civilization.

To try and understand the spiritual event of the 20th century, we must take it deeply into our empty hearts, into the free space in the circle of our moral, spiritual, religious freedom. We have to open this space wide, for the opening up of heart is a fact of evolution. To keep it open means to have the freedom in mind and spirit and in social life to let the true, higher I-nature of humanity begin to incarnate. The old traditional I that was dependent on the blood has been destroyed. It is no longer there. The blood which carried it has been destroyed; it does not exist anymore; not for humanity as a whole, and not as individuals. For humanity as a whole this is no longer a carrying power of the divine, spiritual I of the human image of God, borne in the blood. It must now be brought to incarnation, incorporation or individuation in complete freedom, as people work together in a free cultural, social and economic life.

Looking for a concept to know and understand the event of the 20th century, we have to say that the whole of the human constitution went through a complete transformation, with each of the bodies separating. I cannot go into detail about this now, but the physical body was completely transformed, and the ether and astral bodies were transformed.[20] The most important thing is that the I has now lost its center in the human heart. This is now free, and if the heart system is free this means, of course, that the whole human constitution is completely out of harmony. The heart system brings lower human nature into balance with the higher — physically, etherically, astrally, and also at the I level. Until now this balance was unconsciously maintained. Today this is no longer the case. The balance is no longer there. The human constitution is falling apart. This has extremely important aspects relating to the body and also the soul bodies. I cannot go into it all here, but I will stay with the problem of the I and the self.

When the I was leaving the other bodies, was excarnating in this age, the process was taken hold of by the powers of evil. Evil was thus also able to take a new step in evolution. It was able to enter into the free space in the human heart where the I no longer holds sway but which is completely free. Let me draw this power of evil, which comes from below (see the small arrow on the lower left in Figure 1). We speak of the incarnation of evil, which is not the right term from a spiritual-scientific point of view, for incarnation refers to something that comes from above. Let us call it the individuation or individualization of evil. It is coming from here, from below and in the empty heart center of human beings it can now become something of a reversed human I, cognitively, or more practically, a reversed I. We are the first human generations to have experienced the individuation, individualization of the reversed I. This is given different names in spiritual science. Where it has to do with my individual I, as a temptation, it has been called the Asuras. Where the same principle attacks the I of humanity, it is called Sorat, the beast, the sun demon, the anti-I principle in the universe, the antichrist; the twofold beast, the spirit of the two. If I were to say this evil spirit, the anti-I, became a human being, this would be true; I could say this, of course (but this is the trouble I referred to before: we don't have concepts for what is happening here). But to say this would be a tremendous paradox. For the reversal has happened. Instead of the human being, we have the first foundation of a whole human existence. It is a whole human/non-human, subhuman, anti-human humanity that will bear with it, as a principle of civilization, all levels of life and develop further on into the future. For a time they will still be in humanlike bodies, physical bodies. But in the future this physical body will no longer have the human form we recognize today. What has happened here is the individuation of evil.

This should not be taken as something that happened to humanity as a whole or to particular human beings; we should instead realize that this happens in every human being today. One simply cannot be born in this time without having a copy, an instance, of this anti-I in one's own being. One of the most important inner realities for human beings today is also spiritual research into the spirit in every human being that is not his luciferic or ahrimanic double, but his asuric double. The term is, of course, misleading, for this is not the double. The double is something we can talk about only in relationship to the bodies. One can have a double of the physical-etheric body, and then we speak of an ahrimanic double. A double in the astral body is referred to as a luciferic double. But while it is possible and permissible to speak of a double of the I, we have to remember that this is the I and not one of the other three bodies. The double of the I, this real entity, is a power that seeks above all to destroy the I. It wants to destroy, to disintegrate the I. It has the power to fill the whole of civilization with this element. Whatever comes to pass in this realm from this time on, can again be referred to in terms taken from Rudolf Steiner. But for him, at the beginning of the 20th century, it was only a possibility. At that very point in time, exactly the mid-point of the 300 year release of the whole ether body, he spoke of the second coming of the Christ. He gave his prophesies of what would happen in the middle third of the 20th century. At this mid-point he said that humanity would go either toward Anthroposophy and the world of the spirit or down into the abyss, which he called world kama loka. This world kama loka, which is the reversed kama loka, is the realm I spoke of earlier, where the powers of the anti-I are working and turning all the powers of the I into their opposites. We thus have a reversed social structure, education, medicine, advertising or whatever, everything that has been in progress from the aggregation, the foundation of this world kama loka as a world civilization. Today we have everywhere around us, right down to the physical structure of the physical, etheric and astral earth itself, down to the very foundations of earthly existence, the powers of the anti-I, the reversed kama loka process.

To study this world kama loka concept we would have to take things further, but let me at least give an indication. If you study the real kama loka, which every human soul goes through after death, you could understand the nature of the reversed kama loka here on the physical earth where subhuman forces are working as anti-I forces. It is a highly unpleasant picture. I do not know if some of you have experienced it. This unpleasantness makes us unwilling to look into the depths, to face the evil in ourselves, in our culture. It is an uneasiness that must be overcome for we cannot begin to heal the wounds of our time unless we overcome it. If anything can be said to be important to the powers of the beast, it is above all that this openness to the spirit in our time, the freedom of the I, of the heart, shall be immediately filled and closed and sealed by the other power, the anti-I. This process of filling the heart, now empty of the traditional blood-I, is the main aim, the main ideal of the beast with the powers of evil.

If we can just begin to let the wound of humanity, which is the place where the I no longer works instinctively in the blood, be clearly seen, it appears imaginatively as a wound in the heart, in the central region of the human being. If we can look at it without fear, if we accept the individuation of evil as a fact of human evolution and begin consciously to face up to it, we can confront it with the individuation of the true I, the Christ I, which has appeared at the same time, but is totally ignored by humanity. It is completely ignored because down here everyone is preoccupied with the individuation of evil. No one has time really to begin the Christ principle's individuation process to freedom. The Christ principle is the higher I of the human being and of humanity as a whole. If we allow ourselves to use the expression 'keep the wound open,' we begin to work in the right way against the powers of the beast in our time.

There is an imaginative picture that also speaks directly to the heart. We can bring many concepts together in one picture. Analyzed conceptually, concepts will only strengthen the power of death. But the picture can speak directly to the heart, the empty heart, and begin to fill it with enthusiasm, with the freedom of the spirit, the love of the spirit in which one can always be in this time, if one is truly in the spirit of our time. The picture is a very old one. It speaks of the beast as having many heads. One very special head of the beast was wounded to death. It speaks of the great power of the beast which is apparent everywhere in our time, the great power of the first beast. The greatest power of the second beast is to make a scientific doctrine for the whole of humanity and to teach them about the miracle of the first beast. The miracle of the beast is that it can show, not theoretically but in every walk of human life, that the wound of death, of evil, of karma, of incarnation, of excarnation, of being born, has been healed. This 'wound of life,' as we may call it to give us a picture, has been healed. The beast says that we can be human beings at the present time without having to undergo these things, even without having been human beings; we do not have to incarnate, we do not have to experience karma, we do not have to be born, or to be educated. The beast says that we will overcome death, sickness, growing old, motherhood, fatherhood and childhood. All of this will be overcome because this wound of openness, of incarnation and spiritual development has been miraculously closed. In the place where we have the most terrible burning and the deepest abyss of evil, we therefore also have the teaching: 'The evil has long since been overcome. There was a time, of course, when human beings were primitive. They were born, they grew old, they were still dying and being born. But it is our principal task to overcome this.' We thus have a great image of the head of the beast that was wounded to death. This means human mortality, for it is mortal for humans to open up to the spirit. Now if human beings do not die, they also will not return to the world of the spirit to prepare their karma. They will have nothing to return to then, nothing to continue. The beast teaches: 'Human beings will be immortal in non-spiritual ways — physically, materially, biologically. They will live forever, being unable to be born or die. These things will be overcome.'

This is the nature of the first beast and the teaching of the second beast. This is what we have to work against. In many respects we were asleep to this reality in the 20th century, but it is now our task in the 21st. We may say therefore that the wound is closed, the wound is sealed, and the wound has been physically overcome for humanity. The teaching of the second beast has been completely accepted by humanity. Speaking about people who are seeking in the spirit, including anthroposophists in their professions, we need to understand this picture more and more so that we can let the right kind of powers flow through our work. It is here especially that I see a great potential for the psychological and psychotherapeutic movement. I say movement. It is a movement and what makes this movement potentially important is that it is a latecomer. It came and really developed through the struggles of the 20th century. It is truly at home in it. Of course there were beginnings before this, but in the 1950s and '60s it really caught fire and enthusiastically spread. So we have a latecomer that is there, already sustaining the struggle with the powers that prevail in our time. There is great potential for powers that can stream from this work to other fields of life. These powers do not easily find their way, not even in the psychological movement; it is obviously still just at the beginning. Yet though it may only be in its beginnings, compare it with medicine, education, agriculture, and political and social life. In those fields it is much more difficult, for their traditions have already been completely transformed by the anti-I concept. We have forms there that we may describe by saying: 'you are not able to be part of this civilization, you are not able to buy or sell, unless you have at least one of these three things, in body, soul and spirit: at least the name or the number or the sign of the beast.' All three are already strongly developed. We cannot be a social being in our time, we cannot buy or sell without carrying this threefold signature, of the individuation of evil, down through the spirit, soul, and body of the human being.

Where we are today is world kama loka. This is our civilization. Only people with special grace can begin to do some work here, for to be helpful today, one must have confronted this picture in one's own individual nature and biography, in the individual struggle to become a human being from the very foundation of a non-human being. To become truly human not from the traditional values of society which still had some humanness about them; for example, it was simply accepted from tradition that man was a human being created in the image of god. This was still there until the middle of the 19th century; everyone knew at some level or another, maybe it was completely unconsciousness, but it was still there — the human being was created in the image of god, through Christ. Today, however, we must look squarely at the other picture, the one that is reversed. We have civilization and we have human beings who are already formed in the image of the anti-Christ. This is reality; it is flesh, blood, soul and spirit. It is already here and must be faced. The struggle must begin in the souls and it must go on, a struggle among human beings.

As a last word, I will draw your attention to this mutual human world, the social aspect of the empty heart, and say that psychotherapeutic work can really only be done among people, with other people. As a matter of fact, the work itself is a healing process. This is happening and there is the very beginning of a true recognition through knowledge and through healing power, through conscious human healing. It can only be by working together, to see that work with the patient is as self-healing as the healing of another. Education must be such today that our children will begin to be what they should have been long since. The educating of educators, the healing of the healers, the making social of the social — all this is a reversal of the reversal. For we have to reverse this reversal of the I, and nothing can be taken for granted today, absolutely nothing.

There is no human, positive element in us. If we believe that we have great ideas, maybe even anthroposophical ideas that Rudolf Steiner struggled hard to develop, and that we can heal with them today, then we are completely oblivious to what has already been a reality for decades. We are really asleep to the true reality of our work. There is no field where this can work anymore. It does not work because healing work must today be created out of the purely human element. There are no other powers and the Christ can only work among human beings who are working socially in this reversed ritual again. But here we again come to another concept that will just destroy everything. No more about reversed ritual; just simply the human social element in working with one another. This is an aspect that needs to be emphasized.

We know that tradition must be transformed and Christianity also needs to be transformed in time. The Christ changes his relationship to humanity a great deal more in our time compared to 20 centuries ago. We probably remember the scenes after the resurrection when he came to visit the disciples. You will remember how one of them could not see the Christ in the spirit. He therefore asked the Christ, 'Would you please show me your wounds? For to see you, to believe in you, I must touch your wounds.' And the Christ, always very sensitive to the needs of human beings, went forward and said, 'Ok, Ok, you don't believe and you want to see and touch. I am with you, don't fear.' And he gave him the hands so he could touch and believe. But then the Christ said, 'You had to touch in order to see and touch in order to know, but in the future, human beings will have to believe without seeing.' For the Christ knew quite well that humanity was going into the last two millennia of the great, deep Kali Yuga, where people would not be able to see but must develop the power of belief. The Christ was thus preparing for the age of belief. He rebuked Thomas and said, 'Well then, you could not see anymore, so you wanted to see, but the time for seeing is over.'

Now the reversal is also very important here. Today it is a total reversal. Today the Christ is approaching human beings; he is coming to answer them, 'I would like to show you your wounds. I will show you your own wounds, so that I can be the healer of your wounds.' This is the approach of the Christ today. It is the reversal of the story of Thomas. And He also says, 'I will transform your wounds so you will be able to see.' The healing of the wounds in soul, spirit and body today is the source of seeing, of seeing in the spirit; the new imaginative faculties are those born from transforming the powers of healing, the new healing, the new working of the wound. And the best way to make it clear is to say it in German. For I have just come from a visit to Munich where there is one of the greatest works of a German artist. It is Joseph Beuys' *Zeige mir deine Wunde*. You must of course play this great drama yourself, in the way which Beuys did it. The title shows the right direction. It is the word of the Christ, 'Show me your wounds if you want to see, for the wound is opening the eyes, or opening the heart to new knowledge.' From compassion to knowing, from healing the wound to knowledge, everything must now come from the heart. The head powers on their own are already part of the evil principle. Any concept, even the smallest concept that comes from the head, is already part of world kama loka and therefore not only useless, but definitely harmful. It is definitely a power that hides the wound.

I would like to finish with this picture. The wounds of the Christ (but now the wound of the human being which the Christ makes clear) opens up and heals, so that the eyes of the heart can be opened; the heart of seeing and the wound of the beast. On the one hand, the beast with the wound that was miraculously healed, which is the principle of black magic in our time and in the future; and on the other hand, the Christ with his wounds, but the wounds which are now sealed and concealed within the human heart. I would therefore like to suggest this Imaginative picture as a contribution to the development of psychotherapy in our times.

# Lecture 7

## The Beast and the Reversal
## The Cucumber Law™
## (Gothenburg 2009)

THE BEAST CANNOT BE DESTROYED.[21] It can only be transformed, but it must first be perceived, heard, and grasped. It makes all things "personally mine," but is itself invisible. The Beast has insatiable hunger for true nourishment and nourishment by truth and feeds upon it. However, we should use these gifts that the beast gives us and not reject them. If we reject them we cannot get to know the giver. We should not give up our control or our intellect. We should not go back to the primitive. It is understandable if we are drawn to a primitive, pre-intellectual state, but it is no solution. The final solution is not to go back, though a part of the truth can be found there, but it is an illusion. This is not the way, it is an escape. We need the tools of the Beast. Also the illusion of going back to nature is materialistic as well, and will just enslave us to the Beast. The Beast is the headmaster of gigantic, utopian strategies of the transubstantiation and transmutation of everything human and natural. In the "heart of the Beast," perhaps only in the centre of the spiritual earth (or "Zion," the rescue place of the leftover remnant of humanity in *The Matrix Reloaded* who are hunted by the Machines), the transformation is possible. The Beast doesn't only live and work in the global establishments, but also has found a place for itself in alternative movements, anarchists, NGOs, Anthroposophical institutions, etc. It even provides money and a place for them! It is simply the gigantic idea and practice of making the earth into a totally reversed heaven. There is a difference between creating dreamy alternatives and what Michael is seeking to establish on the Earth through His school.

When we look at the human being as he stands before us today we see the result of a long process of development, a long evolutionary process leading to a strong independent 'I.' The Gods worked on these foundations of the I. The I is now embodied, fully incarnated and strives to spiritualize itself. We have the divine power in the I. It is a singular spiritual being. Through our various bodies and vehicles it becomes separated from the real spiritual world. It found itself as separate but lost its true identity as a divine being. It is created out of the whole universe, containing all the forces of the universe, but received the impulse that separated it — as divine being — from its true source. Its power is divine, but God arranged everything so that it is (mis)guided to divert its consciousness and being to itself and to matter as ultimate realities.

Let us turn to the human individuation of the Ego: the whole of evolution is repeated in each one of us, in our biography. It is natural, instinctive and operates all the time. It can only be reversed through a decision of the free I. But we don't stop it. We continue on the path of individuation started at childhood. We continue it as adults. All Ego forces are there from babyhood on. We become mature bodily and physically but spiritually we remain babies. In childhood individuation is unconscious and therefore pure, in adulthood it become egoistic. But as adults we change the real Earthly world. We create a new world, civilization, out of our continuous conscious egoistic individuation. In this we are "I babies" and it is there that the Beast has its stronghold.

The world is there, it "worlds" and happens all the time in us and around us. But only in rare moments of grace events do we touch reality and come in contact with the real world and real I. Individuation means to forget the world and remember only the untrue I. Grace is to touch the world and be touched by it. It comes and disappears. When it comes it is forgotten. We forget the world because it is in the sphere where we fulfil our needs and desires, wishes, and realize our ideas and purposes in action. We are nourished by the world.

After we are fully incarnated we continue to conquer the world and transform it in our own image as separated egos. This is what material civilisation is all about. We do all this in the realm of Earthly power and freedom. This brave new world is created in my image as unconscious, separated divine being. Physical food for the bodies, love and warmth for our souls, truths for our spirit, these are the ingredients of our nourishment as embodied beings. Any truth we grasp, any experience of grace is sucked in and assimilated. We crave truths as we crave for food and as babies long for milk. The individuation process creates a reversal in the world. Individuation, privatization, is only half a truth. The forces which guide this are the forces which created and guide individuation. The other half of the truth is the reversal of this process, which can only take place in the free work of the Ego. The question is what is the role and vocation of the human? Where is the human being going? We can go either way. A question is real only when the possibility of choice arises; transforming nature and humans through our material knowledge or spiritualizing through our truly gained self-knowledge and spiritual knowledge. God created us in His Image but divorced us and separated us from Himself. We create our world in our materialistic image.

In the *Apocalypse of St. John* there is described a total transformation in either of two ways: 1) towards individuation, a God reversed, as human god, as a real reversal of God, or 2) a reversal of this reversal. Either I recreate the world in my image, under my control, like a machine transforming spirit into matter, transforming everything, every spirit and nature into their opposites, into matter in my image, or, in the other direction, I transform matter into spirit, go upstream. We are so strongly incarnated and individualised, but can we reverse this? Can we go against the Gods of individuation and materialization themselves? Can we transform millions of years of our descent into matter? This seems quite impossible. So we seek "alternatives" and thus try to avoid the hard question.

To succeed we would have to begin to constitute and construct another order of "events." This is also called "Initiation," which means doing the impossible by any normal Earthly standards. This awakening is a new type of event, penetrating to the hard core of individuation, and to our own individualized Beast being. This being makes me into myself and nothing else, precisely at the expense of everything else. It makes me betray all my most sacred loves and truths and reverses them into their exact opposites.

It will be the first — truthful — the truth of the absolute reversal of all truth. *This event of self-encounter cannot come as an event of grace.* We must create and realize it only because we love it. There is absolutely no physical need for this meeting; on the contrary, physical life is strongly disturbed by it. It is the only place I meet reality as myself. We tend to reject this and it appears to be painful, but the forces to meet ourselves can also create real joy, love, truthfulness to our life, much deeper and more ours than everything we may have received through grace alone. *It is a self-given grace — I grace myself with the most painful encounter with myself as the Beast, but I am real in real life with my own true reality, and this opens the gates to meet also my true higher being in the cosmos.*

By individuation, incarnation, and creation of a strong Ego/I, we become masters of the world and create the world in our own image. We reverse God and spirit into matter. Man is the reverse God and now also creates his world in his reversed-divine image. The 2nd half of the 21st century will already witness the first stage of the seemingly conflicted marriage between China, the oldest spirituality that is becoming Ahrimanic, and America, the land of the fullest possible reversal.

This is another major step towards the reversal of the whole of humanity. The merger between America and China will create a mutation of the human on a far greater scale then we today imagine, both quantitatively and qualitatively. There was one lonely person 100 years ago, who opposed this plan all by himself: He was called back then, Rudolf Steiner. Now the forces of hindrance are doing all they can to make sure that he (as an outpost for the cosmic school of Michael) cannot come back. The Michael school can only work, however, if it finds a seed-point on the Earth, a real transformation place within the human. Where can we start this reversal? We must do it, we must practice. Otherwise, Anthroposophy is another rich source of stories to be consumed and assimilated, reversed and used for personal purposes like any other truth. **But where are those who want to reverse this reversal?**

If we succeed in the coming 3rd millennium to do this, then in the 6th root race (or 6th Post Atlantean age) things will not be too bad. In the reversal process during human individuation or development, the child takes the forces of the world and makes them into his own in body, soul and spirit. The laws of individuation are simple, but we forget them and how they work, or we may entertain illusions about ourselves in this regard as adults. The law here is as simple as it is shocking to us personally: **only what we have consciously reversed is truthful.** And the obverse is the same: what we have not reversed is the natural egoistic reversal. It persists, in other words, unless we have consciously reversed the naturally given reversal. But we must know how the natural reversal happens in order to be informed about the true state of affairs, and this is already the first step in reversing it.

I meet a person, an event, a truth, be it cucumber or a friend. Everything that we meet we consume, bodily-physically, psychologically, mentally and spiritually. We can generalise this to include any spiritual, religious, and Anthroposophical truths. I will with due respect designate it as "the law of the cucumber" and baptize it as **the law of reversal.** This is an absolute-universal law, as all encompassing as gravity is in the physical world. I don't meet anything without having a desire or need to capture and consume it. Physically, emotionally, cognitively, spiritually, I meet it because I was looking for it, and I meet "it" from this very personal perspective (e.g. it is useful, enjoyable, feared). Now I am going to have a meeting with a cucumber. If I meet it because of physical-bodily hunger, then it will be physical food. I may meet it aesthetically because it is beautiful. I may meet it as a nutritionist or as spiritual scientist. Whatever the point of view, I am going to use it, to consume it, to satisfy the specific need that led me to meet it in the first place.

Now let us assume that what led me to this specific cucumber is my physical hunger. I meet it because I am going to satisfy my hunger. At this very moment the cucumber is transformed into "that cucumber which is an object by means of which I will satisfy this specific need, my hunger." I am hungry and my body must eat. It is this factual circumstance that defines the situation of our meeting, it and me, to satisfy my (physical, soul or spiritual) hunger, to feed myself. If I am interested in the spiritual being of the cucumber, its relations to the physical and spiritual worlds, then I will meet it as a means to satisfy my drive for knowledge, it will become a means to satisfy my need to know it.

We also have hunger for spiritual truths and it is a spiritual hunger completely identical to physical hunger. We also have hunger for human contact, relations, warmth, love, attention and respect. The human being I meet is looked at, known, recognized, as that which may satisfy my hunger for the human contact, etc. When we now speak about devouring a physical cucumber, therefore, please don't forget that this is a single example of the threefold needy nature of the human being, in body, soul and spirit, which defines its reversing-reversed connection to each and any object and world.

Now let us eat our physical cucumber! First, I must cut it from the living plant, I separate it and disconnect it from the world in which it is rooted, in which it is a living part. I grasp it in my hand, connect myself physically with it, and rip it from the real world. This is the first step: I separate something, a being, object, or a truth, from **its** world — from the real objective world. I declare: from now on it will become part of **my** world (as a separate being). But the cutting from the world is killing. I kill the cucumber. From that moment on it is going to die. It is not reversible, I cannot glue it back even if I would have wanted to do so (which is of course not my purpose). In death the corpse is not living. It only carries some decaying remnants of its real spirit. The soul and spirit of the cucumber are separated from it. They have departed and the natural world is now lacking one incarnated cucumber. When it is killed it now really belongs to me and not to its world. It is dead in and for the world, but it is becoming — and will increasingly become — mine. I now make it my own in thinking, feeling and willing. We cannot begin to reverse anything until we have made it our own. And we cannot start to make it our own before we cut it from the world and kill it. Now we can take it over, conquer it, make it ours. It is the same process with spiritual truths. We pick them up, kill them and make them our own. We subjugate them to our personal need, power and control.

Now comes the time to enjoy our prey. We break the cucumber down, we salivate on it rhythmically and continue to break it down in our mouth and taste it with our taste buds. It is most enjoyable. We liberate the taste hidden in the broken tissue and the flesh of the truths that we continue to pulverize, salivate and break down until the moment we feel that the taste has gone and the material has lost its value for our conscious enjoyment. The transformed cucumber has released its inner life which we now have made our own. I become stronger to the extent I take your physical, life, soul and spirit substance and assimilate it into myself in this manner.

Then, after completing this stage of enjoyment we decide to "swallow." This decision transfers the process of digestion and assimilation from the conscious process to the unconscious. Now what is left from the other's forces and being, cut from the world, killed, broken down and transformed, is pulled down, crosses the threshold from conscious into the unconscious and disappears into total oblivion. We swallow it. Cows can regurgitate and rework what they have swallowed. Humans can also do this with spiritual matters. There is no conscious taste experience in the stomach or the intestines. The rest of the process is unconscious; that is the real part of the digestion, assimilation, in which the foreign being will finally and wholly transubstantiate into my own flesh and blood. Once filtered through the wall of the small intestine, it flows into the creation of lymph and blood. We now build our bodies out of it. It becomes our stuff, our body itself.

We return to the conscious soul life when we return to the outer world. We do this in two ways. We discard the unneeded refuse from which we extracted everything we needed as toxic waste and give it to the Earth, and we use the energies of digestion to fire our will to work consciously and change the external world. With these forces we feel, think, and toil on the Earth to create our civilization. We consciously change the world according to our needs, to create man-made civilization that replaces nature. We are machines that eat, transform, and **sub**-substantiate (as opposed to trans-substantiate) nature (which is permeated with spirit) into sub-natural, sub-physical civilization based on the destruction of nature. But of course we have long forgotten the cucumber, the unconscious process of its assimilation and death. We use its forces but are certain that we use our own. We really made them our own — but we forgot their origin in the real world. Or we may also conceive of the notion that a decent civilization, in order to be human and moral, should make monuments to preserve the memory of and honour the eaten and now truly wholly forgotten **real** cucumbers! And now the cycle starts all over again. The working out of our conscious needs and motives makes us hungry again. After depleting the forces we got from the last cucumber we go back to nature, other persons, and culture, to be nourished again.

The cycle of individuation turns another circle in the spiral of making everything given by God into our own human creation. Up to this point I have given a description of the more objective side of the process of individuation and reversal. It was done more from the point of view of the real world. Now I wish to briefly repeat the same processes and compare the objective and subjective sides of it, in order to make more visible the meaning of the "law of individuation or reversal."

In the first stage, when I pick the cucumber from the plant, I feel really connected to a real world. I hold it in my hand. In my hunger and need I felt separated, lonely, and weak. Now I am connected. This is the reverse of the objective world reality. The world says, "Hey, you cut one of my fingers off! It is now dead and I (the world) experience one of my members dead in me." But I experience only this: *Oh joy, I am connected again to reality, it is mine, soon I will enjoy, taste and eat it and become that much more alive!* I make a physical connection with the cucumber when I cut it off from the world. I become one with the cucumber's corpse and experience myself more alive than before. **This connection with the dead increases my inner life.** It increases through the whole process of digestion. The subjective soul and 'I' experience increases the more the objective decreases, but of course I am only conscious of increasing enjoyment, satisfaction and growing strength, capacity and wisdom. What never comes to consciousness is the real truth: that I am the embodied, real reversing machine of the world. I am not really conscious that I take life and make it my own. For me it is an inner experience of the subjective soul life. Such subjective life becomes a true revelation of being in me, when it is actually and objectively dead.

Now that the being is really mine, I forget it, I "swallow" it and it disappears into my unconscious. The very last conscious experience is the memory picture that I (sometimes) still make and carry within me. This is what is left of the real "it"— **my** picture of you is living in my memory, and I believe that this is the real you and not only my self-made picture of "you." What I received from my friend is made into my possession. The giver is made into a shadowy ghost, (if I still remember — and this is rare — that he exists at all). But in any case what I remember is only what is made into my soul possession. We then say: the dead person lives in our memory, she doesn't really exist after death! We really believe that "she" is buried in the grave we visit and commemorate. I perhaps honestly believe that I re-member "him," that "he" lives in me.

Objectively speaking, any personal and subjective remembrance is the forgetting of the real spirit being. After cutting, killing and hiding the essence from consciousness comes forgetting, and then we erect a monument to the memory. This is a total forgetting of the truth, which we have made our own subjective memory. The bigger and more sacred the monument, the greater the forgetting (objectively speaking), but we say and believe (subjectively) that there is truth in the tomb, ritual, or monument. We say, "I remember him forever," but **in truth** I only remember what I made out of him for my own use as my own possession. Did I ever know who he was in the first place? Of course not! In the first, second and third place I only approached him subjectively, to satisfy a specific personal need. I only met him through this very narrow perspective to begin with. I have greatly enjoyed making him my own possession because it satisfied my own real needs. Objectively I never knew who he "really" was but subjectively obviously I "know him very well," he is my most intimate friend! (But I never really go out of myself to inquire of the late cucumber what **his** take on this declaration of love and intimacy may be. If I did, he would have characterized this stage as a "denial" and later also a "betrayal" of his true being).

This is how we "live together" socially nowadays. All those we have met and devoured in our life make our soul. Parents, teachers, friends, and enemies are assimilated, possessed, forgotten, and then objectively speaking, also denied and hence objectively betrayed (not least perhaps precisely in the moment in which the declaration of subjective loyalty is most intense!) Now in the nourishment process so far, all the forces of the food have been assimilated. They flow in my veins as fresh forces of life. When I go out to realize myself in the world, I experience the joyful and healthy self-affirmation of the moving body, the fired will power working through the limbs, the thought and feeling experiences I have of my really being in touch with the real world — my world — in which my I is becoming real more and more. With all the forces gained and assimilated from the world I become — subjectively speaking — precisely of course most myself! I experience now the powerful self-affirmation, strength, and courage to live and create, to do in the world what I want to do.

This is the most exact reversal of truth there can be in our universe: the self-enjoying, world conquering, individual! And this is not only in America! It is — paradoxically speaking — a wholly justified, objectively given, absolutely subjective truth — the greatest real lie possible! Seriously contemplate this fact. This modern existential predicament, the self-conscious incarnated, joyful and physically, culturally creative human, is **the most truthful denial of truth** that our universe has ever witnessed. So the more I practice denial of the other, the more I experience my subjective loyalty to and affirmation of myself (and if he is still at all remembered, I believe also that I am loyal to him). Objectively speaking, the reversal is accomplished only when I denied the other and wholly forgot its true being, be it cucumber, parents, friends, or ideas. This is an objective betrayal of the real world, the true murder of my father, marriage of my mother, and a blindness of which all spiritual and religious traditions and legends speak. The reversal is complete when the conscious ego appears triumphant and takes over nature, Earth and later the cosmos and realizes **his** aims therein. I do my thing in the world, change the world, I become more powerful. I reverse and transform everything in and through myself and become my-self as master in my-world. I am now able to work in the world, to change the world, to change you, to create "civilization" and create what I believe to be "heaven on Earth." In this paradise, my ideas and my laws will prevail, not God or nature's laws. The original heaven's paradise becomes an Earthly paradise that humans create. (Objectively speaking, of course, exactly the reverse is true: I am lifting Hell from below and not bringing heaven down from above. I am recreating hell on the Earth as civilization, instead of nature and spirit).

You see, even objective grace is given as a free gift, that is, it is given in such a way that humans will be able to, and surely will, reverse it completely. The greatest grace is, as you probably have heard, that God has given his Son (Ego) to us, and we take the Son and reverse His gift of grace as we reverse everything else in creation. Man makes God and God's Son (and his Mother, daughters, in short the whole family) into his own servants. The believer believes that he is a faithful follower, but he is truly only faithful to his own subjective self-enjoyment and satisfaction of his self-affirmation. He worships a reverse God in a reverse temple. All our institutions go through these above steps. Christianity is the archetypal example of all conscious reversals, because it reverses the most sacred into its most reversed opposite and it does it in the name of the Lord Himself. We reverse God into the total opposite because we are God-born. This started in the 2$^{nd}$ and 3$^{rd}$ century A.D. and by the 4$^{th}$ century had developed into the foundation of all coming Western civilizations, in which the most fully matured reversal is celebrated as the highest value and good.

Take a most recent example. Pope John Paul II, who was truly a decent man and an honest believer, really wanted to apologize to the Jewish people on behalf of the Catholic Church for the evils of 2000 years of persecution, crowned with Church's support of the holocaust. Pope Benedict XVI, who was then Cardinal Ratzinger (a Bavarian German), led the Roman Catholic council of cardinals to prohibit him from doing so. (Thus when Pope John Paul visited Israel he was only allowed by the church to offer his personal expression of regret). Ratzinger became the Pope and he systematically worked to dismantle any positive signs of forward steps that the former Pope The shad tried to realize. piritual event that we are looking for is not the one given by God's grace. Not because we deny what God gives freely! God forbid! Rather, because we love it and value it so highly, we wish to really affirm it. But this affirmation can only be done by a self-realization of God's grace. And the self-realization of His grace means to reverse the reversal of His grace. Or what is the same, simply to do what He himself is doing all the time. Any meeting with the real world **is** God's grace, is a given spiritual event. But we immediately reverse it as I showed above. The **real** spiritual event therefore has reality for my world only to the extent that I bring my individuation and reversal process to full self-consciousness and meet myself for the first time as a real spiritual being, that is, the Beast as my real incarnated-incarnating self. The meeting with oneself is therefore my first "epiphany," not the gracefully given, and immediately reversed God-given grace of meeting the given godly world. It is only when I bring the reversal machine into full consciousness, confront it as in meeting a wholly other being, in and through myself, that I have a first, fully individualized and free spiritual event of a real nature. Then I can say, as Paul did (only put somewhat differently in the present context): "Not I, but the Beast (the lower self) in me." This can only be achieved because I use in this work the forces of the higher self through my loyalty and faithfulness to truth. Otherwise the event is given and I immediately transform it into a luciferic and/or ahrimanic individuation.

The same forces which made individuation possible are those which I meet in myself through my truthful self-illumination and reversal. I must however consciously reverse the unconscious reversal in order to see it, because this means that I must become able to love the point of view of the world at least as objectively as I love my own subjective perspective! When I love the objective world's truth as I love my subjective human truth, and when I become as faithful to it as I am faithful to my own needy self, I will surely meet face-to-face the real Beast of my reversals, killings, forgetfulness, denials, and betrayals, and embrace it with a true self-less-self-love.

All spiritual experiences of grace are given to us as sacrificial offerings by our gods and parents so that we may eat and grow and become strong and independent. But are we independent and strong enough to turn around and meet ourselves in the reversal of the reversal? Then there is no longer the need to eat the Gods. We can create gods. We can create through self-offering fresh and original spiritual substance and realize it in the objective world as a **wholly other civilization.** Of course the Beast will fight to the death any effort to realize a reversal of the reversal, because she is protecting its true, God-given nature. At this point I become conscious to what extent I owe the Beast my private "I," and when I look at it face to face I see this fact as a real event in the real world. *Only if you know the Beast in yourself, you can become truly human, because it alone gives you the ability to become what you truly are.* God gives the son to me, but I (the Beast in me) kill it first, and precisely thereby it becomes **my own I**. I owe both Christ (the Ego) and the Beast (the reversed Ego) their-reversed-due. This is the Ur-mystery of all human ego evolution in the future. Until we achieve this, we cannot produce original life-substance in ourselves and offer it to the world. It is like breathing; we breathe in life and exhale death. Can I myself transform death in me without externalizing it outside in the world? Can I create life in me and give it to the world to make it more alive than it was before, not more dead? Can I become a mature Son and self-realize what a mature Son does and not merely reverse what my parents are doing while believing I am their truest follower? Can I begin to kill death instead of killing the being in me that kills death, and begin to create new and original world-life?

Human thinking and human spiritual activity are the purest substance which Ahriman receives with the greatest pleasure. We are machines that transfer the most vital and sacred life, soul and spiritual-esoteric knowledge to Ahriman. Only human beings can do this. Ahriman thinks God is infinitely stupid to have created humans which feed him. And now Ahriman rejoices because he knows well that God promised after the Deluge that He will not exterminate humans any more. Ahriman celebrated his victory at the end of the 19th century, but was terribly disappointed and angry as Rudolf Steiner punched a hole in his celebration. At the end of the 20th century, he heartily rejoiced again. He is still rejoicing. Shall we not do something to disappoint him now? Shall we hand over to him a total victory in this century already? Shall we not try to punch at least the smallest holes in his ever hardening and enclosing dome that he erects over the Earth and over our heads to ultimately separate it from the heavens?

What follows is a summary of the objective and subjective transformative process of individuation:

1. Subjective: I connect to the world in order to satisfy my own need. I am separated from the whole world and therefore need nourishment to keep alive. I connect myself with the world by grasping it. While the baby does this unconsciously, the self-conscious human subject takes this as a self-evident truth: I am connected with the world existentially and I feel connected, stronger, and less lonely when I satisfy my needs.

Objective: I separate a living part of the substance and being of the world in everything I perceive and grasp.

2. Subjective: When I cut the cucumber from the plant and connect with it, I become enlivened, enriched and empowered. I grow stronger. I experience increased life.

Objective: I kill the cucumber when I pick it. The death process begins. (Socially, we "sleep on the corpse of the one we kill" just as our ancestors did in a physical way when they killed their enemy, in order to receive and possess their forces).

3: Subjective: I am chewing, salivating, breaking it up and tasting it in my mouth. I feel intimate with the other during this. I sense and enjoy his inner nature and substance. We say — *now I get to know you from within. I love you in truth*. True love for the cucumber is already culminating. I become ever more incarnated in myself and feel myself becoming stronger.

Objective: After killing the true being of the other, he is separated from his physical body. It becomes a bodiless ghost. It becomes invisible and hidden, helpless to continue its embodied existence in the real world.

4. Subjective: I remember the true being of the other. What we take from outside becomes part of us. We re-member it into our being. The world is in me. I am now my world and the world is my world. I am the world.

Objective: The real being is forgotten. When the human has swallowed the object, the world feels that part of it has disappeared and is forgotten. From the world's perspective, it is livingly killed and consciously painful, because it is dead and gone. The world is really forgotten in the human and therefore the human becomes a place of pain for the world. The world says — *Ach, again this world of pain called "humanity" that we created in our image.* All people who have contributed to our growing up are objectively placed in this world of pain.

5. <u>Subjective:</u> I am free and independent. I feel a confirmation of my own convictions and I am filled with self-affirmation and self-sufficiency. I am the master of my inner world.

<u>Objective</u>: The other is enslaved. The world feels denied and is bound to the site of denial by the force of the self's compelling mastery.

6. <u>Subjective:</u> I am faithful to the human project. I go out to conquer the external world. I feel the power to realize human aims and compel the world to obey my will and wants. We grow more cucumbers in more efficient and more technologically (and ecologically) advanced ways. We are now shaping the external worlds according to our own personal needs.

<u>Objective:</u> We betray the world. In each human transformation of the real external world, the essence of the world is finally fully reversed, and therefore, spiritually speaking, betrayed.

7. <u>Subjective</u>: The human is the sole meaning of the universe. We have unlimited human pride in self-fulfilment and self-realization as the highest spiritual values of civilization, culture, and humanity. Building human civilization is the highest objective value in the universe, because it is a creation of the only intelligent and sentient world in an otherwise lifeless and meaningless universe.

Objective: The empty grave of the killed and betrayed God is made into the temple of the Beast. God meets his total opposite in the human being itself. The human today has become the reversed self-knowledge of God, the ultimate self-meeting of God with himself through the human reversal process.

Therefore this is the question we are left with: "What is the reverse of the reversal?"

The difficulties we can feel in this discussion are that we find it hard to think it through. To think the reversal is already a reversal as real action and deed. It is like speaking in reverse. To think a word in reverse is difficult. It is like going against gravity or against the gravity of time. It is difficult to reverse because we human beings are oriented in one direction ... incarnation ... past-to-future, as our only natural orientation. To reverse the reversal is "time levitation," the same as learning to levitate physically against gravity. It is a conscious dying, but done consciously during life. It is the first and most elementary esoteric or occult stage, and therefore an essentially different event than the most complicated and difficult physical, soul and spirit operations. Why should we at all wish to do it before death? What can be the motivation for such a seemingly stupid undertaking? Who on Earth would wish to produce such an intensely strong desire, need, or motivation to do this, which must be as intense — at least- as the naturally God-given desire for individuation and incarnation? Should we not rather consider such a powerfully unnatural and reversed way to look at and realize life as really inimical to life, against God's given stream of life, an intentional, suicidal, death in life?

Why would we do this before death? Why should we oppose this supreme act of the Earthly free Ego — to be like God, create civilisation, overcome death, create permanent life? The Beast says: 'Illness and Death demonstrate that there is no God, at least no real, intelligent one. Mortal, sick and cruel humanity itself is a fully sufficient proof that there is no God out there. As Mr. Smith tells Morpheus in *The Matrix*, humanity is a pestilence that kills everything and destroys the Earth. It is not like the higher animals that live in harmony with nature. Humanity has much more in common with a virus. The machines will replace it with far better and even more "moral" intelligence.'

The Beast teaches that the human being and evolution are proof that there is no God. Death and illness are imperfections of evolution. Human intelligence can overcome them. The Beast perfectly well demonstrates that the wound of humanness, of mortality, can be artificially (miraculously) healed and sealed. It says, 'Therefore there can be no God, but only chance. We will eventually overcome the flaws of death and illness. Civilization is the final aim. Consciousness can be made immortal, can overcome any biological death. Human intelligence, human consciousness will be saved from the physical, biological world which will disappear when the Earth comes to an end. The Beast is the bringer of true, etheric immortality.'

In looking towards the future, we will look in the reverse. Go backwards. Spiritually speaking the reverse is far truer than the illusions of looking forward. What do we want to do with it, or what is "it" in the first place? In the future, we should try to understand what everything I have said here really means, we must try to find the essence of what we have uncovered. We must create ingenious, unknown techniques, ways to extract the essence of an event that has passed.

The event is covered by itself in the incarnation process as the human essence of the other person is covered by its incarnation in its bodies. We have invested here much attention, love and hopeful energy, gathered it and incarnated it in the ground of our human heart, and the Beast is powerfully awakened and greedy. It is engaged, hungry for the love and truth in-vested! It is so happy we discussed this subject, so that now it will seek us out to have us for its meal, to use our reversals of the Global school's work in order to enjoy a splendid feast. And the capital invested will surely be his or hers and the Beast counts on it, knowing with certainty that it will be so, unless we consciously reverse this process. We have to resurrect these treasures in our life.

We have created once more a reservoir of energy underground, in the Earth, in our Earthly hearts. How do you capitalize on this? The capital is there, but is not used from year to year. It is wasted, given over to the Beast. What shall we do now for a change, and how? Try to use the capital built up in this work. Try to find what it is and then the how. You do not need to solve the how right now. You can do this at home with your friends. The task of the "what" is to look in the right direction. First, make clear what the normal course of going forward is. Then make a conscious, deliberate exception; be sure to notice quickly that you failed, and don't give in to the first illusion. Study the normal forgetting and reversing process, in order to slowly try to go in the opposite way from the normal. Describe what you normally do: *see the seven stages of reversal in your own work.* How do I remember the past? How do I use it? How do I possess it and make it my own? How am I convinced that I am loyal to it, that I am connected deeply with it?

Usually, after having experienced something, we want to do something with it, we want to add our ideas, our practices, to it. Now let us try a different, reversed approach. Let us ask ourselves: *what can I **subtract** from the remembered event?* When I look at the past event, can I subtract and hence somewhat paralyze the operative-functional, instinctive-habitual, individuation or immunization system? But I have already become immune to the essence of this event. The difficulty is that the immunization is precisely assimilation. It is individuated by dint of the destruction of the external truth and its transformation into what builds our own bodies. And this is what is **not perceived**. What we believe is actually the reverse: that we are open, thankfully, and even reverently, receiving the "pure" truth. However, what is remembered is not the real, but only a self-fabricated mental picture, which is conditioned and metamorphosed by subjective needs and desires, and it is this picture that we take to be the "pure representation" of the **real** event. But there are no pure re-presentations in the universe, only pure presentations. A presentation cannot be remembered, only re-actualized. There is a (real) **difference** between the real and the not real, but because the difference belongs to reality, we only remember the not real and forget the difference between the real and its re-presentation. The difference between physical memory and spiritual memory is that each is mutually exclusive. When in touch with the real, we have forgotten the non-real. We have forgotten our self as well, because our ordinary self-consciousness is but another representation of the (real) self. In ordinary memory one not only forgets the real, the spiritual, one first forgets the difference between the real and its mental picturing.

The first element that comes to consciousness when we learn to experience thinking objectively (from the world's point of view) is the death process of thinking. We learn to experience what we do, when we forget the spiritual. We kill it, of course! But now we may start to feel the pain of this (objective) truth instead of simply enjoying the (subjective) illusion. We begin to see and experience the process that transpires all the time in "the night," in the unconscious.[22] The real is a black hole in our daily conscious. Perceiving it cannot be a direct-forward gaze. It can only be a sidelong gaze, diagonal, fuzzy, peripheral; with the corners of the eyes that always look backwards. Begin to remember that I have forgotten that I do not perceive the real. Try to have a feeling of the distinction between the real and the unreal. The real appears as nothing. But it is potent, all powerful nothing. Because of its fullness, it is not seen consciously. Its power immediately puts our consciousness to sleep. The event is concealed behind its own powerful spiritual potency.

Work with this at home. What is conscious? The incarnation process is a real reversal of the true spiritual being. Incarnation can only be reversed through excarnation (dying). Likewise actualization can only be reversed through de-actualization; evolution through involution. This is the truth of reversal. This is also the main practice of Rudolf Steiner's *Philosophy of Freedom*, provided that we understand it. This alone makes Anthroposophy into the real thing. This alone can reverse the reversal of Anthroposophy that is now 100 years old. What is the difference between a living human and its corpse? How do you experience it? Now ask yourself the same in regard to thinking: what is living thinking? What is dead thinking? First, you can be sure about this: what you experience as so-called 'living thinking' is the *corpse of real thinking* which you, in your illusionary reversal, experience as vibrantly alive. Some anthroposophists are particularly fond of this illusion. But if you begin to experience this (and it must be authentic, don't try to suggest it to yourself artificially), you experience a putrefaction process, with smells and tastes, touch sensations and appropriate experiences of coldness, inside your head! When we think normally, we think corpses into being. We produce dead corpses and tremendously enjoy the satisfaction they give us, the fine taste that we call "life," which invigorates our subjective "I think therefore I am" illusion.

But if you truly touch this in your inner feeling and sensation, if thinking becomes an organ of taste and touch, of hearing and seeing, then you have taken the first step towards meeting the real: real death, reversal, "not I but...in me." This is the place of differentiating difference. This is the threshold. Approaching the threshold in this conscious manner, reversing the unconscious reversal, is the very first beginning of the experience of the event of reality or the real event in the objective spiritual world. Feel the inner experience of the concept building up in ordinary thinking. Then the sweetness in your mouth will become bitter in your stomach, but you don't have to wait for the stomach to tell you the whole bitter truth about the metabolism of truth (the truth of metabolism). You can start to feel something grinding in your teeth, we sense it like burnt wood, you begin to say to yourself — *what's wrong with me? I feel as if I have ashes in my mouth!* This happens because only through true spiritual-scientific activity can we discover this secret: that ordinary thinking is dead and this is the very opposite of all the subjective soul experience of the modern human being. Ashes, a metallic taste, similar to eating something sordid, rusty, and dead.

We will begin to suffer, when we merely think. We may begin to feel inwardly nauseated because we discover how much we actually enjoy killing and eating what we killed.

We also know this: the greater and more exhilarating a spiritual event we have, the stronger will be our pain when we decide to think it through and express it, incarnate it in Earthly concepts, mental pictures and words. Therefore, honestly seeking reality must lead us to a true meeting with ourselves in reality, and this is of course the unconscious reason why humans avoid reality at all costs. Meeting oneself leads to reality. Enjoying the spiritual has something luciferic about it. True spiritual meeting, self-knowledge, and meeting oneself in truth, is more real and more painful but also infinitely more fruitful and productive. It is productive because, after all the pain, it is a real (and not luciferic), joyful ascension to the becoming process in the real spiritual worlds. Meeting the event of meeting yourself allows you to also meet the real, higher, eternal "you." It is the gate to finding the true other and brother. I meet myself in meeting you and I meet you, if I meet my real self. The other in me is the ultimate event of truth and reality. Through meeting my real lower self, I turn to you, and since I don't need to project onto you all my needs, desires, and motivations, I can see your true being. I filter consciously, one by one, all my projections, all my reflections. When I cease using you as my screen to enhance myself, lo and behold: I see my true self through your true self. Then if, by a self-created grace, two or three of us are doing the same, the true I AM is there in our midst, and He speaks to us. He tells us about His kingdom, and for a short moment of truth, we can already become in the present what (truthful) humans are going to become during the next 1000 to 1500 years.

# Lecture 8

## The Christ Event of the 21st Century; Intimate Experiences of Christ in Thinking, Feeling, and Willing
### (Stuttgart 2012)

BEGINNING IN 2005, I needed to reduce my public activities in order to dedicate myself to the elementary or fundamental aspects of the School of Spiritual Science. Through this an updated foundation for the School of Spiritual Science came into being, in which I am now working, together with friends and colleagues in several countries. But in 2012, for reasons I will explain below, I resumed my public activity and this is why I can again speak at Forum 3.[23] Today is in this sense a small beginning. And because it is a beginning, I want to speak simply and directly from my heart to your hearts about some experiences that the human soul can go through today.

Before I do this, however, I will give a short extract of what I have been presenting in other lectures this year in the US, Scandinavia, Europe and the UK. What is coming from the future toward us today is enormous. I have myself observed it over the past 3 to 4 years. In the beginning, during 2007 and 2008, it was still very quiet like little droplets that one could feel, very tiny touches that quietly said, "Would you please pay just a small amount of attention to the future?" This grew stronger from day to day and by 2009 and 2010, it was definitely not just little droplets any longer: it had become a river. Since then it has continued to grow. Precisely because of the enormity of what is appearing on the horizon of this century, extending from its very middle, I want to express it so that it speaks directly to our humanity and all that is humane in us.

According to Ray Kurzweil, certain projected technological developments will lead, around the middle of the century (2045), to what he calls the "Singularity." This will be the immersion of the human being as a whole in an infinitely powerful Artificial Intelligence, where the human being will possess unlimited intelligence and an almost unlimited physical life. The colossal acceleration of these technologies is itself a huge topic. If we examine what is coming towards us spiritually, and also what is being prepared on the other side, technologically, then we can already say a good bit about this subject matter today. Those who promote the technological singularity are getting ready to capture the enormous waves of these new life forces so that they can immediately channel and utilize them within the framework of new technologies. I have seen that this enormous wave that will come in the middle of the century is made of the highest creative energy possible. It is a revelation of our higher self, the Christ-self. But people do not perceive this yet, and so it is not yet noticed acting among us, and we are still not preparing ourselves for what is coming toward us! Yet it is already perceptible. Only a very few people are awake enough in our own stream to perceive this. But those who support the technological singularity are already working toward this moment and are amazingly awake, creative, filled with energy, and enthused about what is coming. The difference between these two groups has made me somewhat concerned because the gap is far too large. It shouldn't be so big. And if it remains like this, we will experience the same thing that happened in the last century, which is that the Christ-event was reversed into its opposite. We should at least try everything we can to prevent that from happening. That's what we should try to do!

This is the general picture. Today we are in the year 2012. It has been predicted that the singularity will come in exactly 33 years from now. What will we do today and tomorrow and the day after, to develop the capacities, the qualities, and the strengths that will be all the more necessary to deal with these coming days, years, and decades? What are we doing with the young people? How is humanity going to reach the middle of the century after the next wave? What is going to happen in the next few years, the next 20, the next 30 years? Each century begins with small waves, but each decade receives a larger new wave from the horizon in the middle of the century. In the first decade of the 21st century, we have already felt the first wave and the second is happening as we speak. Already we can feel that it is much stronger than the first. We can already experience that the Earth is beginning to shift under our feet.

But we are only now experiencing the second big wave, then the next one and then another two will come before the middle of the century. By the middle of the century it will be a Tsunami; this is already visible on the horizon. And still we are strolling along the beach, building little sand castles or maybe even a courageous wall of sand, or little canals to channel the direction of the Tsunami. But when we really see what's coming we'll say, "Oh my God, this is a gigantic power!" What is more, if people are unprepared it will be a destructive power. But this is not because it is destructive of itself; rather it is the highest and most positive force that exists, it is our highest creativity. But this means that a massive development is necessary from our side, for if we are unprepared and suddenly a Tsunami rolls in, then times will be really difficult. So what capacities and qualities do we need to develop? What do we need to have in order to receive this power? I would like to describe this in what follows.

First of all, saying that 'everything is alright' is useless. In our time people are still fooling each other, pulling the wool over their eyes. This is the main problem of our spiritual and social life. We must admit that we did not take great steps forward in the 20th century. Furthermore, we haven't developed the capacities for the 21st century. We simply have not developed them yet. That is really the point. It's really not about new programs, or economic, social, political, cultural or spiritual regulations. The most important thing that is needed is attentiveness. One must become attentive to that fact that a great deal is already possible today. Much of what is coming toward us is already here and has been active between us for some time. But our attentiveness has not sharpened enough. So it is not a question of programs, rules, or exercises. It is rather a question of practicing attentiveness. Let us look at this in more concrete detail.

We have a huge intellectual head. It's very necessary and we love this intellect, we love our heads. No criticism will be leveled at our intellectual capacities, as we need this huge head in our technological time to regulate and order our physical lives. But spiritually seen this intellect is something quite different. Spiritually seen the intellect is something which deadens us, which turns us cold as people, and the more we have to use it, to order our outer lives, to research, construct our technologies and so on, the more we have to admit that we do not sufficiently feel the human-spiritual reality behind it. We are so fascinated by the inhumanness, the speed, and the brilliance of this intellect that we don't notice that the very opposite power lies behind it. The first essential thing is to **feel**, to notice, to become aware of what lives in our feelings when we recognize something. I re-cognize my world! Re-cognizing means remembering. It's always the same world, and it has to be, right? When I get up in the morning, I should enjoy the fact that it is the **same** room, and the chairs and table are the same as they were yesterday. When I look in the mirror, I'm happy to see that, with a few exceptions, it is the same face that I see and recognize. That is you, the same person, and the same self! Then when we see our fellow men we say — *There you are again! The same as yesterday!*

We need this sameness. I don't want to criticize our faculty of recognition. But it is dead and can only know that which is dead. When I recognize you as the same person, then it is only that which is dead that arises in me. This dead picture of you is not really fitting for humans or nature, even if it is suitable in the case of other objects. We simply don't experience this very strongly; it's a question of experiencing a real problem. We should reach the point of being sufficiently attentive in the moment when we say — *There you are again, the same old subject or object* — that one feels something and this inner experience comes to consciousness. It's always there! You don't have to do anything to create it. This experience is always present just below the threshold, but we don't notice it and we don't want to notice it? We want things to go on as they are, in the same way. But then over and over again, human society collapses.

If we are attentive and listen to our feelings in this moment, then it's possible to become aware of something different. These are intimate feelings, but it is exactly these intimate feelings that count. It is a matter of not continuing to move toward the future in a totally insensitive, unperceptive manner. These enormous waves from the future are rolling toward us and they need people with open senses and hearts to receive these forces. In the moment itself, I need to **feel** a real problem because I actually can't perceive who you really are, because I constantly only produce the same image of a person according to my habits and my past, and because I cannot take hold of the new moment that is totally alive. People will increasingly experience this as a form of blindness. You will experience something and may hear a voice, it could be a very quiet and gentle voice, in the moment when you recognize and 'know' the other as the same old self. If you really listen to this quiet voice, it will say, 'You have re-cognized and identified this as the same object or person, and therefore you have become blind!' To feel this experience of cognition as blindness, that is what is absolutely necessary. Once you have experienced it and heard this voice that says, 'You have re-cognized this as a subject or object, you have recognized your fellow man as the same being as yesterday and have thus made yourself blind in that moment!' When you experience this, the process reverses and you gain sight. You begin to see. You stop thinking, reflecting, and repeating the same cognitive process. One becomes clairvoyant which means 'clear-seeing.' There are of course different types of clairvoyance. In the social, human, and inter-personal fields it is perhaps the most important strength there is. This also applies to our relationship to nature, but I will remain in the field of humans.

When you really see another person, you experience something cosmic, something unprecedented about the individual that you meet. The other person becomes a real revelation, a real spiritual experience, which acts and creates in a whole cosmos of utmost beauty. The other person becomes a revelation of the highest and the deepest of our world. Because I have experienced and recognized my blindness, I can now experience him with my new vision. In that moment he arises within my own being. He arises within my being as his true self and I arise with him. We both arise. The dead intellect that kills, binds, defines, orders, rationalizes, and explains everything; this same place becomes the place of resurrection. In this place of resurrection where you arise in me and I arise with you, there the human meeting becomes a true revelation. This is the first Christ-experience that comes to us, and actually is already there. It has been there for ages! It is only our attentiveness that isn't sufficiently awake. This has nothing to do with exercises, meditations, regulations or ideals. One should not try to prepare for this in the usual, rational sense as if I could say, "Ahh, that is lovely, I want to see you! I've heard a lecture about it, and read some stuff and now off we go! I'll set up a program, a meditational practice, then I'll do it and tomorrow I will achieve it. I will see you!"

If you do this you are already in the known, in the dead identification. Attentiveness can only be the Event. Attentiveness is Event! I have to experience that something is not right, that there is something untrue in my knowing: there you are again! This has to be experienced, you cannot prescribe this. You must experience it, and then it can be a real feeling experience. I am blind when I re-cognize you. Precisely where I think I know you, I do *not* see you. I am blind and this impossibility of sight has to shock us. Something has to happen within us, which shocks or jolts us a bit, an Event, and then this seeing wakes up, and one really "sees." But this seeing of the other, comes from the tremor, from the problem, that comes with the painful realization: *I am blind, I experience myself as blind!* That is a true Event, and not anything that one can or should enforce.

A second element lies more in the realm of our feelings. How do we experience our feelings with our whole soul apparatus in the physical world? We are modern people aren't we, strong modern people, we have to go out into the physical world to work, to fulfill our duties and in order to do that we have to be physically strong. We must be strong as a self, strong as an ego. I have to go out and accomplish my work in the modern social field. This is not being criticized here. We love our strengths and we love and appreciate our ego. One should not destroy or repress the ego. That would be very one-sided. When we are strong, we go out and feel ourselves to be positively incarnated and physically present with our whole soul. And when we are weak and lonely, we turn back inwardly into ourselves and try to hide from the community, away from others. This is how the split in our whole humanity and in our social lives appears. Only the hardened aspects are turned outward, and we are alone and shut inside with the other aspect, that which works in us as weakness, pain, and loneliness, and where we turn away from other people.

But just in that moment when I want to retreat, I can now also become attentive. In this moment I can also try to listen inwardly. You want to hide because you are wounded, because you are lonely. You have experienced some trauma and you want to retreat from people. Can you hold on to this for just a moment? Is it possible instead to turn towards other people precisely in the moment you feel weak? Turn toward those people who make you feel weak, lonely and helpless, and share your helplessness with them. Open yourself up right at the point where you withdraw, when you are at the point of losing yourself. Turn it around, open yourself up and go to another person and ask her: *are you willing to hear me, experience and carry my weakness, my pain and my helplessness with me?*

But this cannot be a predetermined objective, it has to be an Event, that is, it has to really happen. I have to hear, listen and experience it and only then can it be truly and authentically there. Of course there can be no rule like: every time you feel weak, you should turn to another person and share your feelings! No, not like that! This is absolutely concretely and individually meant. It is a moment where it really happens, not because it would be better if it happened, or not so good if it happened, just do it or not. It is more a question of being attentive and listening to the voice that says: *now, in this moment you can turn it around!* That doesn't mean you'll be able to do it again tomorrow. One should not generalize and say: *Ah, that was so beautiful and good — now I'll do it all the time!* This attitude leads straight back to the intellect, to creating rules, abstractions and generalizations. That is just what we *don't* want to do.

But if you have really heard and experienced this voice in a specific situation, it is possible to alter the meeting, to turn around. And if you have experienced — *I become a full human being when I meet you in this way* — then you can turn to the other person and ask: *Do you want to hear me?* When that happens it is as if one arises in the soul of the other person. In the meeting with the other, I experience my weaknesses as my new strengths, or my helplessness as a source of inner power. This inner power and inner strength comes to me through the helplessness, but through the other, through their love, their attentiveness, their readiness to accept me within themselves. And in this resurrection of the self through the other, I receive a new self. And this self grows together with the self of the other person and a mutual interdependency emerges, or a fertilization between my "I" and their "I" and I arise in their being and recognize myself, as that which I really am, as my higher self. We can also call this a certain Christ-experience in the feeling realm and in the soul. Before it was the transformation or change in my cognitive faculty, that became 'seeing,' now I experience the other, who resurrects through me. Through the reversal of my feelings and the other's readiness to share my helplessness with me, I arise in you and we grow together. A certain common ground emerges between us human beings. This has to be there, and is very, very important for the future.

One could perhaps object and say: *Oh come on, what has that got to do with the future, with the forces that are streaming toward us in huge waves, or a Tsunami that you have said is heading our way? What are we supposed to do with such intimate human experiences in the soul?* But this is exactly it. When the waves come, then we should be strong as a community. We have to consider that as a community we have to build this space. It really is a Sun-space. I said I would try to describe things in a simple way and not use esoteric concepts. But we do create a certain Sun-space, in which new and living forces work from one person to another, and through which the community really grows together. It grows together as a living community and can, through this inner strengthening, lift and extend itself to become an instrument which can receive these new energies. This is exactly what we need in the future. The individual person cannot achieve anything alone. This can only be done by people together, who have connected themselves in these depths. Only in this way can a community receive a large wave and the vitality that comes in with it. This will only strengthen the growing work if it was real and strong to begin with. Some people have already achieved this individually in their interpersonal relationships, they have already built this Sun-space. The highest creative forces, life forces, etheric Sun-life-forces then stream in. Through already having created a certain Sun-space within the community, the inner strengths that live in the community can meet those that stream to us from outside. So the two, the inner and the outer, can grow together and the new wave can be turned toward the good. The beginnings are already there. This lightning, this enormous energy that is coming in can be channeled and made fruitful. In this way, it will not work destructively as it meets the same quality and the same strength in us. Then 'like will meet like' and work toward the good, toward healing and joy.

There is yet a third element. It also has to do with an attentiveness that is not a rule or a regulation, or an exercise, or a new accomplishment. The worst thing that could happen would be if everybody wanted to have new faculties. This is bad. You harden yourself if you desire new faculties. An enormous willpower and an intellectual hardening accompany the creating of new faculties. So, please, no faculties! Attentiveness is not a faculty and it cannot be practiced. If you are practicing, it is not attentiveness. Attentiveness is Event, so it has to happen in the moment. It cannot be planned. It is always a surprising, sudden moment which happens. It is always a miracle, a moment of grace. But here is where our true self works. This is now in the spiritual sphere where these processes and forces are so important. It could also be that you want to do something. You have an impulse to do something. Whether it is my responsibility or my duty, this always has to do with the will and especially with *my* will. *I* have an intention. Something is important for me; I want to accomplish something and in the moment that I want to engage my willpower, I should also try listening. I could maybe hear a voice in this instance, too. It is the same voice, so gentle and quiet, leaving one free. You have to be really attentive to even hear this voice because it is so unobtrusive. If it wasn't like that then we wouldn't be free to ignore it. The main worry that our guiding spiritual brothers and sisters have is that they can become too powerful. They do everything they can in order to remain imperceptible. This is a hard job for such huge, strong beings to make themselves unnoticed.

It is really hard to hide oneself, to reduce oneself, to give the people around you free space and to speak as quietly as you would to a child: do you hear that? Only if you really want to hear it, otherwise you won't. And when you hear this voice or this suggestion you are free not to follow the will impulse you had. You are not forced to carry out that which you wanted to do. You can stop the impulse, look around in your community and ask yourself: *What is happening in my surroundings? Is there perhaps someone in my community that should be doing something, that wants to do something? Is there someone in my surroundings that has an initiative and cannot fulfill it because the social conditions are such that he cannot follow through with it?* Not necessarily because you are the strongest and take up all the space with your energy (although this could also be the case), but it may be that the whole community is so organized that there is no balance or no equilibrium present. There are people on the outside who can't come in or people who belong, but are ignored. All sorts of situations exist like this.

If you have become attentive enough, then don't use your energy to just do what you want, but look for who is there, and find people who may need your energetic will to realize their own will. Then you can feel as if your self has become enlarged and that the true self is a community-self. For our real self, each single person in the community is as important as I am myself. I am really not more important for the community. It seems that way for my personal self, of course, but not for my real self. This is the difference between me as the centre of my world (who says — *my will be done!)* and my higher self (who says — *ok, you are very important, but the community itself is the most important thing*). There is always too much and too little, and you can support the whole in your consciousness, to help each single person find their place within the whole, and so on. This is the third intimate experience that one can have.

If you look at all three intimate experiences together, you can learn to perceive how your own intellect is itself dead and also kills. A joint space can arise if, through this new seeing, the resurrection of the other is experienced, and then you receive through me a true image, a true form, a true self. This happens through *my seeing*, when I really see *you*. And then when I turn to you and say — *I can't do this alone, I am too weak. I am lost and lonely, but through you I can find myself again!* I find myself through you as my true self and we grow together, and then I can make my will available to help the whole. If you connect these three experiences, then something which is communal arises, something future oriented, creative, alive and healing. It is a hopeful space where joy and enthusiasm can grow. Then one can become creative in interpersonal relationships, morally creative with one another.

This community experience is really beautiful and a real zest for life can begin to grow. If this happens, you can meet the people supporting the technological singularity and say, "Hmm, *you have the greatest enthusiasm and passion about this infinite, non-human intelligence. We have a living community. We can go into the virtual world if we want, but we are free to do so or not. We live in two worlds, you only live in one. We can go into the technological-ahrimanic world and leave it again, but we have also created our own world. It is a Sun-life-world and we can be part of this other world. But we have enough strength, enough warmth and enough creativity to also share in the experience of this infinite intelligence. We can help carry it, transform it and humanize it."* For in the future, billions of people will be trapped in these giant machines. This will become the new "unbornness." Billions of people will find this to be the greatest, most humane, joyful and healing solution for everything. They will pin all the spiritual and moral values to the machine. Ray Kurzweil is good at this and he even uses religious terminology to describe his dreams.

All this will come about. 'The blind will see' as Kurzweil said when he invented the reading machine for the blind! The Gospel means however that the spiritually blind eyes will be opened. We're spiritually blind and can see again, and in that event we see the essential being of the other person, we feel with them, we act with them. This is something different than just seeing and experiencing something technologically, as it is brought to us by the singularity. People will be, and indeed already are, enchanted. But our technology is still so primitive. The Internet?! Who could have imagined the internet 20 years ago? You can see how fast things move. Still everything is unbelievably primitive. With Ray Kurzweil you can imagine and project where we will be in twenty or thirty years. When the technology is inside us, then it really begins. We will be totally linked in and made infinite through our bodies. Our corporality itself, with all our physical enjoyments and experiences, will be increased to infinity, to the point where it transforms the human into an immortal, fully healed, un-bornness. This is just the first step, the Kindergarten. We are dealing with the total transformation of the human being, the total and absolute transformation of the entire being of humanity. People are finding this incredibly magical and fascinating. People will put all their trust in these technologies because they see that they will free us from our humanity. It is this liberation that is so magical and glamorous for people. People are tired. From all our news and media we hear this day and night: Humans are evil, people make everything worse, they kill and destroy everything. Humans are really bad and we have to free ourselves from our humanity through the machines, and create an infinite technological paradise! People will not be able to resist this temptation at all. Only a few individuals and the tiniest of groups will be able to resist when this starts. They can then consciously say — *No, we will refuse this offer since we have something better!* Only very few people will do this.

At that time, it will not be a game. Today it is still easy to say — *I choose this and not that!* Today everyone is very smart. Today you can still choose to be a human, whether a spiritual human or something else, but tomorrow you will be able to be something completely different, and experience yourself as infinite, with all the spiritual and physical faculties *given to you*. Soon, you won't have to do anything apart from plugging yourself in and you will be able to heighten all the physical enjoyments and experiences ad infinitum. Then people will say — *what do you want to have? Which physical enjoyment would you like to enhance? Taste? You can heighten it to the absolute.* People will find the so-called physical and sense experiences of their bodies and their environment, totally boring and weak. They will no longer experience anything from "normal" sense perceptions or physical enjoyments, because they will be able to get any kind of sensation in an incredible variety and potency.

But this is just the first level. We don't know what spiritual capacities will be developed by the backward forces and be given to us. But these spiritual capacities will be given to us as physical enjoyments are given. Then the offer will be — *what would you like? Imaginative, inspirational or intuitive experiences?* Yes, this will also come, and when it comes, could you say — *no, I don't want this, I want to continue meditating? I have already meditated 50 years and still not reached any imaginations.* When you can get this from a machine in a totally amazingly, body-free experience, could you refuse? Then you'll say that you don't want this? But, of course, everyone will want to do it! Absolutely, join in! You can then have Christ experiences, meet angels, and more. That will be the next level; all that will be naturally available. There will be very few who say — *no, we want to do this consciously!* Do you understand what I mean? You will have to be in the position of having real experiences yourself. It won't be a question of saying — *I'll read something about it!* It will not be a question of either reading or going into the machines. The point will be: machine-experiences or real spiritual experiences. But only real spiritual experiences count! And these will also only be chosen by a few people. We are moving toward such an era and I wanted to point out that it is time, today and tomorrow, to develop a certain attentiveness, so that we can take a small step forward in our communities.

Now, in our global school workshops we have a strict program that is meant to "develop faculties." We have to practice or we won't be ready! We have to move in a prepared way towards the Event. We can do some little exercises where we try to experience how we work together, so that I experience a certain loosening through you and you through me. By this, a certain sharing that is *with-and-through-one-another* can already arise. These are very elementary, absolutely non-esoteric, exercises for people who are incredibly undeveloped, if not retarded; and who for years have made no progress from an anthroposophical point of view. This is not for advanced students who would probably say — *this is laughable, this is for children!* But this is just what we're aiming for: to become children. My search is towards a *starting point* that is real and authentic and where one can really do something oneself. We can continue to try to understand the anthroposophical ideals that Rudolf Steiner gave to us from now until the end of the world. But it is essential to differentiate between these given ideals and what we can really do and what we really care about. We are trying to meet authentic experiences, to develop real faculties, where you can genuinely say — *this is what I can do and it is completely my own work!* This comes as an addition and does not take the place of studying, learning, and thinking, which retain their importance. In addition, we just have to determine quite rudimentarily where we stand. Is it already Kindergarten or are we still preparing for Kindergarten? There is a huge threshold between preschool and Kindergarten. This is very important and I know that in this area there are lots of different ideas. In my own life and with other people, I really have tried everything. I want to move with what does work, with what is real. In the area of training, be it anthroposophical, esoteric or on other paths, there are many different ideas prevailing. For example, there are people who say — *Rudolf Steiner only gave us the First Class of the School for Spiritual Science, so we have to create the Second Class!* Are these people serious who are trying to take on the Second Class of the High School? I'm trying to make preparations for the Kindergarten! This is the difference and the question is — *what have we really achieved in this realm?*

Of course I said that there are no methods, no rules, and we should not develop faculties. This is connected to the real secret of attentiveness. And then I said that we will do the opposite in our workshops! I said this so sharply in order to lift our consciousness, so that when we practice, we do not try to continue in a conventional way. So I already began with these paradoxes, with this big riddle. How do you prepare yourself to be unprepared? It really is like this! How do you practice, how do you repeat things, without hardening yourself? How does the intellectual faculty that brings death to everything, repeats everything and always recognizes the same thing become transformed? It says — *I know you already, you are the same, and everything is the same.*

When you begin to practice and do not remain attentive, it leads to an incredible strengthening of the intellect, the will and everything else. Someone might think that it would require a tremendous force of will for humanity to wake up and meet the other, but our will is already too strong! That is the problem: our individual will covers everything over. Furthermore, the grace that we need has already been given. In order to receive a gift, one has to be attentive or develop some other faculty that is different from the sheer desire of — *I want it! Give me the present!* The gift has been yours for ages! Please be aware that it has already been given. The will power is directed differently in this situation. It is not — *I want my present.* You have to perceive and be aware that everything is already there, in order to use and work with it. Then it would be possible to receive more. But you only receive more when you have shown that you can economically deal with the capital that you have been given. If you have been given so much and you don't do anything with it, or you make wars, then you don't get any more. It is withheld until you do something more with what you have been given. If you do something creative with what you have been given, then you receive more. But to already get more? There is already more coming anyway, as I said earlier. It is precisely when we have not worked with what has been given and then we get more, where things turn sour. It is like a child who has been given too many toys, but doesn't play with them. He doesn't use them, but wants more. What else do we want? What more do we need?

What we need is awareness. This means to be attentive to how you practice. Then practicing becomes Event. The practicing itself can become Event, if you are attentive. Everything can! But an Event cannot be prepared, you can only wait for it, anticipate it. It boils down to finding this quality of listening in a mood of anticipation, and moving through life half on the threshold, although you have to remain fully attentive in your daily life to the physical side of things. I must pay full attention to the work that I do. It's no good doing my work in a half-dream state. And yet I should at the same time anticipate the moment coming, where I am fully attentive or rather I am prepared to be made attentive through someone else. That someone gives me a sign. As soon as people do something together and want the same thing, are searching for the same thing, and work on these things together, they can become more awake than otherwise, through this attentiveness to the other. That is because we are already connected to one another. We are already in this life together. At this level we are really a community. For, my life is not individualized like my physical body; my life flows through your life and vice versa. In the community all of the life forces flow together. This is a reality that I don't have to generate. It is not my deed, but something already there.

But for this to take place, it is necessary to wake up in our daily life, in the most commonplace things of our lives, in our routines, everything! We have to find these moments where we break through, right in the midst of our daily lives. It cannot occur somewhere *beyond* the daily. Today it is no longer possible to say that daily life can simply continue in such a mechanical way, and then we can simply attend a spiritual workshop on the weekend outside our daily life. To be 'very spiritual' outside of daily life while remaining totally materialistic and mechanical inside our daily life leads to a significant problem in our times. On the other hand, we cannot simply change life; we have to embrace the requirements of our physical life.

The question is how do we wake up during our daily lives, to bring this attentiveness and these transformations in, so that a new living environment is created, parallel and simultaneous? We have to learn to live in two worlds simultaneously: at two levels of consciousness, two conscious lives. Two worlds must coexist at the same time, with two identities at the same time, not one after another, or only on the weekends or even later. I have to develop attentiveness so that I can be fully immersed in the other and at the same time remember who I am. Then the daily intellectual identity will be a memory for the second living-consciousness. The Event-consciousness will be able to remember that there is something like the "I" itself, in the same moment. I will be able to have two simultaneous conditions of consciousness, and that is what I need in our times. The etheric perception has to be there at the same time as the normal physical perception. It's no good saying — *now*

*I'll forget the physical and be active in the spiritual realm, stay there a couple of days and then come back!* That would be too late! For our present conditions we need to have both together at the same time. But this "at the same time" is a mystery. This is why I exaggerate the paradox so much. That is the secret: to be in two levels of consciousness which are actually the opposites of one another at the same time. They are really opposites. One is dead and one is living, and today I need to have them both. I want to transform myself *and* remember who I am. You are the same one you were yesterday. It is so important not to lose this knowledge. It would be unbelievably interesting, but not very practical, if I would really lose and forget myself.

Finally, I want to close by focusing on the Event of the 21st century. You may recall that my description of the last century (in *The Spiritual Event of the 20th Century*), was given at its end. But now we are in the beginning of a new century. These are two opposite time-situations. Back then, I researched and described what had happened. Today, one can only say, it could happen like this or it could be reversed. The reversal of the last century was the most brutal reversal thinkable. The etheric second-coming has begun and its reversal on the Earth is already beginning. Today people are preparing the technological Singularity as a form of reversal. That's why I have said, that the new Event will come about, but at the same time its reversal is being prepared. Just as it was in the last century!

One could also say that Rudolf Steiner was active at the beginning of the 20th century and then others prepared the reversal of his work. They won! Today we have the same problems. The reversal is already underway and we have no Rudolf Steiner. This belongs to the situation too. The possibility was open, through extremely unusual preparations, that in the last century — if that century's Event had been understood and accepted — all the souls who had been there with Rudolf Steiner, would have been able to incarnate and to work with others at the end of the century to give an enormous impulse. That is what Rudolf Steiner described during his last year as a possibility. Here we can see that everything was prepared 'from above' in order to achieve the very best results. Yet, here 'below' people are saying — *Hmm, not yet...later.* People remained asleep. They did not want it and so it didn't happen. The last century was a real disaster.

Now we are faced with a new beginning under completely different conditions, although there is one similarity: at the beginning of every century these big new waves come. This is a law of world development and it doesn't depend on us. But if we are not prepared, well, we live in the era of freedom! As I have mentioned this era of freedom is taken very seriously by the good spiritual beings. They leave people to be free. On the other hand, the not-so-good spiritual beings, also take freedom extremely seriously and do everything within their power to influence people. This creates a huge imbalance. You could complain that this situation is rather unfair, but you would have to discuss this with God, since he made the plan. It's not my plan; it was already laid out. But it's a question of freedom. What can we say about it? We can indeed say many things! Lots! Still, many people object and say — *this is the worst plan of all, and if God made it, he is the worst God there is!*

# Lecture 9

## Israeli Civil Society and the Global Melting Pot (New York City 2002)

WE'VE STARTED A NEW CENTURY, a new millennium. All the present crises, such as those experienced by America, and especially New York, since the September 11th event, are the very beginning of what our time is all about. Our times have to do with the beginning processes of initiation, as experienced through life on the personal, cultural, social and geographical levels. The trials of initiation have to do with the struggle between our higher and lower selves and the reconciliation of the two. Initiation is the process of finding a way to bridge the two, to establish our ground in between our higher and lower selves. All of this, which comes from the most ancient occult traditions, is already becoming common knowledge today.

Nothing happens in the world which is not a rite of passage of sorts, and what remains for us is only to interpret what it all means. Catastrophe is simply part of initiation; it is an act of grace, a beautiful revelation of destiny. We can say that the greater the catastrophe is, the more blessed is the event that the catastrophe rises out of. So what is the appropriate mood for this? It would be a loving, thankful, joyful, serene, heroic feeling for destiny in the face of these catastrophes. In a sense, we have nothing to lose in this rite of passage, because it opens us to the experience of the divine nature of our deepest self, and a divine being can only lose the illusion of separation and loneliness. There are no other basic illusions to lose, apart from this.

When you are confronted with your destiny, when you can identify yourself in the next blissful blowup, this becomes a self-formation of the highest degree. It is the most painful and joyful experience at the same time. It is a direct experience of the knowledge that 'I am a being of the world and all separations have ceased to exist in this moment.' When the blowup or the bliss touches us, we are one with the world, and then we know we are beings of truth, beauty, grace and honor, and we can admit — *Yes, that is what we are. The world is us and we are everything that is in the world.* So whatever we have invoked, whatever comes our way, is what we are, is what we have prepared for so long, as the initiation rites of our humanity.

It's time now for us to be involved with what we are. It's time to grow, to be what we really are, to experience and acknowledge what was undreamed of until now. Whether it is in such great events as September 11th, or in the small tragic details of our daily lives, we take in these experiences as sustenance for the processes of initiation. We have had this in Israel as our daily bread for the last fifty years. When one can approach this in the certain mood of soul that I was trying to express, then the externally dangerous life, the externally painful and tragic life is that which says — *Here, you can use this.* When these events cross the path of our destiny, there is a real chance of redeeming those karmic dilemmas, karmic responsibilities, for which we have prepared ourselves.

So let's look away now from Manhattan and America back to the Middle East, back to Israel. Let's go to this picture now, and bring some of the background to what we know about the time in which we live and how it relates to the past. We know from the basic teachings of Anthroposophy, that our epoch, the fifth cultural epoch, is a recapitulation, a transformation, of everything that happened in the third cultural epoch. The third cultural epoch (the Egyptian, Syrian, Babylonian, and early Jewish epoch) created what would later emerge, during the fourth cultural epoch (the Greek, Roman, Medieval), as the three streams of the so-called Semitic religions. Judaism first gave birth to Christianity and this gave birth to Islam. The third epoch created them and the fourth nourished them. So it is the task of our fifth cultural epoch to reconcile them and unite them.

This of course applies to all the religions of the world, not only to those three. I am just dealing with these now. Creating this melting pot of all the religions is the coming task of every cultural group. These sectarian religions are destined to disappear physically and spiritually in the course of the next millennium. Whatever the nation will become, it will be a totally transformed being from what it is today. The positive spiritual impulse of the future will create a center in which will flow all the past traditions, world conceptions, religious systems, and philosophies into one united synthesis of all the disparate parts. This is the mission of the coming 1000 years. When we see it in this picture, in time and in space, then we can say — *Beware, it's working, it's beginning and everything is already melting*. I mean, at least you can say the fire is burning already and it's pretty hot. And we can see the fire will be fed, because without this fire, no melting is possible.

So looking at the whole, if you dip your finger a little bit into the situation, you can feel the fire working; it's very hot. And you don't have to dig so deep in Israel to feel the molten core, to feel the fires from underneath, the center of which is Jerusalem. Where it is the holiest, there it is burning the most. The whole place is on fire from below. When you enter the place, it's a physical experience. Of course, obviously, it's very hot there most of the year. But even if you come in February, January or March, it's hot, so I don't mean the external fire of summer. We can share some of this fire with you. Come to Israel. You have a chance to dip your finger, your whole leg, your whole body, in this fire. We can share fire with fire, as the destinies of Israel and America, of course, have so much in common. Take some fire home to America to nourish your own big and powerful melting pot.

Fire is something entirely positive. This fire is the fire of the future. This fire has the mission to consume the past and bring those separated, hardened, frozen religious institutions and systems, and all those rocks of Jerusalem, and the churches on top of them, the Mosques, and burn them together until people realize — *Yes, of course we are one. We have the same source, we are going to the same place, and as long as we don't realize this, it's going to burn us.* It will be so painful that eventually we will realize it. That's the only way to experience it.

The places that seem cool today were on fire a half century ago. Middle Europe is cool today, but it was aflame a few dozen years ago, don't forget. Basically, the cool places of today are preparing themselves for another fire, or are cooling off from the last one. Look around the globe. Where is the fire burning? Where is fire latent? Where is it cooling down? Whatever the stage, it's one big volcano. The three branches of this Abrahamic religious and racial element: Christianity, Islam and Judaism, have to come to physical terms with one another in Jerusalem. If I take one stream and diversify into so many different streams or branches, then in the latter days they must all converge back in through themselves to their source. Of course, the time is limited in which to realize a greater measure of synthesis, a greater measure of the ability to embrace the other, the non-self, the oppressed. And these elements, when dealing with one another, converging, colliding, speeding up, heating up, are experienced as conflagration, terror, pain, and blood, absolutely.

These are the pains of convergence. They are burning intensely because there is no way out. Israel is a tiny place. You cannot solve the Israeli dilemma by physical means because there is no place to go. Of course you can try all the physical means — chase as many Arabs as you can beyond the Jordan and further. In the 'good old days' of the independence war, you could do this to a certain extent, but, by and large, this is impossible today. Not in Israel. You can do it in Yugoslavia now because this is in accord with some interests of the global elite. There they can say — *Let's concentrate all the Slavs here, the Muslims here, and the Orthodox over there.* But no longer in Israel. It's completely mixed in Israel. And as I said there is nowhere to go. You cannot really expel the other. You can wish for it, but like in Europe, everything that you are doing to drive away the other brings him back and with revenge. The Germans have noticed this! This is one of the jokes for the Israelis about Germany — *You didn't want the Jews, now you have the Turks!* You cannot do without the Semitic element. Arab, Jewish, Christian, Orthodox, Slav, you cannot do without these. The more you chase them away, the more they are integrated.

In regard to this, read the brilliant American politician, Pat Buchanan. His book, *The Death of the West* (2001), is one of the greatest American "masterpieces" ever. Because Buchanan is not a professor at Yale, he doesn't have to mask so artfully what he thinks. He says what many people think but don't say. Buchanan just says openly what all those professors of policy and sociology at Yale and Harvard are hiding behind in their books, like *The Clash of Civilizations* (Chernow), and *The Grand Chessboard* (Brzezinski).

In Buchanan's estimation the West has lost. We are a shrinking minority of whites. In America and in Europe, immigration has taken over. There is nothing you can do. Buchanan gives the plain statistics, the birthrate, the demographics and details of immigration. He shows a global melting pot, in which the 'white' races of America and Europe are losing the fight. When the one color eventually emerges, it's not going to be terribly white, hmm? And that is a terrible loss for people like Pat Buchanan. He likes this color white. He seems to like it very much. It's a matter of taste. It's not my first choice, but okay... White is definitely endangered and this is a bit of a worry. The American color that is forecast for the middle of this century is not white, with the increased South American immigration, the natural birthrates of the Spanish community here, and the black movement. Whites will become a minority in their own Anglo-Saxon lands and in Europe you have mosques that are sprouting like mushrooms all over now. Islam is spreading itself like fire in Europe.

One can lament the loss of one's own separate racial-religious identity only if one believes oneself to be exceptionally gifted and beautiful. But when one has a more realistic self-knowledge, one cannot lament the loss of one's physical-racial identity. Can it be said, based on physical-racial characteristics — *I am the only representative of humanity? I am here and this is the end-result of human evolution? I am humanity and I represent its destiny?* On the path of initiation, as we have indicated, it is part of the process to lose the sense of self. And the loss of the connection to one specific race is part of that process. To lose the sense of an exclusive race, exclusive national identity, exclusive religion and philosophy, is the greatest release. You cannot find a greater release than that. It is the greatest liberation for the one who can say, 'I am not only this race, I am also yours. I am a human being and a human being is all races. The reality of me, as a human being, embraces all nationalities and spiritualities. I am not only a believer in Moses (with all due respect to Moses) and Abraham and all the prophets. They were great, but sorry, today I know more than that. I have heard about this Jesus; I also heard about Buddha, some good news and some truly fantastic stories. This is all mine, this is all myself. I'm not really my true self, if I'm not one with all teachers and nations and religions and ideas.'

So the same melting pot is for many the most burning and painful experience because they only lose, they don't gain. So they moan and they cry, and they suffer and they kill, and they are killed. They feel only deprivation for something that they love gaining. Dear friends, it's time to expand your being; it's time to expand your consciousness. You can do it willingly through love and compassion and acceptance of the other, and then it's a joy and a release. You can consciously choose to say, 'As a Jewish Israeli, who am I without an Israeli-Arab? Am I an Israeli without him? No. He's part of the land, he's part of the climate, and he's part of nature. He is as myself. In many respects he's more than myself, because my fellows are immigrants and he's been here some centuries. And without him, am I a true Israeli?' You don't have to live with him in the same village and share with him the way he lives. It's not a physical thing and it's not a sentimental, psychological, or mental thing. It's a spiritual thing.

The people of Israel are divided now into seven different cultures. There are only six million of them, but there are seven cultures. The latest research on this is a brilliant effort by our own Israeli version of your Buchanan. Now we have our own book about the fall of our national heritage. The reality of a united, homogenous Israel was never true, of course. It could never be founded in a hegemonic Israel controlled by the elite. So what a joy in this situation, see? This disintegration is only in the eyes of the disintegrated. For the central, elite minority, they were the whole, and now they are disintegrating. They are lamenting the Israeli dream that they loved and nourished, and with love and sacrifice brought into being according to their vision. Furthermore, everything that did not fit into this vision was periphery. In Israel, you also have this 'waspy' element. This term has been coined for the secular, socialist, European, white-skinned Jew. They founded and led the Israeli State from the beginning of the movement. They're the ones, they were Israel, and they were the national-identity. They were dominating the politics, culture and the economy, and they said — *Here we have Mideastern Jews. We will have to absorb them. We will assimilate them as minorities (they might be half the population, but they are second-rate citizens). Israel must also accommodate North-African Jews, but they are not central either. We are the elect Jews of Germany and Eastern Europe and they are the peripheral Arabic or African Jews.*

Yet in this periphery we can imagine there were real Arabs here on the land for some years. But the center could not see them, at least not in the beginning. But after some time, when those in the periphery were shooting harder and harder, some bullets began to pierce through. You couldn't just say it's raining, you had to acknowledge that there were some people around who were shooting at you. So you say, 'Okay, Arab-Israelis are citizens of Israel.' These Arab-Israeli citizens are now eighteen percent of the population, and are growing faster than the Jewish sector. They will be a quarter of the population soon and almost half of the population by the middle of this century. But they are peripheral because they are not waspy Zionists.

Now what about the orthodox element? Some of them in Israel are of Eastern origin and some are of Western origin. As Orthodox Jews, they are anti-Zionist. They were from the very beginning the strongest opposition to Zionism. They were fighting the Zionists in Europe, and only later immigrated to Israel. They became citizens, but were fighting against the state. They only slowly became part of the political-social structure. And now they are more and more influential in politics, but only in order to transform the State into an orthodox religious state. Still, they were always peripheral from the point of view of the Israeli WASPs. So the Orthodox Jews were also not to be considered a part of the identity of the real Israel. Now what about these new immigrants from Russia? This culture is maybe the most surprising of all. One million Russians emigrated to Israel in the nineties. Almost half of them, statistically, are not Jews at all. Many of them cannot prove they are Jews. Many non-Jewish Russians came with them because they wanted to get out of the sinking USSR. There are seven newspapers written in Russian and whole new theaters and literature for this population. They are very proud of the Russian culture. They view the Israeli diversity with contempt or at least suspicion. They are not saying — *We came here to be assimilated, it's something wonderful*. And they negotiate as equals in politics.

So, you see, the center is pushed out into the periphery and all those peripheries are pushing themselves into the center and we have a reversal of center and periphery. Of course, it's not total; it does not apply to all fields. The economy is still in the hands of the old elite; the army is still in the hands of the old elite; the universities also. But the political situation has changed. In Israeli politics, the reversal of periphery and center applies. You cannot consider any Israeli government in the last twenty years without confronting this reversal. And this is eroding the domain of the old elite, slowly. It is falling apart. Or maybe it is coming together for the first time. What is the true picture? If you are identified with the center and are waspy, then your dream is collapsing. The labor party diminished to twenty-four seats in the latest Knesset election, and it is forecast that in the coming elections this party might disappear entirely. The ruling labor party is, of course, the conservative party. It is still the economic, military stronghold of the Israeli wasp. From their point of view, the experience of the Israeli situation is really bleak. If you ask these people, they'll tell you it's terrible. Many flee, many ask for a second passport and buy some real estate somewhere else and invest on the outside.

If you ask the other minority what they think, they say — *Hey, for the first time, we, from the periphery, have a voice in the center. Our voice is heard, we have a political say. This fragmentation of yours is, for us, the beginning of our integration into the Israeli chaos. Chaos in the center is, for us, opportunity. Now we can grab our share of the spoils we never got. So let's share the pie now, according to some new pretense.* Then they share the pie and enjoy themselves tremendously, eating as much as possible and getting sick, from too much of the spoils in a short time. The latest poll has shown that among the Israelis as a whole twenty-seven percent believe in the democratic institution of the state. Twenty-seven! Only the army enjoys the trust of the people: I think the approval rate is around seventy percent. The courts and the legal system and so on, have a little bit more than fifty percent approval. But politics gets the lowest level of respect, because everybody cares only for himself. Different factions take over and take everything for themselves in these completely irresponsible times. Nobody cares for the whole. Each one would like to have only his needs provided for. Each one feels that he is being suppressed. They say — *We don't care for the whole, we care only for ourselves. What is the whole? There is no whole. The whole is your dream. You had the whole. Our concern is for our population, our culture. This is why we are in politics.* So that's it.

The melting pot is very quickly synthesizing and integrating the parts into the whole. It is doing its work very well, but externally the situation appears to be precisely the reverse. Everything's falling apart. It is falling apart because the center cannot hold. And the center which cannot hold, cannot support the whole. What is emerging now as the whole, cannot be anything similar to the centralized forms of the past. If there is to be a whole, if there can be any social form that will express integration, this must be something totally different than what we have had in the first fifty years of Israel's life. Something will have to emerge that expresses a new social, cultural-religious reality.

I have given thus far only the inner picture of the Israeli situation, and have not yet spoken about the Palestinian population outside of Israel, which Israel has controlled with military force for the last fifty years. This is yet another peripheral situation which is so present in the center of Israel now. Present in an explosive way, I might say. We control the Palestinian people in order to control the whole. You cannot criticize this; everybody would like to have the whole for himself. But this means we must use force, suppress the other, and occupy a land that happens to be theirs. The result of this control of the periphery is that the fringe strikes at your center. The Israelis want to have Jerusalem as a whole, for themselves. Who can say that it would not be justified for them to possess the whole city of their fathers for themselves? Everybody wants this. Wouldn't you like to have Jerusalem for yourself?

So we have had Jerusalem, as a whole now, for thirty-five years. In the first ten years it was still okay. The military occupation was okay, in the sense that the Palestinians were a bit slow to realize what had happened. But then the first Intifada (1987 — 1993) came after some time. The young generation of Palestinians who had grown up under military control understood the situation. They grew up with Israeli soldiers in the streets, and one day they said — *No more, we cannot take it!* They started an uprising and now we're in the midst of the second major insurrection (2000 — 2005). Now the result of the first Intifada was that it kept Israelis away from the eastern part of Jerusalem. They didn't go there anymore. Only religious people went there to pray at the Wailing Wall, under heavy military protection. Israelis loved to go to eastern Jerusalem in the first years after the war, when the Palestinians were friendly and happy. The commercial life flourished and everything was fine. But now no Israeli goes there anymore. The east area of Jerusalem has become a closed city over the past ten years. I was there with friends from abroad a year ago. This is a ghost city. Only around Easter and Christmas do you see some pilgrims visiting, but they are comparatively few.

So Israelis have the whole city, but are unable to enjoy it. This is the first step. Terrorism is now striking more and more in the western area of Jerusalem. Explosions are a daily affair in the streets of western Jerusalem. Many Israelis who don't happen to live in Jerusalem avoid the city altogether. We have the whole of Jerusalem, but we lost the eastern part, and now we avoid the western part also. Those who live in Jerusalem try to leave the city and go to Tel Aviv. Tel Aviv is growing in population now, especially on the Jewish side. Jerusalem is becoming a place where only brave Orthodox Jews live, under heavy military protection, and along with them, some very poor Israelis, who cannot leave. Those who can are leaving Jerusalem. The secular Jewish people are leaving the western part of Jerusalem as they are able, because they don't want to live in a city that is being bombed and divided, that is under increasing Orthodox Jewish control, with right wing coalitions.

What is happening? You want to have the whole, but you want to control the whole by force. For the time being, you believe you can make it, but after some time it begins to slip away from you. The periphery appears in the center on all levels: culturally, spiritually, socially, and economically. For some Americans now, after September 11th, this might not sound totally unfamiliar. The great war has come to America, to Manhattan, from across the ocean and has penetrated the center. The whole world is stricken by terrorism. The immunity from foreign threat that America has enjoyed, protected by two vast oceans, is over. America is part of the world. Welcome to the world, welcome to the community: you are not separated! The other, the suppressed, the rejected, is here with vengeance, and will be here more and more in this way, unless we accept him as the other. Unless we embrace him, he will force the embrace. He can do that. Don't entertain the illusion that one can really undermine this force with naked power. That is why Pat Buchanan's ideas are so telling. You cannot forcibly prevent the multitudes of humanity, four billion of them who are not white, and half a billion who are mixed, from invading and eventually taking over the castle of the 'Golden Billion.' The whole idea of the 'Golden Billion,' of America and middle Europe living inside this castle, of separating economically, politically, and culturally from the rest of the world, is a nightmare. The castle is falling, and it will perish under blood and flame in the coming decades.

If you look at those maps that are already drawn and see the design of those who are shaping the global events of the world, you will see a very clear picture, a very dark picture, of the fate of the West. This is the 'West versus the rest,' or, as Huntington put it, the 'Clash of Civilizations.' But a world in which your manifesto states that only you are the 'real' Christian or the 'real' Muslim or Jew or Confucian is a world which has closed its eyes. What nation is not chosen today? Every nation today is the 'only' chosen nation. This has gone on for more than a hundred years now. It devastated Europe in the twentieth century. But please remember that the European World Wars were still European wars. The Second World War was certainly fought in the Pacific Ocean, but the question behind the war was about the destiny and division of Europe; it was still European in scope.

We have entered into a century in which all the reasons for the great wars in Europe persist, but now they are globalized. Which means today, all nations, all powers, all religions suffer under this complex of the being the chosen ones. It was a sickness of European humanity, but now it has become global. The Chinese see themselves as the chosen global leader of the rest of them. But Islam is chosen, and George W. Bush was chosen too. So the first global century, the twenty-first century, is going to face the same challenges that were faced in Europe, but now the challenges will be on a global scale. The opportunities for positive development or mutual destruction are now reaching the global level. The combined opportunities available to Europe, America, and Russia, fifty years ago, are now proportionally increased to embrace the whole world.

In this world, the situation in Israel is very simple, because there you see in a nutshell this global clash of civilizations. In the tiniest land, concentrated around holy stones and graves, people are willing to spill their own blood and their neighbor's blood, to destroy neighborhoods and family connections. We have also seen, in the former Yugoslavia, the full flower of these possibilities. Communities, which were well integrated, were disintegrated within a fortnight because of those hatreds. But the fruits of these possibilities are not limited to distant Yugoslavia. Today no one will be overlooked. I think that when Abraham went out of his father and mother's house and was told to go out and seek land for his descendants, he was encouraged to be aggressive. The aggressiveness of Abraham should not be forgotten. What did the father of all of us do? Remember? He smashed the sculptures and all the paintings of the gods. He physically destroyed them (*Midrash Bereishit,* 38:13). Everything has a flip side; you have to separate yourself in order to take the road towards great promise.

Well enough, but your karma will also come with you. Only for a time can you say — *Okay, we have to separate the Ishmaelites out of this developing Hebrew stem.* You can do it for a time, but don't forget that this will eventually come back to you. Your other is there, it's your double. He was never away. You have forgotten him, but he has developed further. His dream was always to seek you, to chase you. He's your ghost, your double, your little brother, forsaken. He will find you and if you will not embrace him in the moment of meeting, he will take revenge. He cannot control it. I'm not speaking on the level of responsibility, of course, he's responsible. We're all human beings. The stronger suppresses the weaker. The weaker will not take the chance he has to build his own identity, because he is now so fixed on destroying the older brother, that he says — *I don't want to exist alone peacefully beside him, I want to destroy him because only through destroying him will I find myself.* He was educated this way. He is imitating his older brother. This is a typical, vicious cycle. The jealousy, the rejection, the hatred, the hunting of your brother — this is the only way to confront those things, the only way to work on those things, without any great miracles.

The only alternative is that people will be first worthy of their own identity, loving their own selves, accepting their uniqueness. It's not about erasing identity and this melting pot is not mishmash. Differences will be respected, but on a spiritual level. We are human beings sharing this piece of land. We have to find the right political, social, economic, and spiritual arrangements that will allow us to live here, and if we don't, we will continue to bleed.

My friends and I are starting to work on the task of awakening the sense of Israeli Civil Society as an independent third cultural-spiritual center, as a seed for the threefold social structure. This is the sense of our mission. This diverse world of cultural and religious background has no chance without this third sector. We cannot hold all this diversity in this one political center. It cannot provide autonomy for all and it cannot provide the same education for eastern European Jews, Orthodox Jews, Arabs, and Russian immigrants. Nobody can do that. No one should try to do that. This education should be free and it should be given to the communities. Communities should educate. Communities should support their own cultural and spiritual life in freedom. Without a small beginning in this field, nothing can improve in the slightest way. In the political sphere, you cannot even try to touch this. Political solutions cannot even provide a place of minimum sanity, minimum peace, in which people can sit and talk, or at least hear one another and try to understand the other's different world and background.

A space for this in our society does not exist because the political arena is the place for everybody to fight against one another. So Civil Society should first become a place where we can meet other human beings, to be a bit free from the pressing political agenda. It is also a bit freer from pressing economic issues. It's a space to begin to meet. We would like to have representatives from all areas of Civil Society, from NGOs, and from all sectors of spiritual and ethnic life, in order to speak about what needs to be addressed. Each group clarifies its own position, but this must happen facing the other. They don't give up their identity, but they face the other and say — *This is our identity. This is the identity of an Arab-Israeli.* Only they can tell us who they are. We cannot tell them. Then, we can tell them who we are. They have their perspective. This is their vision of Israel, and they are not the periphery and we are not the center. We are all periphery, or we are all center.

One of the more important meetings must take place between Zionists and Orthodox Jews. Who are the Zionists? The Zionists were, and are, secular Jews. They are Jews who have left the traditions of the fathers. Of course, the Zionists wanted a Jewish state, but just the fact that they are secular, makes them automatically the enemies of Jewish tradition. Now they want a state and want to name it *Israel*. Some protested, 'A Jewish state, made by those who have left the religion of the fathers? Those sinful heretics are demanding a state?! Only the Messiah himself, our true spiritual leader, can establish the Jewish state and take us back to Zion.' Now, you may know that Menachem Mendel Schneerson, an old Orthodox guy from Brooklyn, appeared and was declared by many to be the Messiah. This was the most Christian-like messianic movement to ever appear on the Jewish scene. But even he never immigrated to Israel, because he would have been committing a sin to do so. Yet, many Hasidic Jews did immigrate to Israel for various reasons. The fact that Israel was not founded by the Messiah was, and is, the primary reason for their opposition to the establishment of the state in the first place. But now the Hasidic Jews are integrated into the structure of the state and they want their share. They want the spoils in the meantime, but their overarching agenda is to transform the Israeli state into a religious one. Of course, they cannot do this, because they are a small minority. So they hate Zionism and the state. The Orthodox Jew and the Zionist belong to two different worlds.

Now, the orthodox element is becoming more extreme because the time of convergence is here. Because fire accompanies convergence, this convergence is rejected. You see, when you interact with a substance, you and the substance warm up, or even catch fire through your activity. But what happens when there is a collision in the encounter, as is the case here, and it is contained? What happens when you do not become one with the substance, but instead keep it contained and isolated as much as possible? It explodes. Terrorism is therefore just the compressed energy of synthesis, harmony, and love. This is what it is. But terrorism is a physical phenomenon, resulting from suppression and compression. It is the heated gas, which is compressed. So, now the temperature is increasing, because we are in the age of convergence. This is a natural process. The sun is getting bigger, the water is warming up, but we don't recognize the situation that we are in. We light the fire, and after it heats up, we compress it and try to preserve it.

One might imagine that we could build bridges between all of the diverse elements, but the image of building a bridge is a purely external one. It begins with good intentions, but without any real knowledge of the situation. Those who are really involved are themselves stating that they don't want to build bridges. They no longer want to build bridges between Arabs and Jews, for example, because they attempted this in the seventies and eighties to no avail. They went to so many meetings and conferences; they sat in one another's house and ate the pita together. Now they say — *We are sick of hummus and pita and eating together, because nothing has worked so far.* My friends tell me — *Listen, we went to all those meetings; we spent decades coming together with well-meaning Jewish and Arab bridge-builders. What is there to show for it?* But all those meetings, despite the best intentions, were dominated by Jews. So the bridge-building was a lopsided effort from the beginning. The Arabs were always a minority, and since the nineties, nobody has tried to build bridges anymore. This is more of a bourgeois project nowadays; something to do in your spare time. The serious people are just working now to create better bombs.

In the group, *Activists for Israeli Civil Society,* we are not trying to build bridges. What I described before was not about building bridges. I said that each one tries to understand himself or herself better through self-knowledge, and then, without any pre-conceived ideas, without any pretensions of building bridges, listens to the individuality of the other. This is enough, if it is practiced. It will be something deeper or it will be nothing at all. Don't misunderstand me. In its time, much good was achieved with these programs of bridge-building. To a certain extent, people really met each other at those conferences. But this is over, on both sides. The Arab community is building its own Civil Society. Good. If they want us to come to meet their organization, we will come. There is no single organization representing all of Civil Society in Israel. Our small organization is working with our small corner of the whole. We are partnered with *The Jewish Agency*, which is the greatest NGO in Israel, whose sole interest is to develop the Jewish community in Israel. It existed before the state of Israel. There are remarkable powers connected to this organization. We are partners with them and they have developed an interest in the threefolding principles we are working with.

At the recent Civil Society conference that we organized, *The Jewish Agency* and activists for *Israeli Civil Society* (which has an Arab leader) were able to attend together. I just wanted to give this as an example of something that can become fruitful after the end of the earlier bridge-building effort. Bridge-building really always meant that the center would be kind and compassionate. It meant that this center would demonstrate its true goodness toward the periphery, while it maintained the distance between center and periphery. Bridge-building showed some smiling Jews and Arabs together, especially on holy days, and promised to eventually fix the periphery. This was the message and everybody got it. If you were a minority, you even got some money out of it. So if you were an Arab educator, teaching in a school system (which is definitely below the standards of any Jewish educational system) and a bridge-builder came along saying — *Come build a bridge, bring along your hummus and we will give you some money, so that you can plant some trees in the school yard* — maybe you would have gone. But they don't want any trees in the center. Take your trees out to your own home in the periphery.

What we want to do now, first and foremost, is create a roundtable for Civil Society organizations. That's it, very simple. We are inviting organizations and individual human beings, who are part of various cultural movements, to participate in a free dialogue. Of course, we discuss threefolding, as that is part of our focus, but only so far as it is grounded in reality. Does Israel need a strong third sector of society or not? This is our question. First of all, nobody trusts politics. Many people want to transform society for the good, but they know that this is impossible to accomplish from politics. Many of them have been engaged in politics in the past. They have seen that politics has nothing to do with them personally, nor does it reach the other. So many people are seeking another venue to work in society. With these people you can speak about a third sector. It is not business and it is not politics, it is a third. We invite the people coming from this sector to sit down together and speak about the role of this third, next to polity and economy. We begin with that.

There are so many people who are part of this third element and don't know it. In the last meeting, a lady stood up and said that what she heard in the meeting was very significant to her. She said, 'I never knew I was part of the cultural sector. I was always doing my work in my organization, and I didn't know that this was my name. It's great to know that I have a place in society. I was alone in my organization, among many organizations. I knew about these other organizations, but it never came to my mind that we belonged to something together. Before, we were only considered to be appendages to the reality of political life or economic life.' This particular lady started an organization that helps families that have been victims of terrorism. It's fantastic voluntary work. She discovered in this meeting that she's part of a third element of society. If we can infuse Israeli or any Civil Society with this identity and self-confidence, then these people can become conscious of their own sphere of activity, of their own rights, and of their own power. If we reach this, we will have changed reality forever.

With all the variations, the one global question is everywhere the same. The challenge is to work with the other's racial, economic, and cultural element, in micro-social, meso-social, and macro-social circumstances in all places. This is the lesson of the age. The whole fifth cultural epoch, the whole third millennium, is dedicated to the learning of this one basic lesson: to integrate the individual, the national, the racial, and the religious, into one great synthesis, in which we have to learn all the differences and experience all the convergences. This is simply the great and beautiful task of our time. Human beings were not up to this before our times. They were separated in time, space and so on. For example, if you were Chinese, you knew only other Chinese. There were the civilized people that you knew, and the rest were barbarians. One world, one society, one humanity: this is all new. One thousand years to learn this is not long.

However, even at this stage of our intellectual development, we simply cannot conceive of diversity and unity existing side by side, at the same time. We simply cannot. We have to acknowledge this consciously. This means that whenever we speak about it, we fall into one of the extremes, either into diversity or into unity. We can speak about it, but we cannot imagine anything concrete to fill the concept with substance. But this is the first thing that we really have to approach; otherwise our path will be filled with illusions. It is the task of the next one thousand years to combine unity and diversity in a single concept on a human level. The gods learned it a long time ago. In nature, it is masterfully realized. With human beings, it will take time. Individuality and community: we have no concept for what this means. But we *pretend* that we have it. In reality, we overvalue one or the other of the two extremes. We sometimes want the diversity to disappear altogether in the melting pot; but it is really a stew. It is the task to bring these paradoxes together in harmony, in synthesis, without changing one to fit the other. But it will take much blood. God knows the secret. He has created this immense diversity combined with absolute unity. But then he created this other creature...and here, we get into trouble. We are made in His image, yes, but with a snake beside us. So God is very tricky in this regard. Humankind will not only recapitulate all the contradictions of God, they will also have to solve their own unique contradiction by themselves. He was very happy with what He did, without knowing the results. God is really a risky gambler. It's not the conventional God we are used to hearing about. He's a risk-taking, open-minded, adventurous creature. Look what He did. We are here.

# Lecture 10

## Israel in the Midst of the Clash of Civilizations: The Process of the Formation of Civil Society in Israel in the Light Of Social Threefolding (Munich 2004)

SEEN EXTERNALLY AND FROM a global perspective, we stand today in the middle of world-wide cultural conflict. It is a conflict between what comes from the West, the world empire of the U.S.A., which is expanding ever farther in all directions, and what comes from the East, Islamic fundamentalism. Here, Israel is situated right in the middle. Germany, of course, is also right in the middle and every other country too. I would like to describe the Israeli situation from within: as a society, as a culture, as a people, and as a State. For, however great and one-sided the pressures may be that are exerted by the outer global powers, how these forces influence us depends upon our inner situation. Let us first focus here on the modern Israel that arose in 1948.

The Israelis who were born there and the immigrants and refugees from Europe have always experienced Israel as a place of the resurrection of the Jewish people. Externally (historically) and inwardly, (spiritually and esoterically) Israel has been seen as the place of resurrection for a people who in the course of the 20th century had been led to their death. That the State of Israel came into being after the Holocaust, and survived in this form despite all the obstacles it met in this region, including those from the Arab world, is, on the face of it, a great miracle.

If one wishes to understand the Jewish consciousness, then one must come to terms with what I am describing, because it is a profound psychological, mental and spiritual reality for the Israelis. In our time, deeper connections between people can only come about if one takes seriously the inner soul and spiritual nature of other human beings and other nations and gets to know who they are and what they are like. This is what is lacking. For this reason, I will now describe in more detail the essential nature of the Israeli, the Jewish soul. It is a unique mixture of two principal forces, which embody the greatest possible contrast.

The first force is tremendous fear. If you wish to understand an Israeli Jew, you must see the fear that lives and weaves in the deepest regions of his soul. People always say: "What more do the Israelis want? They've got the fourth strongest in the world, they've got nuclear bombs, and they've got everything that constitutes the most modern arsenal of weapons and military power!" And yet, when a Palestinian child throws a stone, the whole nation trembles, falls into a really hysterical state of fear and reacts with unbelievable aggression. This means that outwardly speaking there is no correspondence between the actual power of the Israeli-Jewish State and the fear experienced inwardly by its people. The second force is the power of resurrection. Deep existential anxiety on the one hand, and on the other this tremendous power of resurrection, courage, bravery, creative power and no end of wonderful things of this sort. It is just this mixture of the two elements that constitutes the Jewish part of the Israeli soul.

The Israeli community today consists of a veritable multiplicity of cultures and ethnic elements; here, too, there is a powerful contradiction. On the one hand, the unity of Israel is experienced and the cohesion of the Israeli State is very strong; on the other hand, Israel is divided inwardly into eight cultural communities (but these are only the principal streams). Two of the eight are non-Jewish. First we have the Arab citizens, the Arab minority, and the Arab-Palestinian-Israeli citizenry. I don't mean the Arabs under the Occupation. I mean the Arab citizens (20% of the Israeli population, 1,300,000 Arabs). Two thirds of them are Islamic Arabs, one third are Christian Arabs. And one knows, from demographic projections, that in the year 2050 the Arabs will constitute 40 or 45% of the Israeli population. Already now it is a two-nation State, and this will become more pronounced. So this is the main division within Israel: Jews and Arabs. The other non-Jewish community consists of the foreign workers from all over the world, with their families and children. They have no identity, no place; nobody knows who they are, but they are a community.

What remains are the six main streams of the Jewish communities, which are really different from one another and are in continual cultural struggle with one another: the "oriental" Jews, who were born in Israel as the sons and daughters of Jewish immigrants from Arab countries. Then there are the European Jews, the Ashkenazim like myself, the idealists who came from Europe and Eastern Europe and, from the beginning, built up Israel in the spirit of Zionism. Then the orthodox Jews, who are anti-nationalistic and anti-Zionist, but who have become more and more integrated in recent years; also the religious Jews who have reconnected the Jewish religion with Jewish Zionism and nationalism, the settler movement. Finally, the "Ethiopians," with a Jewish tradition of their own, which they have always protected in their isolation in Africa and have developed over the past 2000 years; and the Russian Jewish congregation which constitutes a community of their own culturally and ethnically, and regards America as their model. All these main and secondary streams come together in the tiny land of Israel: nearly seven million people. Israel is around the tenth most densely populated country in the world and the density is increasing.

When we began our Civil Society endeavors, we asked ourselves: How can we do justice to this multiplicity? For the multiplicity needs to have its own social structures, its own political, cultural, and economic foundation if it is to be led towards the good and not the bad, towards life and not conflict. The global market economy is blind to multiplicity and difference. It levels everything down and it regards every human being as a consumer, rather than as an element of a cultural group. So, we turn to the State, and what do we find there? Each of these communities and sub-communities has formed for itself a political party, in order to get more from the State than the others. The political scene in Israel today is sheer competition, conflict between parties, which are formed according to the different sectors that struggle amongst themselves for the available resources. Each wants the best for his or her own community. Today no one asks any longer what is in the interest of the whole. There are always individuals, here and there, but not as a factor that really counts.

What else is there to do? The only thing that we have found so far is to appeal to the weakest element in us. We have to appeal to free will and the free power of initiative of the free citizen, who is not attached politically or economically. Many people support this ideologically, but say that we should not even attempt such an approach. This is a hallmark of the human beings of our time. People have grown lazy (but not stupid, they are always very clever). When we drew up a perspective called, "The Threefolding of Society and Civil Society as a relatively free third sector outside Politics and Economy," they were enthusiastic. To begin with, we were pleased with this enthusiasm, but now we have learned that people say *yes* on the level of ideas, but then in practice carry on the same as before.

> They say: What you say is true, but we won't join, because it won't work.

> We respond: But you just said that it is the truth!

> They say: Yes, it is the truth, but in the reality of social life, truth is the thing that doesn't work.

This is how many people speak. 'Chosen' individuals (and today everyone is a chosen individual, rather than a chosen people) say: 'We prefer to carry on living with what we have at the moment, in the knowledge that doom is approaching. But we live on with the process of downfall with greater peace of mind, because at least we know where it is taking us. It is better than joining in an enterprise, where we are well aware that it is the only way forward, but where it is uncertain whether it can be realized in practice.'

Therefore, one has to go from person to person and find those who not only know that developing a free, third sector is a true solution, but who also want to do something practically. At first it is only individuals, but we will not really make any headway, if we do not appeal to free human beings. We therefore have to create structures and institutions of the third sector. We call these *citizens' councils* — where citizens meet each other as free citizens. We leave aside political differences, we leave aside economic aspects, and we meet together because we believe that, as free citizens, we have the power to influence and change our society. This is not incredibly extensive, and it is not incredibly hard to understand, but to realize this in practice is a formidable task!

The setting up of citizens' councils — locally, regionally and nationally — has begun. I would hope that in ten years time, we will have a national citizens' council, plus a few local and regional ones, and that the concepts "organized third sector" and "Civil Society" will have found their way into the media and into discussions in Israel. I hope that everyone will be aware that there are places where citizens meet and where the citizenry creates for itself an identity and a voice. Conscience must find a place here, in order to develop what is moral, and where citizens speak together about their own, genuine values and ideals, without political and financial pressure, solely on the basis of shared humanity. This is where our path leads us: not to simply react and demonstrate, but to create something positive and new, with the long-term goal, *that people will place more and more trust in the free and genuinely human element.* But one can only find this trust, if it is experienced directly. In order to experience it directly, it has to be practiced. In order to practice it, one has to believe in it.

It lies in human nature that people can easily be rallied to stage a protest. This is a paradox of our nature: Being opposed to something creates unity, but the positive differentiates straight away. This means that when one has a positive idea, it immediately falls apart. The positive brings our egoism to expression — the personal or the ideological — as well as the egoism of the group or organization. The negative creates a positive appearance of unity. 'The enemy is outside, therefore we are all good!' But if we want to do good, then the enemy is there between us. It belongs to our age, and we do not take it as a tragedy, but as the childhood stages and childhood illnesses of a genuinely new movement. Previously in human history the free individual was not there and thus it was not possible to appeal to the free, ethical individuality. The human being was always a part of a Church, a community, a culture and so forth, and in such a way that he did not need to find and realize, from within himself, his own moral standpoint.

There are Islamic Arabs in our Israeli Civil Society work. They say — *What you are doing here is wonderful. But the way you (the Jewish Israelis) are doing it, doesn't really meet our need, because it is a Jewish-Israeli approach. We have to transform it into a completely independent Arab-Israeli approach.* In the different communities each person must find his own language and the language of the community, in order to bring forth and realize in practice the Civil Society ideals there. This idea of forming a council of citizens is unitary as an idea, but in practical reality it has to be transmitted to each cultural, religious and ethnic community in an individual way.

Also the rabbis have not wanted to meet the Arabs, because they say, 'First the different Jewish communities have to find one another. Our main concern is to bring about a dialogue between the religious and the non-religious, the orthodox and the national-religious, the Russians and the Ethiopians. Only when we have achieved this, when we agree or can at least understand one another, can we then try to also speak to the Arabs and come to an understanding with them. If we as Jews have no understanding for one another, what have we to say to the Arabs?'

This is true: the two groups cannot yet talk to one another. But on the other hand, we are simply going ahead and working with the Arabs already, and both sides are already flowing together. Then the time will come, when a meeting can also take place between real Jewish rabbis, genuinely religious people and real Arabs, genuinely Islamic people. Between human beings in fact! What follows below, shows an example of our proposal in Galilee, and is followed by some frequently asked questions about the councils. Such councils can exist anywhere in the world.

## An Example of a Call to Create a Citizens' Council in Israel

We call the citizens of the state of Israel, that live in the Galilee region, of all ethnic origins, social and cultural backgrounds, sex, religion and nationality, to join the "Galilee Citizens' Council." This is a first effort of its kind in Israel, to create a free and non-partisan gathering of citizens, as part of a nation-wide civil movement, based on a threefolding social conception. Similar citizens' councils will be created in all regions in Israel, as part of the coming together of Civil Society in Israel, as an independent, third social sector, alongside the political and economic sectors.

## Frequently Asked Questions about Citizens' Councils:

*What is a citizens' council?*

A citizens' council gathers the people who seek to be active in a certain locality, for the interests of the citizens of that region, to interact with the local governments, either through struggle and protest, complementation or cooperation, according to the nature of the case. The citizens' council creates its own links with representatives of the political sector, as well as with the producers, consumers, and traders, who operate in the same area, in order to make "the third voice" that is absent nowadays, into a powerful presence in decision making, on all levels and issues.

*Does a citizens' council replace the political authority?*

No. It creates a new social space, free for civil meeting and cooperation, in order to identify the main cultural, social, and economic challenges in the neighborhood. These are problems that fall outside the jurisdiction, inclination, or capability of the elected officials.

*What is the source of the legitimacy and authority of a citizens' council?*

In the third, spiritual-cultural, sector, the sources of legitimacy are called: the freedom of responsibility, conscience, and initiative of the free citizens. They confer on themselves the legitimacy and authority simply by their free initiative. Furthermore, their social initiative is the source of their social engagement.

*Is the council intended only for the residents of a specific regional municipality?*

No. The distribution of the municipal governments is not a civil distribution, but a political one. The practical social problems and all issues of concern are shared by the residents who belong to different municipalities, and cross the borders of political jurisdiction. The council belongs to all the citizens of the region. According to the threefold social conception, there is no "Arabic sector" or "Jewish sector," but a third, Civil Society sector, in which all citizens take part, while also being part of diverse ethnic, cultural, and religious communities. Furthermore, the council is not a body of "representatives" of different organizations, but of free and autonomous individual citizens, who only represent themselves.

*Can you offer an example of the practical work of a council?*

For example, to make sure that the citizens' council participates in all aspects of the decision making processes concerning the managing of the regional infrastructure (roads, electricity, sewage, other forms of energy) and the local natural resources (mining, water, agriculture and food production). The common social practice is that decisions are made about these issues by only two partners: the local politicians and business people, with the exclusion of the representatives of local Civil Society. This applies, naturally, to all social issues: education and culture; relations between ethnic and cultural groups, minorities and religious communities; welfare and healthcare and so on. The priorities will be ordained by the council itself, once it has clarified its identity and its function on the level of principles.

# Lecture 11
## The Global Initiation of Humanity and Education
## (Oslo 2006)

LET US ASK SOME FUNDAMENTAL questions about education within the context of the current global initiation of humanity:

- What is the task of schools, if they are to become a part of Civil Society?
- What are the needs of the young people today?
- How can we transform Waldorf schools or any schools, working only out of the essence and source of their becoming?

What do we mean by a 'global initiation of humanity?' We mean an awakening to the true nature of real spiritual and social change that is happening in our times. I would say that there are five stages to such an awakening, which could lead to a realization of a conscious, worldwide initiation in the 21st century:

1. Seeing the global imbalance and injustice which exist in the periphery
2. Awakening to moral responsibility
3. Try to work for real change at home
4. Confronting ourselves
5. Beginning real processes of community and educational transformation

This may seem to be unusual start for a Waldorf teacher's conference.[24] But in our times, we must first awaken to moral responsibility, which often happens through experiencing the real suffering of people far away from home. If we do awaken, we must then confront the question: what is the true nature and source of real spiritual and social change? There is a difference between helping in the periphery, in the forgotten corners of the world through philanthropy, and then going back home to our own community, in order to work from within. However, we can really make a difference working from the grass-roots up, because we are truly rooted only in our own community and country. It is also the case, that in the Northern and Western countries, we are living inside the international machinery that creates global injustice, poverty, and perpetual war. Therefore, it is at home where real change is necessary and where we can create real change. In the periphery we can offer superficial help, but at home we can work to create and shape a strategic, long-term societal transformation.

But "going back home" and starting to work in our own community means also that we are confronted with...ourselves. In the periphery, we appear as saviours, because we give from our own resources, and confront the misery of others. We may even feel very pleased with ourselves because we help the poor and miserable. But this reverses itself back home. In our own community, the external wretchedness may not be as obvious (though we just have to look, because it is also there, in those neighbourhoods that we don't usually like to visit). Instead, at home, we come face to face with our own shortcomings, limitations and challenges. Therefore, the will to change society at home leads to the need to change your own self. Now we can fill in our overview of the stages of the preparatory stages that may lead today to a conscious experience, research and realization of global initiation:

1. We awaken from our moral-cognitive sleep or refusal, when we see and experience for the first time, the global misery in the periphery in the world of today.

2. We experience a moral awakening of conscience and an inner call for responsibility.

3. After overcoming the temptation to become philanthropists and world saviours at the periphery, far from home, we "return home," because we understand that real change can only take place in our own community, culture and country.

4. Then, after beginning to try and transform society at home, we meet ourselves, our doubles, which mirror back to us the challenges that we must overcome inwardly, if we are to succeed in changing our community.

5. This meeting with ourselves can become a revelation of great significance. It opens one of the portals to the global initiation of humanity in the 21st century. Here we are drawing closer to some of the deeper issues that build the unseen core of the global initiation process. Here we can apply it to the problem of the future of education.

The deeper issues that lie at the core of our times stem from changes in the spiritual world itself. There is a new way in which humans prepare for life on Earth, which began in the middle of the 20th century. It is essentially different from previous times. The invisible, supersensible core of the Global Initiation of Humanity can be described by the imaginative picture of a pre-Earthly "covenant" that each person makes before birth with the Higher Self of humanity (the Christ). This new ritual in the spiritual worlds gives new meaning for modern initiation as a whole and especially in connection with the modern education of children and youth. Specifically, there is a new initiatory experience that happens around the age of puberty in our times, which is a polar opposite of ancient tribal confirmation rituals.

In the past, when elders and priests were the teachers of society and culture, each of us met with the gods and priests of our people or tribe before birth. Before descending to Earth, we were each assigned a concrete task to be realized in the community in which we were to be born. This task was always in line with the main goal of the ancient cultures, which was to serve and keep the traditions of the spiritual will of the community that are transmitted from one generation to the next. For each one this task was given in the form of a powerful spiritual imagination.

On Earth, this imagination had to be awakened at the gates of puberty. This was the purpose of these initiations for the youth, and indeed, for all the ancient initiations of people at every stage of life. When the young person reached puberty, he went through a very powerful (and rather drastic from our perspective) first initiation as a confirmation. He confirmed his identity as the identity of his tribe or nation. The pre-Earthly Imagination was awakened to full Earthly consciousness and memory, and through this, the young person learned how to become an integral part of his community. What was impressed in the awakening soul forces of the young person was his specific task, which had been given to him before birth. Now it became conscious and he was powerfully led to serve his community according to the ancient and sacred, spiritual laws of the tribe or nation.

In our time, as part of the global initiation that started in the second half of the 20th century, this was essentially changed; it was actually transformed. Since then, each person meets with the Higher Self of Humanity and his or her human and spiritual companions. Each soul is given a vast panoramic view the past, present and future of the evolution of humanity. **Then, as a free answer that comes from our own being as a result of experiencing this panorama, we create our own freely chosen task and dedicate this work and ourselves to the service of humanity and the Earth.** We ourselves articulate and create an individual Moral Intuition, an essential impulse or a force, rather than an imagination as a concrete picture of an Earthly task. This moral impulse expresses the meaning that we give to our part in the evolution of humanity in our next Earthly life.

This process, which I described from another aspect in more detail in my book, *The Spiritual Event of the 20th Century*, is experienced as a wholly new "covenant" between our individuality and humanity as a whole. This covenant replaces the old, Mosaic covenant. It is a new, spiritual, "Sinai Revelation," only that today it is created by each individual with the Being of humanity as a whole. Since the middle and especially the end of last century, the Higher Self of humanity can become our individual higher self, and we can begin now, at the beginning of the 21st century, to awaken to this consciously on the Earth. It is humanity as a whole today that has become the "chosen people," as the Israeli folk were in the time of Moses. Then, right after I "sign" the covenant with humanity's true Being in me, I am immediately taken to a special place through which I am also shown the modern refusal and betrayal of the new covenant. We also experience the modern "Golden Calf" ritual and the breaking of our new moral commitment. Each person experiences that, as part of modern humanity, I am also breaking the new covenant. This is a most powerful experience before birth that takes place in the spiritual world which is most immediately linked with the physical Earth.

The pain experienced at this point is very essential, since it will become for many people the very means of awakening a moral responsibility to transform society, to the extent they are morally awakened in Earthly life. The will to heal and reaffirm the broken covenant during the coming incarnation on the Earth may then become a powerful motivation. In the spiritual, supersensible worlds, each person says to herself something like this:

"I am creating a powerful moral impulse, a future seed force, containing the possibility to awaken on the Earth to my future Earthly task, which is now no longer fixed within a tribal or national-cultural tradition. The task is global and must be fulfilled in the first ever, global century in human history, namely, the 21st. Therefore, the future goals are not fixed and known in advance, or "ahead of time." They truly have nothing more to do with "the head," but rather with the conscience and action of the heart and limbs. In earlier epochs, the task was to not forget the past, to be true to the heritage of our ancestors; you had to repeat it again faithfully below. But today, since the middle of the 20th century, the task is to not forget the future, to be loyal to what you yourself have resolved to do, because of your free love for humanity, before you descended down into the 20th and 21st centuries."

The old covenant was written by God on tablets of stone, while the new is written by us on the tablet of our hearts. **It is of great importance today to awaken this "future memory" of the spiritual articulating and Earthly breaking of the covenant. It must be understood as part of the process of realizing global initiation in this century, without which no true new education will be possible.** On Earth we must search to find those people with whom, together, we can remember our future decision, resolved upon before birth, to serve the good of humanity as a whole, to work for creating brotherhood and sisterhood on Earth. We can strive to find a community of mutually awakening humans, a community in which we can realize the new covenant, practically and socially. But this can only be achieved if it is raised to full consciousness. Therefore it is essential today that the social tasks of the future, and especially the educational tasks, be permeated with these updated results of new research in spiritual science.

The task of a timely school for spiritual science, and of a new educational impulse that it can inspire, is to create a human-social-educational "open space" in which this meaning of modern global initiation of humanity will be able, first, to come to consciousness, and second, find its practical realization. This requires that a transformation of both schools should be consciously and also simultaneously realized in the coming years: a transformation of the school for spiritual science, on the one hand and of the school for children and youth, on the other. Both transformations are essentially one and the same: one for adults and the other for adults who wish to serve the new generation. It is a mutual transformation, in which both schools help each in the transformation of the other.

Now, let me give some indications concerning the needed transformation of the Waldorf or indeed of any high school (9th —12th grade). It would be timely and appropriate today to reverse the centre and periphery of any high school, which means a transformation of content and form at the same time. This transformation involves two main stages. The first has to do with changing the main goal of the school. The second reflects this change of goal, in the form of teaching as well as in the organization of the school and its relations to its social environment. All I wish to do at this stage is to give some preliminary indications, in order to stir new thinking and free imagining; encouraging open exploration and courage for deep and essential change. One has to wait for further research and exploration on the side of the educational community at large, in order to continue this later on, as a part of mutual dialogue, research and practical implementation.

The new and central goal of the school in the 21st century should be education for spiritual, cultural and social transformation, and for responsibility and engagement. This cannot be achieved by sitting in classrooms and perhaps hearing good lectures about social issues. This can only be learned through actual daily, moral-social practice, when the school community as a whole — the teachers, students and their parents together — can engage in performing authentic tasks in the community, addressing life problems and community difficulties in real, and not theoretical, social practice. The forces streaming from the awakened memory of our spiritual covenant with our Higher Self before birth, and its betrayal, are our only source of courage and free creativity now. If we truly live through this consciously, we will simply experience this fact: everything that we do must now be reversed inside out and outside in. We will experience it as a natural need, because we will experience that in the existing structure of the school, we cannot breathe at all. Then we will know exactly what we have to do. We have to learn how to breathe freely again!

For example, we will feel the need that the classroom has to be reversed inside out: the social periphery becomes the class-field (instead of a room), and the social tasks should become the "class," or centre of the "curriculum." This must be felt intensively, for it cannot be suggested theoretically. This change will necessarily affect and eventually transform the way we are now teaching our subjects. Today we still work according to a bygone, obsolete academicism that was forced on the Waldorf impulse in the Germany of 1919, because of the conditions of the time. As Steiner repeatedly said, he had to make many compromises, but then people forgot that these were compromises and begun to understand and use them as divine commandments. But today this compromise (and so many others) is neither necessary nor timely in this respect. The academic fragmentation of the subject matters is wholly artificial when it comes to the 9–12th grades and should have long since been discarded in favour of holistic, socially-centred, open-field studies in integrated, multi-faceted, main blocks. Synthesis will replace analysis. In the social main block of "environment," for example, all subject matters will be woven together to create a meaningful whole, that will support the practical-social work that the young people are actually performing in the community. Each main block will have to be planned and shaped by all the disciplines, by many teachers working creatively together with a community that works well as a team.

This community may become in this way not only ideally, but practically and in reality, a community of spiritually creative and socially engaged people.

In this manner, the Imagination of the Waldorf school that Steiner gave a whole century ago, may take a further step in the direction of its future realization. In the near future, if we work on spiritual awakening on the one hand, and are inspired by it to change our practical-social educational work on the other, there will no more be "curriculum subjects" as we have today. Instead there will be major "social problems" as holistic blocks. But this, of course, means that the teams of teachers and community as a whole, will first have to learn how to "breathe together" as a living organism, as a real group of equals. Secondly, they will learn how to plan and execute a full transformation of the high school structure, which will be based on engaged social learning and practice, and then also on the teaching program adapted to serve it.

The work will be holistic, synthesizing, and synergetic, replacing the academic, analytic, fragmentary present curriculum in all schools. A community of teachers will be realized and come to life in a real spiritual-human-social practice, because by means of creating a socially orientated curriculum together, a very joyful and creative exercise in community building process will be realized. From the point of view of a true, rational, future educational and societal strategy, this is the role of the school: to prepare the young people for conscious, responsible participation in 21$^{st}$ century social life. This cannot happen by sitting in classrooms. The teachers will, in the future, be involved in community building processes in the school community itself and in social and cultural practice, together with their students and the community around the school.

These are therefore the essential questions: has the Waldorf school movement gone through essential growth, maturation and metamorphosis in the course of the last century? Did it go through a natural process of spiritual and social growth and *Umstülpung* (reversal inside-out of centre and periphery) that comes at a certain stage of organic-spiritual growth? Or did it actually preserve unchanged what Steiner gave to the world between 1919 and 1924? Are we only getting bigger? Are we like a caterpillar getting ever fatter, refusing the metamorphosis into a butterfly?

This is the real place in which the esoteric aspects of global initiation will be brought together with specific educational tasks. The children meet their future through us. They seek a school a community which can truly remind them of the pre-Earthly covenant that they themselves made with the Being of humanity. This should become the future "Moral Intuition" of the Waldorf School that will imbue it with new spiritual content and inspiration. This new Moral Intuition is living powerfully in the deepest longing of those that choose to become teachers, and in the new souls coming to Earth to seek them. This will fill the Waldorf Imagination given by Steiner before the middle of last century with spiritual and moral substance. It will complement in substance and form the work started almost 100 years ago, and will give it a whole new *Umstülpung* impulse, so that the Waldorf impulse will not die — either with a bang or a whisper. It will enable any education to become fruitful, today and tomorrow, in the 21st century.

# Lecture 12

## The Transformation of Evil in America and the High Tor Archangel
### (New York City 2002)

Introduction:

IN 2002, DR. YESHAYAHU BEN-AHARON gave several lectures followed by question and answer sessions on the spiritual reality behind the unique American legends of Hugo and the Ramapo Salamander.[25] The complete, brief texts of these traditions, from *Myths and Legends of Rockland County,* follow this introduction. These legends from the Hudson valley refer to an event that took place directly after the birth of Jesus, and then to a second event focused on a Spirit of Fire encountered in the iron mining industry that took place in the second half of the 18th century, in the general area of Rockland County, New York. The later events discuss German Rosicrucian immigrants who came to work in Peter Hasenclever's iron mines in 1764.

    Whether or not the leader of the Rosicrucian group, Hugo, who is portrayed as the head of the iron works in the legend, is related to Hasenclever himself is unclear. What is true is that Hasenclever owned about 50,000 acres in the region of Ramapo Mountain and Ringwood State Park in New Jersey. His property extended toward High Tor Mountain (10 miles to the East), from whose height, one can see New York City. Geologists suggest that the rock that makes up the mountains in this area rose from deep within the earth 200 million years ago. Many abandoned iron mines can also be found in

Harriman State Park a little to the Northeast from Ringwood Manor. It was said the Ringwood manor, built under the direction of Hasenclever, was "an iron plantation combining the medieval institution of a manor with the modern iron industry."[26] Another source suggests that Hasenclever was very knowledgeable 'in both mineral and vegetal matter.' His medieval manor along with his knowledge of mineral and vegetal secrets may perhaps loosely connect Hasenclever to the Rosicrucian, Manichean, and alchemic impulses discussed in the legend. For in alchemy, the production of the red and white philosopher's stones is often connected with specific vegetable and mineral transformations. In any case, Hasenclever eventually ran into trouble with his workers, who consisted of German immigrants and Native Americans, among other nationalities, and ran his business into the ground. He published a defense of his actions in *The Remarkable Case of Peter Hasenclever* (1773).

In addition to these short legends, Elizabeth Oakes Smith (1806–1893), a poet, lecturer, and early defender of women's rights, wrote a novella called *The Salamander*, which is obviously heavily influenced by these legends. In some beautiful passages, she relates the terrible temptations faced by Hugo as he comes face to face with the evil spirits in the depths of the Earth, and the profound spiritual connections between Mary, the daughter of Hugo, and the High Tor Archangel in his human form.

Scott E. Hicks

## The High Tor Legend (A): The Ramapo Salamander

A curious tale of the Rosicrucians runs to the effect that more than two centuries ago a band of German colonists entered the Ramapo valley and put up houses of stone, like those they had left in the Hartz Mountains. And when the Indians saw how they made knives and other wonderful things out of metal, which they extracted from the rocks by fire, they believed them to be Manitous or Spirit Beings and went away, not wishing to resist their possession of the land. There was treasure here, for High Tor, or Torn Mountain, had been the home of Amasis, youngest of the magi who had followed the star of Bethlehem. He had found his way, through Asia and Alaska, to this country, had taken to wife a native woman, by whom he had a child, and here on the summit he had built a temple.

Having refused the sun worship, when the Indians demanded that he should take their faith, he was set upon, and would have been killed had not an Earthquake torn the ground at his feet, opening a new channel for the Hudson and precipitating into it every one but the magus and his daughter. To him had been revealed in magic vision the secrets of wealth in the rocks. The leader in the German colony, one Hugo, was a man of noble origin, who had a wife and two children: a boy, named after himself; and a girl — Mary. Though it had been the custom in the other country to let out the forge fires once in seven years, Hugo opposed that practice in the forge he had built as needless. But his men murmured and talked of the salamander that once in seven years attains its growth in unquenched flame and goes forth doing mischief.

On the day when that period was ended the master entered his works and saw the men gazing into the furnace at a pale form that seemed made from flame, that was nodding and turning in the fire, occasionally darting its tongue at them or allowing its tail to fall out and lie along the stone floor. As he came to the door he, too, was transfixed, and the fire seemed to burn his vitals, until he felt water sprinkled on his face, and saw that his wife, whom he had left at home too ill to move, stood behind him and was casting holy water into the furnace, speaking an incantation as she did so. At that moment a storm arose, and a rain fell that put out the fire; but as the last glow faded the lady fell dead.

When her children were to be consecrated, seven years later, those who stood outside of the church during the ceremony saw a vivid flash, and the nurse turned from the boy in her fright. She took her hands from her eyes. The child was gone. Twice seven years had passed and the daughter remained unspotted by the world. For, on the night when her father had led her to the top of High Tor Mountain and shown her what Amasis had seen — the Earth spirits in their caves heaping jewels and offering to give them if Hugo would speak the word that binds the free to the Earth forces and bars his future for a thousand years. It was her prayer that brought him to his senses and made the scene below grow dim, though the baleful light of the salamander clinging to the rocks at the bottom of the cave sent a glow into the sky.

Many nights after that the glow was seen on the height and Hugo was missing from his home, but for lack of a pure soul to stand as interpreter he failed to read the words that burned in the triangle on the salamander's back, and returned in rage and jealousy. A knightly man had of late appeared in the settlement, and between him and Mary a tender feeling had arisen, that, however, was unexpressed until, after saving her from the attack of a panther, he had allowed her to fall into his arms.

She would willingly then have declared her love for him, but he placed her gently and regretfully from him and said, "When you slept I came to you and put a crown of gems on your head: that was because I was in the power of the Earth spirit. Then I had power only over the element of fire, that either consumes or hardens to stone; but now water and life are mine. Behold! Wear these, for thou art worthy." And touching the tears that had fallen from her eyes, they turned into lilies in his hands, and he put them on her brow.

"Shall we meet again?" asked the girl.

"I do not know," said he. "I tread the darkness of the universe alone, and I peril my redemption by yielding to this love of Earth. Thou art redeemed already, but I must make my way back to God through obedience tested in trial. Know that I am one of those that left heaven for love of man. We were of that subtle element which is flame, burning and glowing with love — and when thy mother came to me with the power of purity to cast me out of the furnace, I lost my shape of fire and took that of a human being — a child. I have been with thee often, and was rushing to annihilation, because I could not withstand the ordeal of the senses. Had I yielded, or found thee other than thou art, I should have become again an Earth spirit. I have been led away by wish for power, such as I have in my grasp, and forgot the mission to the suffering. I became a wanderer over the Earth until I reached this land, the land that you call new. Here was to be my last trial and here I am to pass the gate of fire." As he spoke voices arose from the settlement.

"They are coming," said he. The stout form of Hugo was in advance. With a fierce oath he sprang on the young man.

"He has ruined my household," he cried. "Fling him into the furnace!"

The young man stood waiting, but his brow was serene. He was seized, and in a few moments had disappeared through the mouth of the burning pit. But Mary, looking up, saw a shape in robes of silvery light, and it drifted upward until it vanished in the darkness. The look of horror on her face died away, and a peace came to it that endured until the end.

**The High Tor Legend (B):**

A most curious tale is the Legend of Hugo: a puzzling mixture of Indian superstition, Christian faith, and German mysticism. The Indians believed that a great tortoise and a pregnant woman had made the world. To protect mankind, they imprisoned the evil spirits of greed and lust beneath High Tor, the steep basaltic cliff below Haverstraw. Centuries later, the youngest of the Magi heard the story of their imprisonment. He had been deeply impressed by the infant Christ, and determined to test his faith by finding the Tor, and exorcising the evil spirits. In a dream he saw the location of High Tor above a great river in a distant continent to the east of Asia. Traveling across Asia and the Bering Straits, then over the North American continent, he found the Tor.

He built an altar on its peak and tried to convert the Indians and destroy the spirits. His efforts failed and he died of a broken heart. In 1740, a band of ironworkers from the Harz Mountains in Germany heard of the rich iron ore to be found in the county and came to the Hasenclever mines. Their leader was Hugo, a Rosicrucian. Rosicrucians were members of a secret society founded by a German knight, Christian Rosenkreutz. They were alchemists and students of the occult, and of mysticism. They believed that base metal could be turned into gold and that evil could be turned into good. When Hugo heard of the tale and the Magus' efforts, he too dreamed of the evil spirits beneath the Tor. He ordered his men to build a forge where the Magus' altar had stood, and began to pray over them as the Magus had done, trying to turn them from evil to good. The spirits answered. They told him he could set them free by reading aloud the letters on the back of a giant salamander that lay beneath the forge fire. If he did this, they would give him unbounded wealth and power over the world.

He refused. His men became alarmed. They begged him to put out the forge fire and leave the cursed mountain. He continued to watch and pray over the fire even though his wife and children, a boy and a young girl, begged him to leave. One night the salamander rose out of the flames. The huge lizard fatally burned Hugo's little son and shocked his wife so badly that she died. Hugo went mad with sorrow and wandered raving through the woods. Mary, his daughter, was left alone in their small hut. A few days later a young man of unusual beauty came to the hut and asked Mary for shelter. She made him welcome, then in great distress told him what had happened to her family. He promised to help her, and knelt with her in prayer for her father. Touched by his kindness, she began to trust and love him. He returned her love, but one night he confessed what he really was.

He was the Angel of Fire sent down by God to help mankind. Instead of doing so, he had allowed himself to be corrupted by the evil spirits. They had treacherously changed him into a salamander with secret letters on his back. If the letters were interpreted correctly and the words spoken aloud by a human, the evil spirits would be set free. When her father had refused to read them, the spirits had ordered him to destroy her brother and mother, drive her father mad, and in the shape of a man corrupt her. As Hugo wandered nearby, he heard the young man's confession and came to his senses. With a loud cry, he pushed the young man into the blazing fire. But because of his love for Mary, he was transformed into an angel again and, drifting upwards through the sky, vanished from their sight.

**Dr. Yeshayahu Ben-Aharon:**

We will speak mostly about version (B) of the High Tor legend today, which is more clear and suitable for our purposes. It is the second, shortened version of the legend. In some respects it is different from the first version (A), but we are not going to enter into a study of the two versions here. As with all myths and legends involving esoteric content, it is important to consider the place and the time to which the legend refers. I chose this legend of High Tor because it especially illuminates the questions involving the destiny of northeastern America, with its connections to Europe (but it is also, of course, an illustration of America's destiny as a whole). For those who are on the East coast of the US, this legend definitely symbolizes the potential, nature, challenges, and esoteric tasks of New York City and the larger New York area including New England and the Mid-Atlantic States. Before we choose certain details of the legend to discuss and interpret, let us widen our scope in connection with the legend, which should help to put it in context.

The three Magi or Wise Men followed a star to the birthplace of Jesus of the Solomon line, to Jerusalem, and there they offered him gold, myrrh and frankincense. These three, esoterically speaking, are great teachers of humanity. They had been pupils of the Christ being before. Zarathustra, fifty centuries before the birth of Jesus, spoke about the Sun Being who was approaching the Earth. So the Magi followed His star; they followed His reincarnation process and they came to honor Him. Then they died very shortly after this meeting took place and were immediately reborn. They were reborn quite rapidly in order to make it back in time to be on the Earth again with Jesus. They reappear again for us in the great miracles that Christ performed. The first one to reappear, Lazarus, is the Christian Rosenkreutz individuality. The second one reappeared in the woman who was bleeding for twelve years and the third one reappeared as the young man from Nain, who, if you remember the story, was dead and was being carried out of the city when Christ approached the crowd and awakened him back to life. The young man from Nain is always young, as we say, spiritually. He was the young man in Egypt, who lifted the veil of Isis and died. And he was the being who incarnated in the third or fourth century, known as the Mani, the founder of Manichaeism. We hear that the youngest of the Magi, called Amasis in the legend, came to High Tor right after the time of Christ. He settled here, built the first place of worship, and sought to redeem the evil in the depths, which was locked down and bound. Of course, this evil was destined to be released, spiritually speaking, one day. He came in order to transform the evil spirit into good. Obviously he failed and he died here of a broken heart.

In the other version of the High Tor legend (A), it is said that he made contact with the Indians and they wanted to convert him into a Sun worshipper. But being a disciple of Christ, he knew He was here already. Amasis told the Indians, "My dear friends, you have not been updated. He is not out there; He's here. I've met Him." We also hear that Amasis married an Indian woman and had a child. So he saw the vision of the evil in the depths. As he was trying to redeem these spirits, the Indians tried to destroy him. When they came to kill Amasis, a tremendously powerful gust of wind came sweeping over them. Everyone in the area, apart from him, his wife and his child, went under in this gust of wind. What we see today as the Hudson valley, especially around this area of New York, is a result of this gust of wind. This is an important aspect of the legend. It gives a spiritual-geological element to the High Tor legend. It relates the forming of the Hudson, and the opening up of mysteries of the depths, to this gust of wind.

This is Amasis, the youngest of the Magi. I would identify him as Mani himself, the founder of Manichaeism. And this explains also why the Rosicrucians came with Hugo in the eighteenth century. So twice, in a relatively short time span, a strong Manichean element is involved with the High Tor. Although Manichaeism is not necessarily introduced in the legend as having a connection to Rosicrucianism, we find support for this in the Manichean idea that evil can be turned into good. This is pure Mani. We read, at the end of the next passage: "trying to turn evil into good." This is Hugo's task. He came here in order to transform evil spirits into good. So this Rosicrucian element is definitely connected to the Manichean stream we are talking about. Of course Rosicrucianism is a continuation of Manichaeism, as is Anthroposophy, but it is not always that we see such a strong connection of Rosicrucianism to Manichaeism. But here it is expressed openly and it is the main focus of the whole legend. The evil spirits of the Earth were bound. The Indians knew about this secret. And this becomes an interesting story of a two thousand year process of trying to transform this evil into good through the new Christ impulse.

So what is the story? It's very simple. It's a story of Earthly power, that's it. The one who sets the spirits free (as opposed to the one who transforms them into the good) will be granted the greatest imaginable Earthly power. The spirits offered this power to Hugo and he rejected it. Of course, he was too pure. He wouldn't read the symbol, the triangle, on the back of the salamander. He didn't do it. He said no. But we can say that beyond this, Hugo failed, because he could not transform the evil into good. If Mani failed, then Hugo failed also, for he was just a humble pupil of Mani. But one hundred years after Hugo lived, the evil spirits were set free. This means that eventually human beings came who did read the letters in the triangle.

We know, esoterically speaking, that this form of evil, having to do with the Earthly power of the depths, is connected with America. We also know that this is the reason why western humanity was kept away from America until the fifteenth century. For those who are not aware of this, Rudolf Steiner said that western humanity was kept away from America until the voyage of Columbus in the fifteenth century, because this continent contained this secret of evil. This is exactly what the High Tor legend is all about. In this legend, we can see that the spirits of evil were bound, were not released, and were not free. In the time since, these forces would come to be released and this question of evil would then have to be confronted. Hugo represents someone from the tradition who is trying to transform the evil to good according to the Rosicrucian-Manichean impulse. He did half the job. He did not read the letter, but he also did not transform the evil.

Then other people came to Manhattan (this is not part of the legend, but popular history). They were the ones who set the evil spirits free. They were the ones who came here and used the Earthly power of the depths in order to rule the world. This is basically the story of the rise of the financial and industrial powers of the East coast. But this also extends to America as a whole. Of course, on the East coast, it is much deeper. If you go to the West coast, the evil is, let us say, more human, more ordinary. There you are connected to Mexico and to South America, and to the mysteries coming from there. Mexico is another story altogether, where you find a lot of evil, black magic, and decadence connected to its past. In High Tor there is a specific American kind of evil that is not related to the past, decadent, Indian or Mexican mysteries that we encounter more in the Southwestern US. This High Tor evil is something which belongs to the future. The Indians were not touched by it. They were protected. To speak about the West coast would involve the whole perspective from the South, the Mexican mysteries and the Spanish element. All of this is important, but that's not our task today.

The situation is such that from the end of the nineteenth century, from the end of the Kali Yuga, those spirits are no longer bound. They were set free. And those spirits, who were not transformed during their time in captivity, are now free to influence human consciousness. America was discovered. The white people came. It's colonized. They begin to work with the forces of the Earth. And, as non-initiated, ordinary human beings, they are under the influence of the forces of the depths. They can use this power for anything on the Earth. So the possibility of world domination by the American people comes from High Tor. These spirits of the Earth are the spirits of gold, jewels, and all the metals. Through these forces, they gain unlimited control of human consciousness and spread this ahrimanic spirit throughout the globe. We have here, in this legend, the story of America. It is an esoteric interpretation of what is essential for our time, essential for a simple understanding of Manhattan. This legend is central for the understanding of the challenges that we confront in this evil power, in trying again to transform it into good.

From the work we have seen of these two great leaders of humanity: Mani himself and Hugo, we can assume that for two thousand years there have been other forces working here. This is the story of the transformation of evil into good, of success and failure. It's part of the history of America and of Europe since the mid-to-late part of the nineteenth century. In this one legend we see the work of several spiritual impulses: Mani, pre-Christian spirituality, post-Christian spirituality, and then the work being done in the consciousness soul age. The Indians were immune to the evil of the depths. For the Indians, the evil spirits were bound. The Indians were guided by higher spirits and could not be tempted by this power. The evil spirits were bound because the Christ was not yet on the Earth. The Indians could not have dealt with those spirits, as this was not part of their destiny. They were still sun-worshippers. The sun was outside, not on the Earth, and evil was not to be transformed yet. Then after Christ, the first thing that happened was that the youngest of the Magi, the Mani himself, came right here. The legend implies that it was immediate. He was so impressed by the infant child that he physically traveled through the Bering Straits to the home of the American Indians, where he had seen the vision of evil. So the Christ impulse was immediately here, without interruption.

In addition there was a different element among the Native Americans on the East coast, because of the Iroquois confederacy. This confederacy resulted from a strong impulse of spiritualization in the ninth to tenth centuries, and by the fifteenth century it had developed into a six-nation confederacy. This was a transformation of consciousness preparing for the confrontation with the white man, preparing for the coming of the European. The Iroquois confederacy was highly modern. They already had the consciousness soul in an inner way. When you ask an anthropologist who studies the Indians of Manhattan and New York, you find that those Indians outside this confederacy were not as friendly to Europeans, since the Iroquois were more prepared for the confrontation.

Until now, in anthroposophical circles, we have spoken only of the European and Asian streams in relation to the Christ. No one has spoken about the Christ impulse in relation to America. The only place, to my knowledge, that immediately connects the Christ impulse to America is in this High Tor Legend. And if this version of the story is correct, Mani came in connection with this impulse first. My own research of this legend is, of course, historically and culturally, not incredibly advanced yet. We have not looked for verification or similarities in other legends or historical accounts. Even experts on Indian culture, New York historians, and anthropologists have not worked with this legend. It is one small legend that appears next to many. It was through the High Tor Organization, that I came to know about this legend. They told me when I came to America in 1997, "We named our organization High Tor because of the legend. Read it. Can you tell us something about it? It must be very important." We have here, as far as I know, the only direct connection between the mystery of Golgotha, America, the Manichean impulse, and the Rosicrucian element.

First, the legend is of universal significance for any spiritually striving person, and so also for anthroposophists working in America. It is very important to try to understand this legend. Ordinary human beings who are now here: we are the ones to do this work. We have to do this same Rosicrucian-Manichean work. We are confronted by the same temptations. We are the power-seekers and the world-conquerors, filled with the impulse to go out from America to conquer the world, to create our empire. We have to transform the American empire, the power-seeking impulses of those evil spirits of High Tor and of Manhattan. As true students of Manichaeism, we must try to transform this into good. It is important to know the legends which relate to your country. These stories are not simply reminders of past events. Rather, most legends pertain to the past, present, and future.

For example, when you begin to experience Israel, you begin to experience the land of the Christ. You begin to relate to the land through the stories, not only as tourists, but inwardly. It takes time. Myself, I could never try to do it until recently. It was not my interest to feel my homeland in this way. It takes time until your spirit is so near that you can approach your neighbor and ask: 'What's next door (spiritually)? What events took place here?' To study the spiritual archaeology of your own home takes some time. Even in Manhattan, this is quite a task. This is true as well in upstate New York, in Saratoga Springs, where the Iroquois made this holy healing place the center of their nation.

We have a unique position and a unique approach to evil here in the US. If you want to be evil, this is the place. Don't go to Israel. Israel is small in comparison. Of course we do a lot of evil, but you are outdoing us! Ours is harmless compared to what you are achieving here. This is a world evil. This is the real thing. If you want it, it's here. If you want to be good in Manhattan...first, your chances are very small. But let's imagine you say to yourself, 'No, I will persist, I really want to be good. Through all these temptations, I really want to be good.' If you persist, despite the temptation to go in the other direction, if you choose to try to do something fruitful with those forces, you are then directly confronting the vast possibilities of power in ahrimanic domination, for this is what it is all about. We have to understand that the destruction of the Twin Towers is not in itself, a cause of anything. This is not something that will change anything. It's just an effect, just a symptom of conditions that were emerging throughout the eighties and especially in the nineties. This event is not a cause for great change. It can only be understood as part of a change in conditions that took place on all levels during the nineties.

But symbolically it has a great value. It is a tremendous consciousness-raising event. This is what makes it very important. It speaks to human consciousness. Now people can become aware of the conditions that were already manifested. With a more awakened consciousness, in light of this event, we will be able to appreciate where we are and where we are going. But let me say now, that exactly two thousand years before September 11th, 2001, we had this tremendous Earthquake described in the legend, which created the Hudson River and destroyed those Indians who tried to interfere with Mani's work. What happened now, exactly two thousand years later? It was a similar Earthquake. When we look at 'Ground Zero,' when we look into this hole, we look deep into those mysteries of the Earth. So now we can actually look into the depths. This is a rare opportunity to look into those depths, as Mani did two thousand years ago, during the First Coming; and now we are with the Second Coming. He began the work here, of the transformation of evil. In this second time now, we have the light to look into the depths. We can go to 'Ground Zero' physically, but spiritually also, and see now much more clearly the nature of those evil forces in the depths, and upgrade our consciousness. It is our task to awaken our consciousness, to confront the challenges of the next millennium, and to restart our anthroposophical endeavors on a completely new level, with the problem of America's global influence in the forefront.

The awakening power of this time holds the promise of at least planting the seeds of consciousness, which can penetrate further into the depths of the secrets of America. This is truer today than before because of the symbolic character of this catastrophe on September 11th. The evil spirits were very influential from the Earth going upward toward the sky, but this was taken away, and this negative empty space was left behind. In this empty, negative space we can see the nature of those forces of the depths. It is time to look through this hole and search for the meaning of it. This is the legend of High Tor. Study and meditate on this legend. Work with the symbols in this legend and of this place and go then to Ground Zero. Relive the events of our time against this background. Then I think we can really be updated for the contemporary world. We then have a strengthening beginning for the tasks in this next millennium, which is really right for our whole time and for our future. Let us say again that this is not only a local event but this is relevant for all of America. I believe our friends from the West coast and from the South will find this of interest for the destiny of America as a whole, in spite of the differences of location.

Also, keep in mind that the work involved here is not just starting now. It is already two thousand years old and will continue on into the third millennium. This is an ongoing confrontation with evil. To the failures of Mani and Hugo we are now adding our own failures, and will add many more failures in the centuries to come. In each century there will be another significant failure; hopefully another significant effort to change our failure into heroic good. So let's be prepared for the coming failure. Let's prepare to fail in a real sense. Let us find a worthy confrontation, a worthy enemy. In truth this enemy is right here and is already worthy. We are not worthy yet. So I cannot really say, 'Let's find the worthy enemy.' Let's create worthy opposition to this most worthy opponent that spreads its net across the globe, using the great ahrimanic power of our time.

Where materialized spirit has been captured by the Earth-forces, where human consciousness is fixed to the physical-materialistic level, this is where the spirits of the depths have done their work. If you look at this place, Manhattan, this place of the depths, you will see the evil spirits that I described here. They are the keepers of jewels, precious stones and metals. They are transforming spirit into metals and so on. This is the accumulation of wealth. They take universal, free, cosmic energy from the stars, from the planets, from the universal ether, and they are continuously condensing it into jewels, money, gold and silver. Metals are condensed star forces and spirits. Ahrimanic beings condense them and accumulate the universal spirit and transform it into Mammon. They are the Mammon beings. This is capital. Mammon is the evil god of the future; he is the inspiration for the whole monetary system. This ahrimanic spirit works within gold. Mammon is the greatest adversary of Michael in this particular Michaelic age and Mammon's place is here. It is through Mammon's work that universal spirituality is transformed and condensed into metal, and is accumulated as capital.

The uniting of these forces into a World Trade Center is something that is really taking place globally. Many centers around the globe have been built by the inspiration of Mammon. There are world trade centers in Israel and in Asia who are serving the same network, doing the same work. So the gospel is spreading, it's not only in the US. If you go out into the rest of the world, you'll see that they practice the same art of *transforming spirit into matter and binding human consciousness to metal*. But this originates in Manhattan. This is the secret of Manhattan, and this is what the High Tor legend is all about. So if we want to penetrate into this empty space left from the destruction of the Twin Towers with consciousness, we can study this legend and see what became of the fire spirit.

What happened here to the salamander fire spirit? The essence of our interpretation involves the work that the evil spirits are doing. What are these deeds that have bound the salamander? They transform spirit into Mammon; they tempt the spirits of the stars and transform them into evil spirits. This is what befell the salamander. But this is only the first part, for the story then tells of his redemption through human love and purity.

Let's look at how the salamander described himself. He said that he was an angel of fire sent down by God to help mankind, but that instead of doing this, he allowed himself to become corrupted by the evil spirits. The evil spirits changed him into a salamander, and inscribed secret letters on his back. It was said that if these symbols were interpreted correctly and spoken aloud by a human, the evil spirits would be set free. In exchange, the one who read these words aloud would be granted unlimited material power. The evil spirits, once free, could then invade human society and consciousness and create havoc on the Earth; they could control the Earth. Until the fifteenth century, western consciousness had to be kept from America, because only initiates could survive the conditions prevailing here. Mani then tried and he failed. Hugo tried again after the fifteenth century, but he was still connected to the old traditions and had only mixed success.

This legend is concerned with the temptation of the fire. The fire was magically transformed into the salamander, with a secret letter inscribed on his back. This is fantastically correct, esoterically speaking. If you speak it aloud as a human, evil spirits are set free. Note that the secret letters are written on a triangle. You may recall that in the Temple legend, Cain gave Hiram Abiff the hammer and the golden triangle and the metal. He gave him everything he needed to master the Earthly forces. Hiram needed these to build Solomon's temple and he became the founder of everything that comes out of the master builders' traditions. This is an aspect of Manichaeism, that out of it springs the Rosicrucians and the Freemasons. The people of this stream are to learn the secrets of building the temple of humanity, which means using the Earthly forces for the good and building a place for the spirit to live. They are to learn the secrets of the Earth, but remain pure. They always have to go through the temptation of those experiences where it is said — *Look, here is a triangle. This is a means to power, if you read it aloud.* What does it mean to 'read it aloud?' It means that a human being takes it in, raises it to consciousness, and then employs it for his own power. This stream is involved with a very specific path of knowledge. They study geometry, mathematics, and all of the sacred tools. These are sacred, but they can also be used for evil, by using these forces of the Earth to control human consciousness. This is the secret of the sciences. When we speak about jewels, gold, silver, and other metals, these are all connected to the powers of Mammon. And this power involves both capital on the one hand and the sciences and technology on the other. This is the unique power of America: to combine them together.

No nation on Earth can combine capital and metals, this materialized spirit, with the prowess of the science and technology that America utilizes. When you combine capital and science in America you have this tremendous technology that nobody else can even try to imitate. If you try, as a non-American, you find that you don't have the capital to invest. If you have the capital to invest, you find that you are not so efficient. And if you are efficient and have the capital, you still won't find the right combination to make it into a world power. Only America can use this totally new combination that the Europeans cannot even attempt to emulate. So now we will see what kind of evil and good can come of this situation. Both are possible, and on a huge scale. Everything is huge in America. Can we compare it to Israel? Take the attacks of terrorists, for instance. They count the dead by tens in Israel, but in the US it's in the thousands immediately. You can understand the big forces here, everything moves on a greater scale.

In any case, Hugo refuses to read the triangle and because the salamander is still under the control of the evil spirits, he is ordered to destroy Hugo and his family. So the salamander killed the mother and the son and Hugo went mad. Then the salamander went after the daughter by taking on a human form in order to corrupt her. It is told in the first version of this legend (A), how love developed between Mary and the salamander, who had taken on the form of a human man. It is told how the redemption of the salamander's spirit occurs through Mary's purity and through the salamander's overcoming of the temptation to establish a physical relationship with her. This occurs exactly twenty one years after the whole story began. She was twenty one and the Salamander was twenty one. Everything happens according to the seven year rhythm. So it's a whole biography of this being. After she is three-times-seven years, Mary comes into her age. She meets him, and through the purity of their love, this corrupt being is transformed. The salamander is transformed, thrown back into the fire as a human, becomes an angel of fire again, and ascends to heaven.

Esoterically speaking, the spirits of fire are archangels. Fire spirits of the sun. They went through their human evolutionary stage in the Old Sun evolution. So we are dealing with an archangel. Remember the Christ himself was an archangel. He is an archangel, a being from the sun. All of these beings, including Lucifer, reached their human stage on the sun, in the Old Sun evolution. But this legend is concerned with a really unique fire spirit, who had a quite specific task to come down to Earth to help humanity. He said, in the first version of the legend (A), "Know that I am one of those who left heaven for love of man... Beware of the subtle element, which is flame, burning and glowing with love... Here was to be my last trial and here I could pass the gate of fire." Then he was thrown into the fire by Mary's father. It's interesting, no? He described that he fell from heaven, but that he originally came to help those corrupted by the Earthly powers. He's a fallen angel. After he had fallen, he wandered around and found High Tor, the place in which he might be redeemed. He did not fall into this specific location, but he chose to come to

High Tor, where the evil spirits took hold of him and transformed him into this salamander. For him, this was another trial and another chance to return to his source, if he could keep true to his task. So we see this archangel transformed into a salamander, fighting for his own being.

Remember as well that salamanders are the human beings of the future, the human beings of a future Earth, the New Jupiter. They will reach this stage on Jupiter. The elemental beings become human through us, with us. Hugo is also fighting for his own being and Mary saves them all. But the archangel does not give in to the human love. He says, 'If I loved you, physically, as a human being, then I would be enchanted forever.' He goes through human existence and temptation, but by overcoming this temptation returns to his source, to his hierarchy. The first version (A), the meditative version, is all about the relationship between Mary and the archangel, and is elaborated at length. It speaks of the transformation of fire and water, which is a basic alchemical transformation that he performs with her. This is the whole thing. But if you leave aside my interpretation, you can also read the legend as an initiation story with all of the 7 year rhythms. This is an incredibly fascinating story for this aspect alone. Then we can also discuss those details of the communications between the persons: Hugo, his wife and their two children: a boy and a girl. The Mother dies, the boy dies. Mary becomes twenty-one and meets the young man and so forth. So the legend recounts the secrets of the "I," the secrets of the birth of the self.

Don't forget that the self is also a fire spirit. The self, the ego, is the spark of the Spirits of Form; all the mysteries of fire are of the self, of the ego. This is the reason why the twenty-one year initiatory process is part of the legend. What happened after the first seven years, in fourteen years, in twenty one years? Kindly note that we are also living in the 21st century after Christ appeared. It is also the ego-stage. But this is the Michaelic age as a whole. The birth of the "I," of the higher self, of the Christ, is related to the fact that evil cannot be hidden anymore. Because the good is exposed, evil is exposed. Not vice versa. We can begin to confront evil now. But we cannot confront evil with Earthly power; we can only confront it through the Christ.

So this being of fire, an archangel, one of the gods, came here. Mani arrived here first to save this particular angel, but did not succeed. Hugo tried and his family succeeded, which shows us that the Christ impulse was strong already. So two thousand years past the dawn of the Christ impulse, the salamander is released and becomes a fire spirit again, a free archangel. This, in itself, is a significant story. He was released and became an archangel in the end. Then, sometime later, the evil spirits were released to influence and tempt human consciousness. But this archangelic being is now free as well, and he is free to be contemplated by human consciousness. You see here the two liberties. Here is this being no longer bound, back in his original, pure form. *He can inspire human consciousness, especially as it is connected to this place and time.* He fell to the Earth, he was corrupted, but then he was redeemed by the Manichean-Rosicrucian impulse. We can contemplate this.

The salamander was saved by the Mary principle, not the Hugo principle. Hugo helped but he did not fully redeem him. We see that the Mary principle, the feminine, is the only hope at the end. In America this feminine principle is utterly essential for any spiritual transformation. Of course in other places, such as Israel, we can't do without the feminine principle either. But in America, never even try to do something without Mary or you will fail. In America, you will fail before you start, because in America only the feminine can overcome the ahrimanic forces. If you are a male incarnated in America now, you need the Mary principle — sprinkle holy water all day, night and day. As is explained to us in the legend, Hugo became fascinated with the ahrimanic, and his daughter did later. It's not easy reading, it must be judged carefully. The language and the style are quite complex, but the story is very clear. The story speaks of the seven year period of the initiation of Hugo, including the essential third, seven year, will-initiation, of Mary. Mary undergoes this will-initiation, which is completely beyond words in its scope.

But let's go back to the story as it is told. The salamander was released. He became a spiritual power, free from the Earth, an archangel who went through this whole initiation, a unique initiation for an archangel. He fell, he was corrupted, bound to the Earth, and then he was released. Let's take this aspect of Christ as an archangel. He came down, became a human being, remained connected, and did not fall to temptation. Christ went through all the trials of temptation, but did not succumb to any of these forces. But this salamander being was tempted and fell. And then he was released by the Mani-Rosenkreutz impulse and returned. That such a highly-evolved Christian being from the sun, came here to help humanity and fell and then was redeemed through his particular Manichean destiny makes this being a special source of inspiration.

Failure and success, what are they? What did it mean for him to fail? Yes, to fail, for he was corrupted. Mani was the young man instructed in the Egyptian temple, the one who came and saw the statue of Isis, which proclaimed — *I am Isis, past, present, and future: no mortal shall lift my veil.* So what does he do? Swish! He lifts the veil. So he died immediately. What a failure. In this sense it was a failure and this being is an expert of failure. He failed then as a young man from Nain. He was slipping away to death so early in life, and was only saved at the last moment when he was awakened to life by the Christ. Then he was born as Mani and later as Parzival. Remember that Parzival travelled a long path, with so many failures on his way. So this is the being that always fails, because he's the youngest. What does it mean to say *the youngest*? It means the closest to Christ. In the hierarchy of those beings who are closest to the source, he's the highest human leader. All the big names that you have heard of are his pupils. You always hear from Rudolf Steiner, 'Mani gathered his pupils: Christian Rosenkreutz, the Buddha, and Scythianos.' These are his pupils! So he is a higher messenger of the Christ. In this incarnation we are concerned with, he is the youngest of the Magi, Amasis. The legend says he was 'impressed by the infant child.' It's a very specific expression. Why is he impressed by the infant child and not by the other forms, the Crucified or the Resurrected Christ? Since Mani was reborn as the young man from Nain, he was alive to experience the Mystery of Golgotha. But it's not said that he was most impressed by the Resurrection. He was impressed most by the infant child and because of this he came to High Tor. Then, his failure in High Tor is redeemed by the child, Mary.

What do we see here? We see here some different levels for the interpretation of this legend, specifically as it regards the feminine, youth, and failure. It is significant that this Mary is described as a child. And we see that because the archangel is connected to a Manichean impulse, that failure is involved as well. Mani is the one who fails. The mission of the Mani in the future is to transform evil into good. If you are to transform evil into good, you have to know evil. You have to go all the way down to evil. You have to become part of it. You have to be tempted by evil. So the way of this archangel who became a salamander, is the Manichean way. He came to High Tor for his last trial of temptation and for his salvation. Furthermore, this is why the youngest Magi came here. He was not interested in the Middle East; he was not interested in India. He wanted just to come to High Tor directly. The other Magi went to the Middle East and further into Asia. Mani came right here.

So, we have three levels of destiny working here: the destiny of the gods represented by the archangel, the destiny of the highest teacher of humanity in the Mani, and the destiny of ordinary human beings in Hugo. Let us add something else to this interpretation. When we speak esoterically about Cain, we know that he was born directly from the sub-spirit. But Abel was born from Jehovah and the spirit of the Christ. These two streams are represented in these individualities. Now remember how strongly Cain is connected with Mani and Rosenkreutz: they are one and the same element. What is more, remember that they are not of the stream which is born directly from the sun. The sun beings came to the Earth and could not find a way to progress in the beginning. This comes to expression in the story where Cain kills Abel: Cain kills the proper human being of the time. He kills his brother because Abel could not yet develop those powers that could be integrated into human life. So Cain is the master of all things Earthly: he works with metals, science, technology, and art. So what do we have here? We have the archangel, which is connected to the stream of Cain, as it is connected with the stream of the Mani. This Cain stream is responsible for the cultivation of all the riches of the Earth, all the results of science and technology, and for using all of these for good or for evil. The legend and the contemporary story of Cain have behind them the Mani and Rosenkreutz, the healers of the Cain Mysteries. All of these have their center here, in the East coast of America.

From the colonization of America up until now, the work of this place has strongly involved Earthly materials, death forces, electrical energy, atomic energy, magnetic forces and the power of Mammon. America can make use of these forces in an evil Cain's way or in a new, transformed, good Cain's way. So, if you read the Temple Legend, what happened to Cain after he killed Abel? He was imprisoned in the center of the Earth. Cain was imprisoned as it was not yet his time. His power would have wreaked havoc on the Earth. So Cain was imprisoned as the evil spirits were imprisoned. America was not to be discovered until Cain could be released and the evil spirits could be released. Cain represents our human power to control the riches of the Earth. In America this is something totally different than is found in Europe. In Europe, Cain was never bound under the Earth. There, Cain was the master-builder; he was the founder of the liberal arts. Cain cultivated and civilized Europe. He could not do terribly evil things there. To do real evil, Cain had to come to America, because only through the forces of the depths could this great and fantastic evil, that we are encountering now, be achieved. So if you want to talk about unconsciousness, materialism, and being separated from the spirit entirely, this cannot be done in Europe; this must be done in the United States. The reverse is true as well. If you want to change these dark impulses into the good, this can only be done in the United States.

And Cain, through his offspring, taught the arts and technologies to humanity. This includes Hiram Abiff, the master builder of Solomon's Temple. The initiation of Hiram, Lazarus, and Rosenkreutz is the Cain initiation. This tradition was passed on to Hiram when he was killed by Solomon's deeds and went down into the depths where he met the father figure of his stream, Cain. Cain gave him the hammer, the triangle and metal, and sent him out with the three gifts to finish the temple. This is the origin of the Freemason and Rosicrucian traditions. This is all so clearly echoed in this High Tor legend. So, especially for us today, this archangel, as he belongs to these Manichean mysteries, is a real inspirer. He's a being that can really help us, especially here in the East coast, in New York. We should communicate with him — *You were a salamander. You know the evil in the depths. You were released. You know what is pure, what love is, what quenches the fire. You know the secret of Mary. You are the archangel.* This can be a strong inspiration for us.

In addition, this is an abnormal archangel. He is not a member of the ordinary hierarchies of these beings. These abnormal beings have special missions; they have specific powers and they can do great things that normal archangels cannot do. Here we have a fire spirit who went in the opposite direction. He actually did not properly finish his human evolution on the Old Sun. You can only be tempted to become human in this way, if you haven't finished something. We know that the luciferic and ahrimanic beings are approaching us, because they haven't finished their own human evolution. The class of luciferic beings belongs to the rank of angels. They have not fully completed their human ego development. So they come to us now, to complete it through us. We have here a sun being who did not complete his human stage on the Old Sun. It was because of this unfinished business that he came down to the Earth to become human. The salamanders come from below, and are on their way to becoming human on Jupiter.

Here is a sun being, an archangel of the sun, who came down to complete his humanizing process. But he descended even further than the human level, and became a salamander. So his ego development occurred first through the experiences of being a salamander, then through becoming a human being, and finally through entering into a human-to-human ego relationship with Mary. He became a human being: that's his secret. Why should he have done this? Because he didn't do it before. He became a human being, after twenty-one years, for Mary. He said — *Ach, I finished my sun evolution, better late than never.* And he was freed, but not normalized. He's not an archangel in terms of his evolutionary stature. In terms of power, he's an archangel, but he hasn't achieved the complete goal. So he, like so many of those we know as spiritual, ahrimanic beings, works with evil. You could say that this was an ahrimanic archangel. You could say this because he became a salamander. He was tempted by the evil spirits of the Earth. He became an ahrimanic being. This salamander is portrayed as a hostile, destructive being, who attacked Hugo and his family.

There are many different aspects to this. We said the luciferic spirits are tempted in us, to be evil. But they are finishing their human evolution in this way, in a good sense. They receive their experience of ego through our egotism, which they inflame. So it's evil on one side, good on the other. Without them, we couldn't develop a strong sense of self. Without such a fire spirit, certain qualities, which are especially significant for the mysteries of Earthly secrets, could not have developed for human beings. Good and evil together — all of this is connected to what we described in this being. It all depends on how you relate to this being. It is not a question of what he is, but how you relate to him. Through the relationship to Mary, the salamander becomes good, but Hugo could not relate to him in this way. The salamander would only remain evil, or become more evil through Hugo. Don't forget what Steiner said: all the gods of ancient mythologies are retarded beings. All the Greek, Norse, and Germanic gods were abnormally developed. They are all luciferic beings. These are our highly admired gods.

But there are also good spirits, who are not normal, working for good and not evil. So here we have an example of a being who is retarded but who is also good. This is part of the essence of the story. We see that he completes his evolution through his human incarnation, and that he becomes a full sun being, an archangel. He achieved his human ego stage on this Earth, with us. So you can imagine what an interesting spiritual being this must be. He's an archangel, but became human like us. And this development process began, more or less, in the time of Christ, who is also a sun being that became human. This is something which is not completely unconnected to the sun mysteries of today and of the future. This relates to the question of evil.

# Lecture 13

## High Tor, Part 2. The Fallen Angels and the Alchemical Processes in Initiation (Saratoga Springs 2002)

THE HIGH TOR LEGEND HAS a very specific task to show how the American spiritual impulse is connected to Anthroposophy, Manichaeism, and Rosicrucianism, and also to this geographical location that has significant spiritual forces working in it. I believe it would be of the utmost significance to the anthroposophical world if this could be assimilated in an inner sense.

At the end of our own human evolution, only part of humanity will have reached a fully developed ego consciousness. Some will have gone far ahead and some will have fallen behind. Those that stay behind do not finish the class. They have to repeat the same lesson in the next class, in the next evolutionary stage, but under different conditions. Let us look at this process as it applies to the angels. Many of those angels who developed ego consciousness on the Old Moon are the proper, good angels of today. They reached their human stage in this prior stage of cosmic evolution. They are now one level beyond the human being. These are the good, properly advanced, angels. They've been fully human, and now they are proper angels. But among the whole company of angels, there are some who did not reach the fully human level on the Old Moon. These beings are angels by evolutionary stature, but since they have not become fully human in the prior evolutionary stage, they are known as 'retarded angels.' In being, they are less than angels, but in strength they are angels. This means that now on the Earth, they are making up for a part of their ego development that they haven't experienced before.

How would they accomplish this? The most promising way to do it is through the beings that are now currently going through their human evolution. So what would they do? They would look to beings on the Earth that are at an equivalent stage as their own, at a stage where they had left their evolutionary progress in the prior evolution. In short, they look at us. These retarded angels have developed a very intimate connection to our ego consciousness as it develops. When you look at a human today, you can say that each one of us has a proper guardian angel, a real angel, one which was fully human in the last evolutionary stage. This angel is doing her job in the best way according to our karma. Don't blame her! She is doing her best to help us fulfill the destiny that we chose for ourselves.

But, we are surrounded by many other angels who are trying, through us, to make up for what they missed out on in their human stage. These angels are not guardian angels, they are selfish angels. They don't care about our karma. They don't do only what is right for our karma. They look at our karma and say, "Okay, that's his fault. We have our own human agenda. We have our own goals to attend to." They are selfish. They don't care for our development, as our guardian angels do. Of course they are held in certain bounds; they cannot do whatever they want. But they can, to a certain extent, intervene and experience, in us, a level of egohood that they didn't experience in the prior evolution. And we, without them, would have a very sleepy ego consciousness. Without them, we would be childlike, quiet, angelic human beings, very obedient to the will of God. An awful picture, the worst imaginable! These retarded angels are the serpent from the Bible, we know this. They are the luciferic angels. They came along in Paradise and brought a rebellious element. Because of them, we suffered the fall from Eden, and now we enjoy this heightened sense of egohood, of selfishness. But these are all good things. There is no doubt that if you are more religiously, spiritually, or creatively inclined, the spark of luciferic pride and egotism is also there.

We are talking about the hierarchy of angels, but the same principle is true of all stages of evolution. So in the Old Sun stage, which preceded the Old Moon, other beings went through their human stage. These are the fire spirits, the archangels of today. In the High Tor legend, we are dealing with an archangel, a fire spirit. Now what is interesting about this being is that he's incredibly retarded. Some beings don't make up the lesson, even when it's repeated in the next class. They may try their best to make it up in the next class, but they may not quite make it. So they have to continue onto yet a third session. You will find beings intervening in our ego evolution that do not only belong to the rank of angels. The retarded angels give us the joy of selfhood, of creativity, an enhanced sense of self. Now these twice-retarded archangels have double the power of angels. These fallen archangels also want to make up their ego evolution through us.

Here we are not just the petty, selfish, I am that I am, living through my daily life, crushing individual competitors on my way to bliss, which are the normal gifts of intervening luciferic angels. Here comes something totally different. Here you find those great individuals who are leaders of nations, corporations, and soccer teams. For these great ones, they have a fallen archangel working through them. Their selfishness is a group selfishness of party, nation, corporation, not merely an individual one. In these groups you find the fire spirits working, trying to go through their human stage, in which they failed on Old Sun. To allow fallen archangels to express their ego through us, it must be done through a group, through a group egotism. Through this group egotism, the fallen archangel can gain, for the first time, a strong enough sense of self. The individual sense of self, that we experience, is nothing to these beings. These fire spirits need a corporation, an institute, a state. This is a general abstraction, this is everywhere, but nowhere. ?

In the High Tor legend, we find a being who tells us that he came down to Earth to help mankind for his love of mankind. There's nothing evil about this being. He cannot fit into the category that I just portrayed. I want to emphasize how varied these individual beings' experiences are, as they would occur to us. Here we have a sun spirit who is here to help humanity. That's his self-profession. He's not saying that he's a fallen archangel or that he didn't make it on the sun, that he's terribly selfish, and that he wants to make up his human evolution through the experiences at High Tor. He doesn't say this. He says that he came here for the love of humanity, sent by God to help mankind. But here we see the other side, which he does not, and cannot, explain. Instead of helping humankind, he was corrupted, he allowed himself to be corrupted by the evil spirits. We cannot just go with our familiar concepts about good and evil, and say that a fallen angel is, by definition, evil. He was sent to help; God sent him to help.

You will find indications from Rudolf Steiner, to the effect that, the luciferic beings were sent by God to help. So is this a contradiction to what I said before? It seems to be a contradiction. But don't rush. It seems that retarded beings who come here to experience their egohood through us, are completely selfish and create evil by this fact. To think that they were sent by God to help humanity seems like what a proper archangel would be sent to do. Michael and Raphael are archangels in the true sense, and these beings are sent to help humanity. But they are not, thereby, corrupted by evil spirits. How can you be a properly sent archangel and then be corrupted by evil spirits? What on Earth can corrupt you, if you are a fully developed archangel? That's the question here. This might explain the contradiction. He's been sent, but he's also a retarded being. If he were not a retarded being, he wouldn't be corrupted. But the evil spirits took him over, and they transformed him from a divine, archangelic spirit of fire, a sun being, into a salamander.

Salamanders are the fourth class of elemental beings. We have gnomes, undines, sylphs and the salamanders, which are the fire elementals. When we count from below, Earth spirit, water spirit, air spirit, and fire spirit, these fire spirits are the highest category of elementals. So the evil spirits transform the fallen archangel into a salamander, and use him in order to tempt Hugo, the miner of iron ore, and all seekers of this sort. The letter is drawn on the back of the salamander, the triangle, and if Hugo can decipher it, and read it aloud, the evil spirits will be set free to do evil on the Earth. We already heard what happened. Hugo refused to read the letter aloud. The evil spirits then commanded the salamander to destroy Hugo and his family, and to take on a human form and corrupt Mary.

So this is an archangel, coming from the sun, to help humanity. What this shows us is that this is not a regular archangel, if only by the fact that these evil spirits have power over him. But he, nonetheless, has a mission to help humanity. Now what can his mission be? If he's retarded, he must fulfill his human stage, since he has not fulfilled it on the Old Sun or later on the Old Moon evolution; he still has to become fully human. But, at first, he is too weak to withstand the power of some of these demons from the depths, which are very powerful in America. Let's not underestimate the situation here, he's not falling to a bad gnome here or there; he's falling prey to something quite a bit bigger.

A proper archangel cannot be sent to help humanity and be transformed into a salamander. This is not a proper way to do things. This one has an affinity for the Earth, he needs the Earth, he still needs to become human. And he will look to human beings, so that he can become human through them. Because of all of this, he is open to temptation. He's tempted and he's transformed. He is then, finally, saved by the initiation of Hugo and his company. So the first aspect of the High Tor legend, as an initiation story, a human-divine initiation story, already has a double-aspect. The evolutionary process of a divine being, an initiation of a divine being, is taking place in the legend. Furthermore, this archangel is still very closely connected to human destiny now. This is why he can be such help. If you meet this being, you can ask him a great many questions about those beings of the depths. He was in their company, as a salamander, for quite some time. He remembers. Now that he is back to his original archangel purity, he now has an enhanced beingness for his particular level. He is not just an ordinary archangel, how boring. He was an archangel who was retarded, but who won back his sense of self under such radical circumstances.

Think about the normally developed archangels. They were flower-human-beings, who enjoyed light and warmth in the heavenly world. They were divine human beings on the sun. What a different destiny to receive your ego through the greatest spirits of evil and a

Rosicrucian pupil of Mani. Such an archangel is much more than an archangel. He's a human, but much more than we are. And yet he shares so deeply our destiny. He knows something about us, and our future. He knows about those things from so deep below. He knows this from firsthand experience. So when we become salamanders, when we become enchanted in this way, we always pray to him. So I think he is the guardian being for the East coast. He is a real master of evil: he knows of the depths, he knows the secrets. He was an elemental being. For an archangelic being, to be transformed into an elemental being, a salamander, and then to become a human, all in the same evolutionary period — what a wealth of experience and wisdom for the Manichean mysteries!

As you know, the initiation of the gods themselves is at the origin of all mystery places. In older times, all the mystery places were those where the gods had gone through their own development, after which, they passed it on to humans. Humans have walked the path of these gods and have participated in the destiny of these gods by following their example. All the mystery centers are built around the destiny of a god. As I mentioned earlier, all the Greek gods were luciferic beings, all of them retarded. Don't be shocked. I understand that I said something terrible. So let us pause. All the Greek gods that we admire so much, the beautiful Apollo and Dionysius, Jupiter himself, Mercury and all the company of Olympus were luciferic beings. Judging by their behavior, we can see that it's true. Until now, we might not have dared to say what we felt about them, but now we have a concept for it. They are all luciferic beings. Greek mythology, rising from the most advanced human culture ever, recounts nothing other than fallen angels trying to advance in their experience of egohood.

So what's good and what's evil? How are these forces working in the world? Whenever we hear about something significant having to do with human evolution, especially the closer we approach modern times, the more the abnormal, retarded beings, play a significant role. I don't want to draw any hasty conclusions here. I don't want to lead into a discussion about proper children, and non-proper children, about who is more advanced, who is more retarded and so on. I don't want to get into trouble with this. But on the level of spiritual beings, something very significant is happening. This is almost a rule, that when we draw close upon our times, the more those abnormal beings intervene and become incredibly influential in our history of development. This is for good reason. Time is running out. These retarded beings have to make up their evolution. This is their last chance now. They are doing whatever they can to become human. From our side, we are coming to the human level, and they can really use us. This is the reason for the luciferic and ahrimanic chaos of our times. Luciferic and ahrimanic beings are mixing together with the activities of the good beings, inside of us. In spiritual science, the most essential teaching is that the individual human is a composition of luciferic, ahrimanic, and good beings. This is the human today. When you read such stories, keep in mind, that we are this composition of evil and good.

This High Tor legend is a very appropriate teacher of this. We have an evil being, a fallen archangel. We call such beings, in Anthroposophy, ahrimanic beings. But we don't want to call this one an ahrimanic archangel, because he is made of the gentle fire of love. But from the gentle fire of love, to the burning fire of hell, which is the home of the enchanted salamander, there is a difference in quality. Compare the divine fire of the sun, of love, and the fire from below that burns and destroys; this is fire in its divine aspect on the one hand and its Earthly aspect on the other. This being is an ahrimanic archangel, who was corrupted by evil spirits; he became a salamander and then he was transformed, through the human love and warmth of the Mary child. This is obviously a very important mystery for future times. We see here that the divine (or superhuman) and the human are working together.

This being was freed by Mary's deed. But it was just one of many of the remedial classes that he has to go through. If we learn to work with such beings, we come into contact with something highly relevant and strengthening for today and tomorrow, in many fields of our life. These are the beings that animate our group egotism. If you want to deal with the being of a corporation, an institution, or a soccer team, you are dealing with ahrimanic archangels of this sort. So they are part of our life. But even more than that, in terms of the intimate process of initiation, we can refer to the High Tor legend, and say that a divine being, an archangel of this ahrimanic nature, became an ahrimanic salamander, and was used by ahrimanic spirits. As an archangel with tremendous power, he was not, of course, an ordinary salamander; he was a huge, powerful salamander, an awful, big, ugly being. He came out of the fire to kill Hugo's family and corrupt his daughter. This being, then, through Hugo's insight, courage and purity, was transformed. Note that here we are taking all of Hugo's family as a representative of one being, of Hugo himself.

As it follows, twenty one years after Hugo first encounters the salamander, the salamander becomes human. He meets Mary in this human form. And thanks to her purity and love, and the salamander's purity, he is transformed into a redeemed archangel. Why has he become pure when he reached his human form? Because of the help he has already received up to this point from Hugo. Hugo refused to fall prey to the evil spirits. He refused to read the letter on the salamander's back. This is why the evil spirits commanded the salamander to destroy Hugo's family. But the salamander did not completely obey them. How did the salamander summon the power to not obey the evil spirits? It was through the partially successful initiation of Hugo. This gave the salamander the power to avoid completely destroying Hugo's family, especially Mary. He was able to release Hugo and his company, to become transformed through his relationship with Mary, and return to the ranks of the archangels, purified.

Since the end of the eighteenth century, there is now an archangel who has gone through all of this. He can be called the guardian of a very specific Manichean initiation. If you want to find a good source of inspiration for this kind of Manichean-Christian effort, to work with the evil in the depths, to work with this specifically American form of power, here is an archangel to turn to. He came from the sun, he came to help humanity, he was transformed into an evil salamander, he was redeemed through human love, and he is there, now, as a pure archangel. This archangel is one of us, a human, but still on the archangel level. He is very close by. He was here on the Earth; he knows the secrets of the depths. He's a master of evil. If you want to be good Manicheans, and transform evil into good, he's a great help. Hugo first made his salvation possible. Hugo's initiation as a human and the salamander's initiation as a god, meet here in an archetypal initiation. This is especially significant for spiritual work here in America (but, of course, this does not only belong to Americans).

Especially on the East coast of the US, when you deal with these sorts of mysteries, this being and the story has a special significance. The East coast, with its great centers of power, connects us back to Europe, directly to the spiritual stream of Christianity. The power of money, the great power of the Earth, from the nineteenth century onward, could no longer be withheld from human beings. We do not have to limit him to this specific place, but the nature of the spirits of the depths work in this place, in High Tor. Something of this very specific nature is working in Manhattan, on Wall Street. This is it. This is the modern form. This is the same as those spirits of the depths if we understand it in human social terms. We know what it's all about. Wall Street is not a mystical allegorical picture. We know exactly what these evil spirits are all about, when we see how many human beings are used by them, as tools of power, control, and greed. Ahrimanic consciousness = Manhattan. This could not have happened anywhere else in the world, only here. You see this Magi, the Mani, came directly here. He came all the way here, after he saw High Tor in a dream. Hugo, from the Harz Mountains, also had to come here to High Tor. This is the place. Wall Street could not have happened someplace else. No way. Manhattan is Manhattan. Physical locations are spiritual locations, and the evil spirits have their center there. Their inspiration can work through us everywhere, but their center is here. All geological formations and substances are connected with the primeval Ur center or foundation of the Earth. Manhattan is pure, solid, primeval rock that was connected with the fires from the very beginning. Think of what beings come from these beginnings, from the primal fire.

Luciferic beings enliven our egohood. Quite exciting. Ahrimanic beings develop this group, national egotism. More than exciting! Now the *archai*, those beings who did not attain egohood on Old Saturn, also called the *asuras*, are tempting the ego on cosmic proportions today. The asuras were kept away from us for a time. The luciferic beings were the first to approach us, because they are the smallest. So God said, let humans first be tempted by the luciferic beings, give them the individual ego. But don't tempt them with the ahrimanic archangels. Then came a time, when human beings were strong enough, when the ahrimanic archangels could intervene. When it was not enough to have just individual egotism, the archangels joined the play.

Only in the last century, when the time of their captivity ran out, could this last group join in. The American Indians knew about them. These are the Titans bound to the Earth. These are backward archai beings from Saturn and beyond. They are huge beings. They are cosmic beings, terrible, horrific monsters. These are the High Tor beings. And they can definitely take an archangel and twist him into a salamander, no problem. They are beings that can destroy planets. When we speak about atomic energy, the capacity for destruction and corruption on such titanic scales, this is beyond group egotism. This is a planetary egotism.

This is global vision. For example, Bill Gates does not speak about his corporation. He is a global visionary. He is developing tools for global transformation. Bill Gates does not represent the consciousness of a simple archangel. We are speaking about the archai, about the asuras. We are dealing with beings that control entire planets and world evolutions. Even Michael himself is finding it hard to fight with these beings. They are on the same rank as Michael. We are very humble beings. We are starting with everything that the luciferic beings are doing. We cannot advance further than this challenge without first confronting it. You have to come to terms with your own soul, and all those luciferic temptations associated with your immediate egohood. This is the first task. Then you approach the challenge of Hugo, the institution and social community, this is the realm of the archangels. Family is already at the archangel level. But when you are dealing with globalization, with its evil and good sides, and of the fate of the world, then you are entering into the realm of the archai.

With my own soul, and its temptations, I am really the master. This doesn't mean that in one incarnation I can overcome all of my inner struggles, but it is still within my own soul, alone, that I deal with these challenges. The temptations of the self are on the human level. When you enter your group, you are not the ruler of what is happening. You are part of the group. Your power is already limited by the fact that you are one among many — unless you are the head of the institution. If you are the head of the organization, then you are directly connected to the archangel, but then you are a tool. So you have to transform the group structure, the group community life, all this.

If you look at groups and institutions, they are less inspired by the new spirituality than at the individual level. To transform the group, to integrate new spiritual impulses into the institution, this is our task going into the future. We have highly developed individuals belonging to groups, which are totally ahrimanic. This is natural for our times. I can do something for myself. But I cannot yet change my institution. Not because of other people, but because I don't have the power. When we go beyond the group, the institution, the nation, to global proportions, here we touch something that has, still, a different quality. Here is a wall, here is a giant force. This is something that I cannot even try to touch. The struggle, for our immediate time, has to do with the institution. We work and grow through these challenges. We begin with individual life, proceed to community life, and only then do we approach the global life.

But still human beings should have been ripe enough to deal with these spirits face to face. These spirits have now been set free. That's where we are today. The whole last century is already a century in which evil was set free. The evil spirits' captivity in the Earth, which the American Indians knew about, has ended. Since the end of the nineteenth century, since the end of Kali Yuga, evil has been set loose. Human beings, even if unconsciously, are being tempted by this evil. But human beings are also free to transform this evil. These evil spirits are no longer kept from us. They tempt us, every day, freely. And what was in Hugo's time a mystery, are things of daily life today.

The High Tor legend is dealing with Rosicrucian-Manichaen initiation. Hugo is, at first, not pure enough of soul to completely transform the salamander. He cannot do this. But he's pure enough to refuse to read the letter on the back of the salamander. Actually in the novella version, *The Salamander*, it says that he's not pure enough of soul to give an interpretation of what's written on the back of the salamander, so he tries to compel his daughter to speak the word. But in our version (A), we read that he was pure enough not to read or speak it at all. Both relate to the same aspect of this stage of the initiation. In any case, we are dealing with an initiation that begins with the luciferic initiation. So we are first dealing with the angel group and then the story advances to the second and third groups in further initiations. The archangel fell prey to the evil archai spirits in the depths.

So we are dealing with the secrets of everything that has to do with power.

In this legend, we find the seven year cycle described precisely. The wife of Hugo plays a critical role in the first seven year rhythm. It is with her sacrifice that the first seven year period is consecrated. The son of Hugo has to do with the second cycle. And Mary appears in the third. At age twenty one, at Mary's 'I' birth, her ego comes together with the salamander's human ego. Again, when we say 'Hugo,' we are combining the whole family, as they represent distinct aspects belonging to one being. So Hugo's initiation began with the journey from Germany to America, up until the first encounter with the salamander. After this work has gone on for 21 years, we have a beautifully described process of initiation that takes place.

It is described that Mary is mature after 21 years. She is, in the deepest sense, human. Mary represents that most mysterious part of the initiation process of the western mysteries. This aspect of the initiation must be developed in three times seven years. This configuration and duration is required, in order to connect the fire birth of the 'I,' of the spiritually divine 'I,' with the fire of the depths. The fire of the salamander connects with the fire of the sun. The human connects with the archangel, into a single threefold-fire, its two elements joined through the 'I.' This is the essence of this initiation. It is an archetypal initiation, but with completely unique particulars. The fire of heaven and the human fire join together, consecrated by the purified ego element embodied in Mary.

And we know that in America, only the woman in us, the feminine, can approach the spiritual path. For one to say, "The masculine and the feminine must work together, and only when the two come together, do you really have the whole," is fine for social studies class. But the reality is much harsher. You cannot take the first steps along the spiritual path without the feminine in you, without the Mary impulse. You cannot deal with the ahrimanic-asuric fires of evil, without the deepest and purest feminine qualities. In the individuality of Hugo, we see that initiation is impossible without the mother, the son, and Mary working within him. It's only his feminine qualities that can balance and transform such powerful masculine principles. Ahrimanic principles are masculine, luciferic principles are feminine. Only in the Mary principle can the 'I' be born, only through the Mary soul can this happen. Mary is, of course, also the name that belongs to the mother of Jesus. We might take this as a description of how the Jesus 'I' incarnates, according to the requirements of the American East Coast mysteries. It is Mary that gives birth and redeems the salamander, changing him from a human back to an archangel. This speaks about a human initiation, on the level of Lucifer, dealing with the human ego, and, at the same time, an archangelic initiation, dealing with the ahrimanic forces. Hugo cannot transform the asuric forces, but he can redeem the group, the organizational element of these spirits. This is possible for the future because these global issues are just beginning. Don't pretend that you will change the forces of globalization overnight. This will be a struggle for a thousand years, or more.

But where we can fight is within the institution, at the group, or even national level. There we can work. There is much to do here, even if we are working in just small groups; and here we can achieve some success. We can redeem archangels; we can redeem groups and institutions, to a certain extent. Of course, you may come face to face with individuals who are representing global interests and then you can say to yourself, "Relax, it will take some time." What would you say to Bill Gates? "Give me one billion for the Waldorf schools." That's what you should say! But of course with his billions, goes his archangels.

Remember that Christ is the archetype of the entire process of Redemption. He went the whole way from the beginning to the end, through the middle. He's a sun-being also, an archangel; this is one aspect of the Christ. He was the leader of the humanity of the sun, He and Michael. And Michael came down as well. And Lucifer was still a brother, he was one of them. Christ was also far, far beyond that stage, as we know, but this is one level. So they were one company. Then Lucifer fell, Christ came down, and Michael followed the Christ. But this salamander that we've been hearing about has a completely unique initiation story. I don't know of any other gods who have a similar biography. In Greek mythology, the gods have gone through many transformations, but this is the luciferic level we're talking about, not the ahrimanic. Lucifer belongs more to the past. In the present and into the future, the confrontation with Ahriman and the asuras will happen. Lucifer is becoming more and more the good guy, as we experience him, in us. If we change those qualities of egotism in us, then this fire is added in a good way, to our ego. This is not far-fetched, this is possible. So then, we have Lucifer with the Christ to transform the ahrimanic beings and the asuras.

The Christ is now looking in this direction all the time. These are the mysteries of the future. This is the Manichaeism of the future. Mani came to America, directly after completing his mission in the East. He didn't stop in Europe; he didn't stop in Asia, no. He came directly here, to fail here. Why? If you look at the destiny of Mani, in connection with High Tor, you see that he prepared, two thousand years in advance, the seeds of redemption, just as Christ was touching down on the Earth. This was done, so that we can, now, in Manhattan, begin to struggle with these challenges. Mani's participation demonstrates the depth and magnitude of this project for the future.

Remember that Anthroposophy speaks about the seventh cultural epoch, after the Russian, as being the American epoch. This will be the end of the post-atlantean age. This will be the most materialistic, preposterous, occult downfall, of this whole age. And this great downfall is named after America. In this epoch, all those dark forces will reach ultimate concentration and influence. For the non-spiritualized part of humanity, those connected to the dark and retarded forces, will come to full-flower in the seventh epoch. In the sixth post-atlantean epoch, begins the real work of the transformation of evil into good, under the leadership of Mani. So here we have some perspectives on the future. These are all immediate tasks, daily confrontations, and they are distant goals at the same time. Daily life and the future are the same.

But what does it mean for a divine being to go through a human stage? I have been wondering about this. I myself have not yet reached my own human stage! It's hard to imagine an archangel becoming an evil salamander. Let's look at it from another side. Salamanders are the fourth class of elemental beings. They are the most human of the non-human beings. Salamanders have a sense of an ego. The other elementals, the gnomes, for instance, are human-like in many respects, and they make fun of human beings, but they don't have a sense of ego. Nor do the undines and sylphs, but the salamanders connected with fire, which is also connected to the ego, are beings with a sense of self.

And we know that they will become the human beings of the Jupiter evolution. Among them, the human egotism of the future is developing.

So here we have another aspect to the whole mystery of the ego evolution. Regarding our time, Rudolf Steiner said that human beings are developing 'right interaction between one another.' In other words, if I develop the right love towards all the natural kingdoms, and to other human beings, so that I love not only my pet as myself, but also my coworker, then a fire spirit develops between us, of a human-like quality with a sense of self. And such fire spirits will become the human beings of the next cosmic evolutionary stage. This brings in another element to the mystery of archangels, fire spirits, and human beings. For example, what happens if you develop an intense relationship with an animal? An animal doesn't have a sense of self. But we know from our individualized pets that an ego develops and a salamander emerges. So salamanders develop in the love between me and my pet. And this salamander becomes a future ego embodiment for the pet. You don't have to take this to mean an individual dog, but for the species this means the next step in its evolution towards egohood. Salamanders, since they stand between us and the animals, are a prophetic indication of the direction that animals are going towards in the development of egohood. On the other hand, bad relationships with animals create terrible salamanders, and other elemental beings, which become pests. These are the parasites, microbes, and viruses for the generations to come. This is what happens when we deal with nature in a selfish way. When we degrade the stature of the animals, we create illnesses that will attack us in the future. But they can be redeemed! This is the karma of illness. So, exactly what we do to the animals today, will come to us.

Therefore, we will have to develop counter-programs, where these beings are treated in accordance with their future development.

New elemental beings are born out of our creations, good or bad. In the Jupiter evolution, everything that we do now for good and evil, will become nature. There will be no mineral substance, but the lowest kingdom will be the vegetable, the etheric, and all of nature will be the result of human creation in our present evolution. The moral-spiritual results of each word that we said, each deed that we performed, over millions of years will become nature, in the Jupiter evolution. In this future nature, you will see the most pure and loving things coming towards you, and you will say, "Ach, these are my nicest, most beautiful thoughts and loving deeds, from the Earth.' And then coming after you will be some of those great dinosaurs of Jupiter, which will be much more ferocious than any of the physical creations we have seen here. What is nature today, but the most loving creation of the gods? We didn't create this beauty. These are the creations of beautiful spiritual impulses of the past. We can still be as evil as we are today, and continue to enjoy a sunset and beautiful gardens. If you visit places today, even where the most terrible atrocities have happened, you see the area is blooming. But morally speaking, the astral element of these places is most horrific.

The moral creations of the human are invisible at this point. But spiritually, it's terribly visible. Of course, in our own evolution here, it will become more outwardly evident, as time progresses, but it will be an influence on existing nature, not a creation of something entirely new. We have, in the High Tor legend, some unspoken indications about the relationship between humans and animals, and humans and salamanders. The whole question revolves around the mystery of fire. America is in the western half of the globe. It is the volcanic, fiery, half. The eastern half of the globe is the spiritual half. Spiritually seen, the eastern side of the globe appears as a bluish-purple, and the West appears as a fiery red-yellow. The West radiates fire from the depths out to the world. The East reflects the cosmic spirit. Everything of the West has to do with those forces of the depths: original fire, original electricity, atomic power. This is why those people with western consciousness were not allowed to come to America until the fifteenth century. They could not deal with those atomic, electric, magma-forces (but magma, in this sense, refers to moral qualities).

What's morally here in the west is the original evil. Steiner said, for example in 'Geographic Medicine,' that most people were not allowed to come and live in the west, but medical experts from the mystery schools, came especially to America because they could only study certain illnesses on American soil. In the Greek expeditions from the mystery schools, one could only study those things having to do with the double, electricity, magnetism, and influences from the Earth on the human being, on western soil. In the East, one could only research cosmic illnesses. So, those initiates came to America and studied the phenomena of electricity, magnetism, and atomic forces. Now today some of us live here permanently, and some come as guests. The people who live here permanently are irrigated all the time, with these forces from the depths of the Earth. And those forces, transformed into consciousness, are evil spirits. When they only work as natural forces, their consciousness is not yet released. But when they do become conscious, they become this power-seeking, global-empire-establishing, type of thing. When we look at these powerful primal forces, we also have to consider the moral qualities that belong to them. Electricity is a sub-natural power, which we use, but a real being stands behind it. It is a being which is close to our wills, our fiery desires, our power seeking impulses and all these beautiful things.

You could also interpret the High Tor story as a path of initiation of the self, as the initiation of the ego through fire, as a Manichean initiation. You can take this whole legend as the 3 seven year periods in the process of initiation. The transformation and redemption of this being clearly happens 21 years after Hugo first started his fire. When 3 times 7 years passed since Hugo started his fire, the salamander began to grow. So you have these fiery beings, and after twenty-one years, the salamander is an ego, naturally. You light the fire, and after twenty-one years, your spiritual ego is born. It's an initiation process. Furthermore, the principle of fire is rhythmical. It is controlled in your will activity. It is controlled in the taming of your desires. And Hugo was a bit sloppy in this regard. But you see, again, the story is very precise. It's indicated, in short, that he forgot his peaceful European manners in coming here to America. This happens to most Europeans on coming here: they lose their good manners!

His mentor told him that there is a law: all alchemists, after seven years, must put out the fire. It's an ancient law; you can find it in the Bible. For example, after seven years, you don't till the Earth anymore, you leave it uncultivated. So this was the basic law for the alchemists and all those who work with fire. In seven years, the fire-spirit grew to such an extent that if the fire wasn't put out, it would become evil. This means that through your greed, you want to cultivate the land, you want to have more fruits to continue whatever you are doing. You need to mine more iron, more gold: you're greedy in the fiery processes of your will. Your ego development becomes selfish. You have to be able to control your evolution, see? This is a basic law of spiritual development. Hugo couldn't follow the law because he was already tempted by the fire. The temptation begins when he refuses to put it out. He wants to achieve something, to work iron, to redeem the evil spirits — and this is a good spiritual ambition. For example, in our own lives, we begin to meditate. We want to be initiated. This is a good intention, but full of self-seeking and desire. If it's not purified on the way, in spiritual training, we become like Hugo, and lose our wife and daughter, our future. We have to awaken to the consequence of our actions.

This is what God does on the Sabbath. At a certain stage, He stops, looks back, contemplates the past creation, and begins a new creation out of it, learning from the mistakes. He says, "Ach, what a terrible thing that I created humans." We have to learn to put out the fire and contemplate. This is the meaning of the Sabbath. What is achieved by looking backward? Peacefully pausing, giving up struggles and desires, all of this is connected to the meaning of the Sabbath. The first version of the High Tor legend relates that one of Hugo's first challenges is to comprehend the letter on the salamander's back. Hugo, because he lacked a pure soul, failed to read the words that burned in the triangle on the salamander's back. You will see that the first version of the legend gives you a more human Hugo, in that he is not pure enough to give an interpretation of the triangle. He was not pure enough to solve it. So, you see, he didn't put out the fire. Therefore, the will-element, the desire, grew and grew. The salamander grew and became evil. When we begin to meditate, we have a salamander. This is our ambition, power, intentions, our ego, ourselves. It's burning in our blood. All of our desires are growing together around our spiritual goals. We want to be advanced, good, whatever. Each one of us desires. This is always said: spiritual training without purification is dangerous. And this is Hugo's story. It's dangerous.

Hugo didn't purify himself, and therefore he became tempted by power. But he came here in order to redeem the forces of power, of ego, of fire. With Mani before him, Hugo is a founder of the initiation of the will for America. Coping with all the tragedy, Hugo begins treading a new path of initiation, adapted to America. To leave Europe in the eighteenth century, to come here, to found a Rosicrucian colony whose purpose is to turn evil in America into good — this is already, in itself, a sign that we are dealing with a completely unique individuality, with a completely unique mission. Hugo came with a purpose to America, which was not merely physical. He saw the vision of the evil spirits, and came here in order to continue the work of Mani. So Hugo goes through the same initiation, with all the conflicts and tragedies.

Since we have discussed so many different kinds of beings, one might ask at this point how we can differentiate between good and evil beings. Not through reflection, for sure, but through spiritual intuition. You have to be transformed into the being which you are contemplating. You cannot judge something from the outside. If you want to know another human being and judge him morally, what do you do? You can, of course, stand back, look at him and reflect. You can come to a judgment of the human being in this way. But is this a true judgment? If you want to know him as he is, in his being, you have to take his place. You have to enter into his world and see it through his eyes, experience things through him. Then you can say, 'Ah, of course. You are a murderer. I would be the same in the given circumstances.' It's a moral judgment, but it's from within.

What's evil and what's good? That is the question. Conceptions of evil and good follow from external judgments. Spiritually, one does not do this. There are different levels of judgment. Physically, as human beings, it is justified to say, 'The serial killer is evil.' If you don't say it, there is something wrong with you on the physical level, because you don't recognize him as a dangerous person to society. What can you say? That he is not a serial killer? He is. Being a serial killer is good? No, it's evil. So there are different levels of judgment regarding evil. Spiritually speaking, those ahrimanic or luciferic beings are doing a very important job. Without them, nothing would have changed. They've been asked to do the job. They've been commanded. They were told, 'You, you are going to be retarded. It's not a choice. Do it. Don't ask why; you'll know it at the end.' And we now go and say, 'Ahriman, you are evil.' He was commanded by God to do this, for the sake of evolution! Does this make him good? Evil?

However, we have to be careful not to throw these considerations out the window in our daily lives. If we say that there is no good and evil in daily life, then we are in trouble. But if we carry this judgmental position into the spiritual world, we are in trouble as well. We should not confuse them. When we return here, we should return to our normal judgments. When we go there, it's another story.

# ENDNOTES:

**Editor's Note:** Although the sources for all of the material in this book were ultimately lectures given by Yeshayahu (aka Jesaiah) Ben-Aharon, all of the lectures have been reworked, truncated, and revised to one extent or another by transcribers, translators and the editor(s). They therefore may differ quite a bit from the original lectures heard by the participants. The author also was able to revise and extend some of the lectures. Thanks to Cathy Sims-O'Neil, who was able to read through most of the typescript and give further corrections and suggestions. (S. Hicks)

[1] Spoken to members of the Anthroposophical Society in Alsace-Lorraine, in Colmar, France, on June 1, 2007. The occasion was initiated by the late Christine Ballivet, and its publication is dedicated to her. An earlier, very similar version was published in *Being Human*, the magazine of the Anthroposophical Society of America. It was revised by the author and edited by John Beck and Scott E. Hicks.

[2] See Rudolf Steiner, lecture of 7 October 1922, Stuttgart; published in *The Younger Generation*, pages 61-3.

[3] See Rudolf Steiner, *A Way of Self-Knowledge*, p. 69.

[4] In GA 137, Lecture of June 12, 1912, Oslo.

[5] From the essay "Immanence: A Life" in *Pure Immanence – Essays on a Life*. New York, 2005.

[6] Järna, Sweden, February 20 – 21, 2004 (revised by the author)

[7] See C.G. Harrison's book, *The Transcendental Universe* and Rudolf Steiner's comments in GA 184, September 7, 1919, and GA 174a, March 18, 1916

[8] See Robert I. Rotberg, *The Founder: Cecil Rhodes and the Pursuit of Power,* Oxford University Press, 1988

[9] The World Social Forum shows the weakness of Civil Society. There is still a strongly inherited tendency towards Marxist thinking, which is folded in with politics as the ruling force and Civil Society as mere social "superstructure." (author's note)

[10] January 1988; see www.voltairenet.org

[11] February 20, 2004 in Järna, Sweden (revised by the author)

[12] GA 110, lecture of April 12th, 1909 and GA 107, March 22nd, 1909. See also *The Karma of Untruthfulness*, volumes 1 and 2.

[13] February 21, 2004, in Järna, Sweden (revised by the author)

[14] Ferguson, Niall (1999). *The House of Rothschild: The World's Banker, 1849–1999.* New York, N.Y.: Viking and Ferguson, Niall (1997) or *Virtual History: Alternatives and Counterfactuals.* New York: Basic Books.

[15] Orust, Sweden, August 2-4, 2012. All three Orust lectures were originally transcribed by Claire Toril Alex and Martin Alex. (revised by the author)

[16] Given in Orust, Sweden, August, 2012. (Revised by the author)

[17] See Rudolf Steiner, *Esoteric Lessons, Vol. 1*, Lecture in Munich, December 5th, 1907 (GA 266a).

[18] Given in Orust, Sweden, August 2012 (Revised by the author)

[19] This lecture, given at the World Congress on Psychotherapy and Anthroposophy in Driebergen-Rijsenburg (near Utrecht), Holland in October 1997, was published in a slightly different form in *Psychotherapy and Humanity's Struggle to Endure, Persephone*

*Vol. 13*; edited by Dekkers-Appel and Meuss, Verlag am Goetheanum, 2001.

[20] See *The New Experience of the Supersensible*, Temple Lodge, 1996 and *The Event in Science, History, Philosophy & Art*, VBW Press, 2011.

[21] Notes from a workshop of the School of Spiritual Science, in Gothenburg, Sweden, 2009. Transcribed by Hester Renouf.

[22] For more on the Spiritual Event of our time, see www.event-studies.org

[23] A lecture given in March 2012, Stuttgart, Germany. Transcribed by Gaby Morgenthaler and translated from the German by Carol Bergin. (Partially revised by the author)

[24] A Seminar for the Waldorf Schools Oslo, Norway, October 19-21, 2006. (Revised and supplemented by the author).

[25] February, 2002. Thanks to Paul Zachos for the transcript.

[26] http://www.nynjctbotany.org/njhigh/ringwood.html

# A note from the publisher

For more than a quarter of a century, **Temple Lodge Publishing** has made available new thought, ideas and research in the field of spiritual science.

Anthroposophy, as founded by Rudolf Steiner (1861-1925), is commonly known today through its practical applications, principally in education (Steiner-Waldorf schools) and agriculture (biodynamic food and wine). But behind this outer activity stands the core discipline of spiritual science, which continues to be developed and updated. True science can never be static and anthroposophy is living knowledge.

Our list features some of the best contemporary spiritual-scientific work available today, as well as introductory titles. So, visit us online at **www.templelodge.com** and join our emailing list for news on new titles.

If you feel like supporting our work, you can do so by buying our books or making a direct donation (we are a non-profit/charitable organisation).

office@templelodge.com

*For the finest books of Science and Spirit*